Melnika

Tale of the White Crow

Tale of the White Crow

Coming of Age in Post-Soviet Latvia

Iveta Melnika

ELLIS PRESS 2003

Tale of the White Crow copyright © 2003 by Iveta Melnika. All rights reserved. No portion of this book may be reproduced in any manner, printed or electronic, without written permission of the author, except for brief selections embodied in reviews or articles.

Cover: "Tisnikar's Raven" by Norbert Blei, used by permission.

Published by Ellis Press, P.O. Box 6, Granite Falls, MN 56258.
Photos by David R. Pichaske.
Printed by Admon Printing, Ulaanbaatar, Mongolia.

ISBN: 0-944024-46-7

1 2 3 4 5

Publisher's Preface

I spent academic year 1996-97 in Riga, Latvia, teaching American Literature and American Studies on a Fulbright fellowship. I met many good people and many dedicated students from many different disciplines: my course in American Cinema attracted pre-law, pre-med, business, science, language and culture students... anybody who wanted to watch and discuss English-language films.

Oddly, the most fluent student I encountered during the whole year took none of my classes, not even the movie class. She was a German major whom I found waiting in the back of the hall one Friday afternoon in early spring when I'd finished showing *Bull Durham*. She introduced herself, apologized for not taking the movie class (a conflict with something else), and asked for some help with a project related to the English language component of her German major. She later told me that she had almost chickened out because I looked kind of grumpy—"not like those other Americans who are always smiling."

Her name was Iveta Melnika. I helped her with whatever it was she needed help on, and in my last months in Riga, Iveta and I became good friends. English, she told me, was her real interest, but she'd been directed in the Soviet times into Nordic Languages and Culture, Swedish actually, and drifted into German at the University. We stayed in touch over 1997-98 (her senior year) through the wonder of the intenet, and 1998-99 as well, when she taught a year of secondary school in Riga. I made a couple of visits to Latvia; we translated—via e-mail—a few films for Latvian television: *Fletch Lives, Trespass, Rain Man*. 1999-2001 Iveta spent at Minnesota State—Mankato doing a MA in TESL. She married a former Marine, now a lawyer in the JAG Corps, moved with him to Germany, had a baby daughter. This story turns out okay.

My Fulbright years in Poland had produced a book, *Poland in Transition*, and I went to Latvia thinking "book" right from the start. I gradually discovered, however, that Iveta had a better story to tell than I did. In some ways she was a better satory-teller: fresh, enthusiastic, a good eye for detail and a good ear for speech. I had a ton of photos, but Iveta had the life. And the stories. So a plan emerged: she'd write the book, I'd edit and add photos, arrange publication. "Do it as a journal," I told her; "just tell the story of your life in journal entries."

We stuck with that plan. Given Iveta's studies and teaching in Latvia, her M.A. at Mankato, her marriage and baby, and the distractions of my life, this book has been maybe too long in production, but it is a book at last.

And an interesting tale it is. Iveta's experience is in one sense prototypical, in another sense particularly Latvian. And not just Latvian—eastern European at a moment of crisis and transition. *Tale of the White Crow* overlays an almost archetypal coming-of-age story with the fascinating particulars of life in Riga, Latvia, in the 1990s—from the communal apartments through economic and political turmoil to the aggressive recruiting of American religious cults and the Russian disco scene. I saw all this happening from the outside; Iveta lived it. And she not only survived, she prevailed. This book is a testimony to courage and determination.

The photos in this book speak for themselves, but I want to say a few words about the editing. The original texts were transmitted as they were written by e-mail. Vestiges of garbled transmission may remain, although I think she and I have caught most of them. Almost all were written before Iveta came to the States—early entries are a bit after-the-fact, but later entries were written as they happened. What you read here is about 66% of what Iveta wrote: she and I both cut some entries. Over the course of her writing, her style matured. She dropped what I found to be colorful stylistic features like "a lot of bullshits," British spellings like "neighbour," German-Latvian constructions like "let's better go," and German-Latvian expressions like "don't take this too close to your heart." In revision, Iveta and I went round and round on this matter, she favoring normalization, I favoring the original. What you're reading is a compromise of style as well as content.

This book as published containes a final overlay of possible linguistic/editorial/trasmission confusion: it was printed in Ulaanbaatar, the capital of Mongolia, where I am completing yet another Fulbright experience. I think I can get good color reproduction here on the pohotos, as well as good printing. We'll see. Maggie Perry has sent an electronic file of Norbert Blei's painting for the cover; Iveta has sent e-mail editorial changes; I'm "typesetting" on the Educational Advising Resources Center computer. If all this works out, you're holding in your hands a truly remarkable artifact—the story of a girl coming of age in Riga, Latvia, written in English, edited in the United States, printed in Outer Mongolia. Who in the year of my birth, or even in the year of Iveta's birth, could have imagined such a thing?

—David Pichaske

Tale of the White Crow
Coming of Age in Post-Soviet Latvia

1. My diary is the only thing I can completely trust, my only true friend. I am glad I started this friendship a month ago. Now writing my diary has become one of my favorite occupations during the day. When I am done with my classes and home works, I sit down on large, old couch and open my diary. Not that anything exciting ever happens in my monotonous life, but even the sad things seem less miserable when I put them down on the pages of my diary. And — who knows — if I ever die in my young age, maybe somebody would find my little black diary with checked pages. Maybe that somebody would tell somebody else about the miserable teenage girl, and then that somebody else would tell somebody else, and then somebody would decide to write a story about my life, and then it would be that I had been at least of some use for this world.

There are so many things I would like to tell my parents and my teachers. I feel them deep down inside. They are beautiful and painful and so strong that sometimes it seems to me they will tear me apart. However, I know pretty well that if I told them, they all would think that I am just a sensitive little hysterical teenager with a tendency to black thoughts and melancholy, and with a very low self-esteem. So I have decided I'd rather trust my secrets to my diary.

2. Today, during the unbearably boring chemistry class, I was busy observing the gray skies and the first snowflakes falling down on the dirty sidewalk. By the time I went home, already the old women with their wooden shovels and brooms were cleaning off the sidewalks, pushing the snow onto the streets, where it will melt when the weather gets warmer and disappear between the cobblestones. Or it will mix with dirt from the road and turn into gray ice. The late fall and early winter is called the gray time of year, only this period between November and Christmas. Then comes the turn to the light again.

In my life, however, the gray time doesn't end with spring. I have almost no friends at school except for the girl with glasses and incredibly thick legs (it's amazing, for she is not at all fat herself) named Urzula. I am an outcast at school, a white crow among the black ones, an ugly duckling, for I am tall, skinny and clumsy. No style, no grace. The girl with thick legs is outcast too. Besides, she is hopeless at German. I am always helping her out. That's how I earned her friendship.

I hate going home after classes, but I have no other options. Even though I live in the very center of the city in an old, beautiful house designed and built by the German invaders, I hate our stinky staircase where the old people and drunkards come and pee, and our small, communal apartment, crowded like a train compartment: only fourteen square meters for my mom, dad and me. This apartment was probably a big, beautiful place for one German family to live, but it is not good for three families living together and sharing the same bathroom and kitchen. My dad has a serious heart disease and he is in line for a new SEPARATE apartment for at least already ten years. However, it doesn't seem we have any hopes of getting it.

I have no privacy at home. I can't even make my dinner without suffering the scornful looks of our neighbor Anastasia. My mom hates her heartily, and I guess for a reason. Anastasia is a pain in the ass. It is not enough that she needs to put her finger in every pie, in every little personal affair of her neighbors. She is convinced that she is actually the boss in the whole apartment and everyone else should submit to her plans and arrangements. When she is at home—and she is at home always—nobody else is able to use either the bathroom or the kitchen. She always manages to occupy them both, and that is what drives my mother nuts the most.

I know Anastasia hates me too, for I am tall and healthy, but her own son Mitja is short and kind of a weakling. She hates me also because she is Russian and hates all the Latvians. I do not know what crimes the Latvians have committed against her.

When Anastasia is at home, I hide myself in my room. I try not to use even the bathroom. Not that I am scared of her; the very thought of seeing her is repulsive to me.

3. Music is my only joy in life. I had always wanted a tape player, and mom bought one for me just recently. Now it has become a source of my happiness, especially since I have got that new "Modern Talking" tape. Mitja had it already a long time ago. Since tapes with the foreign music are so difficult to obtain, I didn't hope of ever getting it. However, sometimes miracles happen even in my life. My aunt got it from one of her friends, whose son works as a DJ. She knew I would be in raptures about it. Yeah, every dog has its day, even a mutt. I could listen to that type of music forever. I like the blonde German singer. I think he is cute. All the other girls go crazy about the other one, the one with dark hair.

My dad often doesn't feel good, and he can't stand loud music when he is sick. The real misery starts, however, when my mother comes home from the work. She is very nervous; I guess it's due to Dad's illness. She is in constant fear about him, and then she is always grumpy with something and somebody. She quarrels endlessly with Anastasia. Mitja is nasty towards me. He is three years older, but he is shorter than me. He and his friends bully me all the time. Whenever I have to go to the kitchen, they are always standing in the lobby waiting for me. Usually they call names and try to pinch or push me. I try to go through that embarrassing situations with as much dignity as I can; I dash into the bathroom, lock the door and burst into tears. I cannot weep in front of my parents; they wouldn't understand it. I do not know why people bully me all the time. The kids at school call names and mock me because I am tall, clumsy and insecure. When the teachers ask me to talk, I start to stammer and blush.

I guess I probably know why Mitja hates me: his mom taught him to hate Latvians. It doesn't matter a bit that the Russians have occupied our land and are destroying our culture. They hate us because we are small but tough. They want to trample over us like over the worms; however, they do not succeed very well. We are crushed and humiliated, yet we are still alive.

4. Tomorrow we are having a math test. I am hopeless at math. I will definitely get a bad mark and Mom will be upset. I try to study. I put in a lot of effort, but then it's all so complicated and I never quite get the point. My teacher has told my mom it's not a problem of not understanding; the problem, she says, is that I am too absent-minded, totally locked up in my own dream world. I guess she's right. Since my real existence is so colorless, I take a refuge in my imaginary world, and most of the times it helps me feel better.

Maybe I shouldn't have been born at all. Does God sometimes make mistakes, creating good-for-nothing people like me? I think about God a lot, even though at schools we are being taught that such a God doesn't exist, and it's all just imagination of dull and primitive people. God had been created by the feudal government in order to keep the people in obedience by threatening them with God's wrath and revenge.

In the kindergarten we were taught to worship our grandfather Lenin, thanks to whom we are having such a wonderful life now. When I told it to my mom, she said it was a lot of bullshits. She refuses to believe in Lenin. Actually, she could have gotten in trouble for that, but nobody heard her rebellious words.

I do not see anything wonderful about my life at all. I am not even sure if I am going to be accepted in the communist party when I grow up. I think I lack zeal and enthusiasm: I am considered to be an insecure and quiet mouse. Then also my parents have never been involved in any communist party at all. I think that's a pity, for if they were, we would have permission to attend the communist shops, and we could get the bananas there. Getting bananas nowadays equals the difficulty of getting the moon itself. They appear in some shop maybe once a year, and then you have to stand in a huge endless line of furious people pushing and cursing each other for at least five hours. When your turn comes at last, the sales woman with a guilty smile announces that she is very sorry, but the bananas are already sold out. Sometimes they offer you to buy carrots instead, with an encouragement that the carrots contain more vitamins than bananas after all.

5. On Saturday one of my classmates, Samanta, is having her birthday party. It is weird: we were born on the same day, yet we are so very different, like the sun and the moon. Samanta is only thirteen, but she is already a success. She is so popular and so beautiful that the guys at school, some even from the twelfth grade, are all crazy after her. Samanta is also rich. Her parents for sure are in some communist organization, and they are getting bananas every week. Samanta is bragging about that all the time. She is so spoiled with attention and care from the people around her. Samanta has invited to her birthday party the whole class, except for me and Urzula. Of course, everyone would be happy and proud to attend Samanta's party. Who would come to my party? I guess nobody. I will not risk to ask. Besides, I am so deeply ashamed of my train-compartment room. I cannot ask anybody, even my few girl friends, to come over after school. I think I could invite Urzula. She, by the way, doesn't seem to be upset at all that Samanta hasn't invited her.

Sometimes I admire Urzula. She doesn't seem upset about her thick legs either. She is happy with herself and with life in general, even though her parents aren't in any communist party either. And the whole family is living in a communal apartment in a room no better, maybe even worse, than is ours.

Samanta is in love with Svens, the handsomest guy in our class. Svens has a special hair style like a punk, and last Saturday on the excursion to Sigulda he was wearing torn jeans and had a little walkman with him, which was a miracle equal to heaven itself for all of us. None of us had ever seen a walkman before. I heard that his parents have some relatives in Sweden and even in the USA.

Svens was holding Samanta's hand. Nobody has ever held my hand. I haven't even danced with a guy once. I remember the last disco party for our class only, and it's painful. We have these class discos quite often. The girls usually put on nice dresses and even some make-up they manage to steal out of their mothers' cosmetics bags. The guys are usually wearing jeans and T-shirts. Jeans are also difficult to obtain: normally there are none in the shops. Then they in a miraculous way appear, but it's the same situation as with the bananas.

At the last disco party the guys were fighting with each other for Samanta. Yes, Samanta has everything: jeans, bananas, Svens besides her, and guys fighting over her. She is teasing them mercilessly, yet they seem to adore her anyway. I sometimes do not understand what they find so special in her: she is nasty, wimpy, and fussy. Besides she is dull and superficial during the classes. Yes, but she has the looks, and she is popular. At the last disco party I was sitting in the corner being a total wall flower as usually. Even fat-legged Urzula was dancing with somebody. And I was sitting and fighting back tears. It was my favorite song from "Modern Talking." Everyone was dancing, only I was sitting alone.

6. Sometimes at night I sneak out of my room with a book under my nightgown. I hide myself in the storage, where each family has its shelf of jam, potatoes, and dried fruit. Sometimes I stay in storage until 3 or 4 o'clock in the morning. I love to read. Books are a shelter for me, a world where my teenage dreams become a reality. I read all the books I can get in our school library. Most stories are about courageous communist girls who fought and gave up their lives for their country.

I sometimes ask myself, if I had to fight, would I have enough ambition and courage to fight for our country? I guess not. First of all because I am not a fighting type of a person. I am always blamed for lacking energy and interest in the social events. I would be more enthusiastic about all these events if the people themselves didn't make me feel like an outcast. Some people say it's all my own fault: if I had more self-confidence, other people would have just to accept me the way I am. But I still haven't figured out how to gain that self-confidences. I have already tried to be brave several times, but it ended as a complete disaster. When I try to speak up in a company of people or try to start a conversation, everybody stares at me as if I had committed some crime.

Second of all, I would have never fought for the country because I do not get the point what's so special about this country. I personally do not experience that wonderful a life at all. Should I fight for our communal apartment, for that mysterious dead figure in Moscow mausoleum called Lenin? What has he ever done for my life or the life of my family? I do not care for him one bit.

The day I was first accepted into Pioneers, I was so proud of the red tie that although it was a bitterly cold winter day I came home with an unbuttoned coat so everyone could see who I was. I was 9 or 10 then. Now the red tie has become an ordinary thing. It's more of a nuisance now than a joy. I have to wash it and to iron it every day, and eating soup for lunch in our stinky school kitchen I always have to watch out that the ends of the tie are not swimming in the soup bowl.

That feeling faded away already a long time ago, and I do not think that losing my life and becoming a hero after my death is a good idea at all.

Sometimes I read romance. I love to read it. Stories about love make my heart beat faster. I have no love in my life, like Samanta, but I like to dream. I guess I must be a very big fool, but then who cares? I tell my secret thoughts and my fantasies only to my diary. My only true friend.

7. Yesterday I was visiting my aunt Olga. These visits are horribly boring for me, for all my aunt Olga does is talk with my dad about the tough times we are currently having: the endless lines after food, the lack of our good Latvian pork and beef in the shops. People say all the good production from the country collectives is being sent to Leningrad. People who have been to Leningrad have seen it there. My grandma is especially upset about the lack of pork and beef. She is a meat lover. Butter is also difficult to obtain. My dad, since he does not work, is the one who has to stand in all these long lines to get some food for our family.

Recently our current president Andropov prohibited the production and the use of alcohol throughout the whole Soviet Union in order to lessen the drunkenness among the Soviet citizens. The fool, however, didn't realize that by prohibiting it so strictly he will bring enormous trouble upon the whole country—at least such is my aunt's opinion. Many have started to produce the spirits themselves illegally. Then they are not only getting drunk themselves, but also selling it for enormously high prices. Since materials for producing alcohol are so difficult to obtain, people are using anything that works, sometimes even the stuff you normally use for cleaning windows or cars. Some drunkards have already died drinking that stuff.

Women drunks have started to use perfumes in a great amount. Some get themselves drunk by smelling all kinds of weird stuff, like the stuff for killing cockroaches and poisonous bugs.

My aunt Olga seems to be greatly distressed about that. I just do not get the point why. Is she worried that all the sugar in the shops will be sold out to people who try to make spirits themselves, and she will have none left for her beloved cranberry jam?

Well, I do not give a shit about that prohibition. As long as they sell candies and ice cream, I will be fine.

People in this "wonderland" are not so happy after all. Even people who are not tall and not failures, people who know what they want from their lives, are not happy. Very often I hear my aunt and my dad (since I am forced to be a part of these family gatherings) saying lies and ambiguity are ruling all the areas of life. We have this so-called central planning system, which means the government is going to plan all your life ahead for you. While you are a kid you are supposed to attend the school. When you get done with the school, you get enrolled in some university regardless of if you want it or not and regardless also what your marks are. When you are done with your studies, they have already found a place for you to work. Maybe it's the work in the collective. In the best case you are the boss of some collective, which means you are carrying out the orders from above. You do not really have to think for yourself how to manage things. You just do what you are told to do, or they will make you a worker in some factory where you will work hard all day long—a monotonous boring work, but you will be working according to a schedule set by the central planning system. Every five years they set certain goals which you have to strive to fulfill. If some organizations do not meet their goals—which is most of the time—they write in their papers they have succeeded anyway.

My dad is skeptical about the Soviet government, and in my opinion it is nothing more than some old incompetent drunks. But hush! Nobody is asking me. Dad keeps quiet too. He is too old and too ill to get himself into trouble. Aunt Olga is skeptical, too. However, my other aunt Zelma (dad's older sister) is with all her mind, heart, body and soul into all the party activities. She believes in the Soviet government and in their promises about a better future for everybody, and she is ready to give up her life for them. All she gets for her devotion is some 50 Soviet rubli and a little stinky room without a bathroom and with a shared kitchen.

The other thing that really puzzles me is the noble ideas on which the whole Soviet Union was built, the ideas about equal rights for everybody, equal rights and equal amount of money. We were supposed to forget about the wild and exploitative capitalism, and we were to live all together in agreement with each other, sharing everything we may possess. That was the main reason why the communal apartments and collectives were created. The people who owned more were robbed of their property and deported to Siberia. When somebody inquired about them, they were called damned capitalists to whom the punishment suited right. Now we have everything equal, yet such Anastasias are trying to act superior over others. If we are equal, then why are all the communists and the government people having better summer cottages than we the common people, and none of them is sharing the apartment with another family? I think they are not setting the best example of equality for us.

My mother and most Latvians get really concerned about our Latvian language, which slowly starts to disappear. Absolutely everywhere, starting with dental clinics up to the governmental organizations, the Russian language and unfortunately the Russian culture too is dominating. Latvians are even not permitted to celebrate our summer fest Ligo, which has been an annual tradition since the times of our ancestors. Russians make fun of our national songs, and I do not remember when was the last song festival we had.

The old people who remember Latvia before the Second World War say that Russians have made Latvia as one of their big Russian villages full of fights, disorder, and poverty.

Even though our people are not accustomed to thinking much, not everyone is dumb or blind. Some see the rulers' lies and injustices. They see the double standards the government officials are setting for us.

However, we all have to keep quiet. Otherwise we may end up in jail. Like the guy called Gunars Astra. He got in jail only because he was trying to translate Orwell's *Animal Farm* into the Latvian language. All the foreign literature and music that, in the government's sight, could be provoking, or could arise suspicions in our people's minds is prohibited. All we are allowed is to read bittersweet French love stories, or listen to banal German songs.

Most of the population, however, is simple minded. They take what the government has already digested for them and just swallow it. Why bother? If you try to rebel or decide thing for yourself, you just get yourself in unnecessary trouble.

8.

Most of all in my life I hate Mondays. As soon as I open my sleepy eyes, I am faced with the harsh reality of life: Mother is yelling at me, "Get up and get yourself washed and dressed; at 7 Anastasia and Mitja are getting up. Nobody will be able to use the bathroom then."

I drag myself out of my warm bed, put on my shabby morning gown over my pajamas and start my way to the bathroom. Shit! Anastasia is already up boiling water for tea. Despite her resentment towards Anastasia, my mother is always forcing me to say good morning to her. I can never do it. I open my mouth, but no words are coming over my lips. My tongue feels like paralyzed. I just wrap my morning gown tighter around myself and dash into the bathroom. I feel Anastasia's mocking eyes burning my back.

In the bathroom I take my clothes off and observe my tall, skinny body in the large wall mirror. I am too tall and too bony; besides I am so clumsy, and my face and my forehead are all in pimples. My eyes have that scared, troubled-animal look. I am ugly, there's no doubt about it. My mother's friend told me once that I have beautiful hair. I think it's ugly too. It feels like a horse tail. The other family has woken up too; I must hurry up. I take my soap and throw a quick glance at Anastasia's shelf. She's got all kinds of aromatic shower gels, which make the skin soft and silky. All I have is a soap that makes my skin dry and rough.

On Mondays the first class is math. I guess that, so far, is the biggest misery of my life. I can never get rid of that sickening feeling in my stomach when I am waiting for the teacher to call me to come to the blackboard. I hate to be the center of attention. Samanta is even more hopeless than I am; however, she doesn't seem to take it too close to the heart. Her thoughts are too occupied with other things. She has no time at all to brood and ponder over her bad marks. Regardless of her marks, all the boys are at her feet. I watch them secretly passing little folded paper notes to each other. What are they writing to each other? A real love letter, like the letters in the romance novels? I try to imagine what could be said in a real love letter.

Today is the worst of all. Of course I got a bad mark on the math test, and as if it wasn't already enough of a misery, I have torn my pantyhose too. Mom will yell at me as if the house was on fire.

Samanta was sharing a blue chewing gum with everybody but Urzula and me. Obviously her relatives from abroad had sent it to her. Not that the chewing gum is a big deal, just I cannot help having that strange and heavy lump in my throat again.

9.

I love my dad very much, and I am so scared he might die any day because of his heart disease. That's what all the doctors have threatened to him after he refused to have a surgery. But all the people who agree with the doctors about having a surgery usually die shortly after the operation. I pray to God for my dad every day. I do hope that God exists, despite the claims of all our teachers that He does not; otherwise, I do not know to whom else I could turn to, for our grandfather Lenin is not going to help my dad at all.

When I was a small kid, my grandma used tell me not to steal candies while she was away. She told me God in heaven would see everything, for God can see everything and everybody at the same time. I never questioned the fact. It was enough for me to know that God saw me. That's how I came to believe in Him.

I remember my grandma telling me that God could see my heart, and if I had a good heart, He would reward me.

She told me also that looks don't matter to Him. Yeah, not to Him, but they definitely matter to people, and very very much, by the way. People, at least my classmates, love you for your good looks, not for your good heart. Who cares about Samanta's heart?

Sometimes I feel sorry for my mom, too. She has always that panic-stricken expression on her face; besides, she is unnecessarily nervous and over-concerned about everything. I guess it's partly because she, too, is worried about Dad. At least she has a good job. She can get foreign candies and sometimes even some clothes from abroad. However, she can never get jeans, and I want to have real jeans so bad. Maybe if I had jeans my classmates would look differently at me.

10. I think I am having a crush on a guy from the ninth grade. He's got the funny last name Cook. I know that Anda, a very fat and very conceited girl in my class, is having crush on him too. Now me and Anda are sitting at the same desk. When she told me about Cook I was stunned, for I thought she was still hopelessly in love with the nasty Uldis. When I reminded her about that, she just rolled her eyes as big as a frog's, spat on the ground so vehemently that I had to jump aside, and said, "Pee that jerk. I think my tongue will rot if I dare to mention his name one more time." I do not know what has happened between them. I guess Anda found out that Uldis is mocking her in the most insolent ways behind her back.

Anyway, Cook is the handsomest guy in the whole school. Of course I know I have no hopes concerning him. I didn't even plan to have a crush on him. But it all just happened. Last week at school I was left alone in the clothes closet. I was buttoning my coat and ready to leave . . . when suddenly I noticed my hat was missing. I wouldn't have cared about the hat much. However, I knew very well I could never appear in front of my mother and still hope to stay alive after losing my hat somewhere. I desperately started to search for my hat; it was nowhere to be found.

Suddenly, there was Cook standing right in front of me with my hat in his hand; he was smiling at me. I was so embarrassed I didn't know where to look. I was blushing horribly. I silently cursed myself for blushing, but I couldn't help it. The stupid moment seemed like eternity to me. Cook was twisting my hat and smiling. I stretched my hand to grab my hat and then run away and slam the closet door and leave him all alone there. I was about to grab my hat, but he put the hand with my hat behind his back and then—Oh!—then he leaned his face so incredibly close to mine and whispered, "What favor will I get for finding your hat?" I could feel his breath on my cheek and my nose. I was about to stammer something like, "thank you," when he laughed and put his hand on the door knob. "Never mind, you will pay me back some other time," he said. I still do not get the point about what he meant by repaying him. I do not know how it all happened, but I was totally helpless under his spell. He is so handsome, especially the way he smiles. I just can't get that out of my mind.

Of course I didn't tell Anda about it. I think if I told her, it would ruin our friendship. She is so jealous. I cannot share my secret with anyone, but that makes me so happy I am the only one who knows it. Sometimes I am so happy that I smile during the class, and when I meet Anda's questioning gaze, I put on an even broader smile. Anda says Cook resembles a little bit the movie star Patrick Swayze from *Dirty Dancing*.

I do not know how to define these strange feelings I have for Cook. Is that what's called love? I guess Samanta could enlighten me about these matters, but I never speak to Samanta. Or let us say she never speaks to me.

Anyway I feel weird when Cook passes me by in those long, noisy school halls. My heart starts beating faster, and I feel the heat running into my cheeks and I cast down my eyes and I cannot even look at him and—oh!—I behave like a ninny and a fool!

11. Since in our country God does not exist, we are not supposed to celebrate His birth either. No Christmas. New Years is all we have, but we can celebrate two times. If you are Russian, you raise your glass at 23.00, which is midnight in Moscow. All over Russia, people raise their glasses at midnight Moscow time. This is what Anastasia does. Latvians raise their glasses at 24.00, midnight Riga time. If you are that great miracle, Russians and Latvians who get along, you can celebrate twice.

But there is no Christmas celebration. I remember my grandma telling me about the birth of Jesus and about some mysterious salvation Jesus brought into the world.

Well, to be honest it doesn't make much sense to me. I even do not have a complete understanding of who is God and who is Jesus. When my grandmother was young, they had to study scriptures from the Bible and go to church. It was a mandatory thing, for such were the requirements at their schools. Now we are being taught that there's no God and that we humans have developed from monkeys. I cannot imagine that one of my great- great- great- great-grandmothers was an actual gorilla. I think it's funny. Neither can I imagine Jesus Christ and that mysterious salvation he is supposed to bring to us.

Most of our churches are closed anyway. Many of them have been changed into museums and shops and even, in the country, places to store the grain. A few are still open, but only old people attend them. If young people go there, they risk to be kicked out of Pioneers or even out of the communist party, and in that way they lose all the advantages the communist party offers them, like, for example, the communist shops, or a better apartment, or summer cottage by the seashore in Jurmala.

I remember a story about one teacher who went to church one Sunday. After that she wasn't allowed to teach anymore for fear that she might poison the heads of the young and promising Pioneers.

Nevertheless, our family is always celebrating Christmas. Usually we even manage to have a real Christmas tree. Even though it's pretty small, it makes our train compartment room look more appealing and welcome. My mother is also baking some pastries and cookies.

My dad always looks sad on Christmas Eve. Sometimes I think I am hurting him too much. I am being obstinate and disobedient, but I hate it when he forces me to eat vitamins and wear mittens and a hat until the month of May. My horrible hat just gives more bread to my mockers.

Once he told me that I am being too thorny for a girl. Thorny? I don't know. I guess I am pretty nasty, but even if I tried to be more kind and gentle, nobody would like me anyway. I like to be nasty, for that's the mask covering my vulnerability. I usually make a grumpy face when I have to pass through the crowds of my mockers, like the guys at school and Mitja's friends. There's a Russian saying, "One becomes a wolf just because the life is hard on him." I guess I am thorny because of all that hurt and unhappiness inside me. If you are not happy you can't help being thorny.

I guess I am often nasty, too, because I am defensive. I am fed up of everyone attacking me and correcting me. I often burst into tears. I hate myself. I can stare at my reflection in the mirror for hours, and it makes me hate myself even more. My legs are too long, my arms are too thin. I have no waist. My nose is too big. And worst of all, I have started to develop breasts. My classmates call me "sausage" and "beanpole." I do not like my house, my train compartment room, or my class. And I do not like the changes in my body.

12. During the holidays, I am going to be at my grandmother's. That's been already decided. I hate it there. There's never hot water, and the kitchen is dirty, stinky and cold.

My grandmother is a weird woman. She cannot get along with anyone. Actually, she's at war with all her neighbors, for she is living in a communal house too. Well, it's the county collective's house. All the people live together. They work together in fields and barns, and get some copper money for all their hard work. Most women milk cows, and most men drive tractors. Such is the future for every girl or boy growing up in the country.

My grandma used to work for the collective, too. She was a shepherd for cows and pigs. Now, however, she is too old to do anything besides nagging her neighbors.

When my mother comes, they fight all the time. I do not understand why they hate each other so much. I remember when I was a little kid and they were fighting, I couldn't endure that. I dragged myself into some remote corner and cried hysterically until there were no tears left. Usually after such crying I got fever. I wonder if these fights and my desperate weeping in the corner has affected me somehow, so that I am kind of psycho now.

Now I do not give a shit for these fights anymore. When they start yelling at each other, I run away from the house. I go to the big oak tree right next to the wheat field, climb at the very top of it and hide myself into the branches and leaves.

In the winter time I simply go out and wander around in the fields until I am exhausted and my feet are wet and cold. I feel lost at such times.

In the country I have some friends. Those are the kids at the age of 6 and 7. I play with them, and they seem to like me. Since I do not have any real friends of my own age, I enjoy their company. Together we climb the trees and swim in the little dirty duck pond near the house. Sometimes we sneak away to the woods and pick the wild strawberries. I love the way the wild strawberries smell. Their smell reminds me of something far, beautiful and unreachable—something of the beauty of life I am missing, simply passing by.

13.

The winter holidays were quiet and peaceful. I suffered through the time at Grandma's easier than usual. She was real nice to me. Actually she is always nice to me. Of all the people in the world she seems to love me the most, and that's amazing.

On Christmas Eve after everyone had gone to bed, I was sitting alone in the kitchen and thinking. I do not know what it is, but I feel sorry for people, for all people. They seem so helpless and frail and vulnerable confronted with calamities and disasters. I feel sorry for my loved ones first. For my dad most of all. I can see he's suffering, and I cannot help him. I am constantly terrorized by fear that he may die. I feel sorry for my mom, too. Even though she's got a nasty nature, there's something about her that touches my heart to the very depth.

So the holiday is over, and today is the first school day in the new year. I had a resolution that I would be a better student in the new year, but already after the first class I realized how empty and hopeless such resolutions are. I get so easily bored in classes. I cannot concentrate on what the teacher is trying to say, and then I do not care much. There's nothing that will ever change my life anyway.

14. Tomorrow I have to work in the kitchen. Everyone in eighth and ninth grade has to work in the kitchen one day in the month. Tomorrow is my turn. Fat Anda will be there, too. In the recent times we have become friends. She is conceited and thinks she's better than me, for at New Year's party she was dancing with Uldis; it was the first time in her life she was dancing with a guy, and now she is putting such airs about it. She doesn't know, of course, that Uldis behind her back is calling her a fat cow. I know also that he was dancing with her only because he had a bet with one of his nasty friends. I know also the reason why guys are not dancing with me is because I am one foot taller than all of them, and they feel weird about it. Well, there's that handsome guy named Kristians— he is as tall as me and he is staring at me all the time, yet he has never asked me to dance with him. Urzula thinks he is in love with me. What a nonsense!

Kristians is going to be in the kitchen, too, tomorrow, and I am afraid so is that nasty Uldis.

Usually I like to be in the kitchen. It means you do not have to be in the classes for the whole day, and you can get as much dessert as you want.

We are supposed to help the kitchen ladies: fat, rude and dirty Russian women beyond the middle age. They cook the food and serve the tables. We are supposed to help them to serve the tables at each meal time and also to take all the dirty dishes away after eating.

During the other time we are to watch that there are no other kids in the kitchen except for us. Usually we have plenty of free time, and all we do is fool around. We play hide-and-seek, or try to catch each other, or sometimes have vegetable fights. We pick all the vegetable that are left and throw them at each other. This drives the kitchen ladies nuts the most.

15. Today for the work in the kitchen were assigned four guys from our class and only two of us girls: me and the fat Anda. I knew from the very beginning it meant trouble. Me and Anda are among the most scorned people in the class, Anda because she is incredibly fat and I because I am tall. I knew guys were going to bully and attack us in all the possible ways.

We defended ourselves like heroes today; we fought with rugs and vegetables and Anda even splashed grape juice on Uldis's new jeans. Uldis was throwing at Anda the tray with bread, but instead he hit Kristians, who kicked him in the ass.

I had a personal fight with Uldis, too. He was calling me a sausage again (which I hate most of all). I hit him in the face. It's not very ladylike, but I am so fed up of people calling names at me. He was trying to break my arm. I started to pull his hair . . . in the end I saw I wouldn't be able to get rid of him that easy, so I kicked him hard in a private place. He got mad like a bull, and I knew I was in the trouble, so I ran as fast as I could, knocking over the table with vegetables, and hid myself behind the back of one of those fat ladies. The lady was exasperated, of course. She threatened to go and talk to my teacher. She said, "All the girls are like girls except for this one; she is so boy-crazy that she cannot maintain a proper behavior even in the kitchen." Boy-crazy? I have never been crazy after anyone. And no one has ever been crazy after me.

16. Oh, what a day! I do not even know how to tell it. I am so overwhelmed, so excited and so incredibly happy. I guess for the first time of my life I feel genuinely happy. Today after the math class, the teacher sent me to fetch some books for the literature class. I was walking down to the library when suddenly the doors of one of the classrooms opened and Cook came out, and we met in the middle of the hall. I stopped and for the first time I stared straight into his eyes, and he stared back and smiled. At me! At the ugliest of all ugly white crows!

When, in my stupidity, I told the accident to Anda, she just shrugged and said, "It's a nonsense; you've got to be dreaming. Do not ever mix your dreams with the reality. Didn't you know that his favorite is Sanita from the ninth grade?" Well, I do not care if Anda believes me or not, but I know for sure I wasn't dreaming. Anda is just jealous, for despite her fat body she is considered, at least according to her own understanding, to be a better quality than I am.

17. Yesterday night I couldn't fall asleep. I tried to, but I could not. I was too excited and too happy! Now, whenever I close my eyes, I see Cook's smile, and he looks so cute when he smiles, and I feel that surge of happiness running through my whole body. This feeling is so new and fascinating to me. I wonder what color his eyes are: brown, hazel. Sometimes late at night I hear my parents snoring, but I cannot think of anything but him, and I cannot even fall asleep.

I cannot talk about my happiness to anyone, least of all to my mother. Whenever I mention some of the guys' names to her, she gives me that severe look and says, "You'd better concentrate on your math tests." Of course it's all foolishness to her, the guys and falling in love. She herself was damn boring and so industrious at school that one can get sick of such people. I know, for my grandma told me that. She never went out or did anything that wasn't connected with school or studies. Besides, she wasn't even a bit interested in guys. I wonder how she got married to my dad at all. She cannot understand me, for I am so different than her. She's so dry and practical and insensitive about most matters of life. I, however, am over-sensitive about all matters, especially what concerns love and all that comes out if it. I have been always dreaming about having a boyfriend since I turned eleven. If I had a boy friend, we could go for walks, we could hold hands, we could go to the disco and slow dance, and nobody would be able to mock me anymore. This all would be if I had a boyfriend.

18. Currently we are having great crisis at school. Some people from our class have refused to wear the red ties. The teacher is in distress. She may lose her job if somebody finds out about it. More and more boys, instead of wearing the little badges with Lenin's head, are wearing the badges resembling maroon-white-maroon flags. They risk to get beat up by Russian kids. Russian and Latvian kids seem to hate each other as strongly and as bitterly as their parents do. I had heard the rumors also that instead of the odious school uniforms we will be allowed to wear whatever dress we wish.

The new president of the Soviet Union, Michael Gorbatschow, in the latest forum has declared that each Soviet Republic can freely discuss all issues and freely express their points of view about certain happenings in the country and certain governmental institutions. He has come to conclusion that we cannot go on like before; we need some fresh and radical changes. The "new era" started by Gorbatschow is called *Perestroika*. More and more newspapers have started to sharply criticize the Soviet government and their ruling methods. On the street corners people whisper that *Perestroika* is the beginning of the collapse of the Soviet Empire. Gorbatschow has even allowed people to start their own businesses. The so-called cooperative businesses have started to grow like mushrooms after summer rain.

Unfortunately the majority of these new businessmen do not seem to have honest intentions. People say that the private businesses are in the hands of the offsprings of the mafia. There's robbing and stealing throughout the whole large Soviet Union. All the natural resources are being drastically devastated. People, along with my two aunts, Olga and Zelma, are wondering how far it can go and where it will lead us all.

The majority people are just weeping and wailing because the government has stopped taking care of them. The situation in the country gets more and more tense, because the inflation is increasing rapidly. Many useless Soviet-time factories are at stillstand. The former workers of these factories are in despair, for they are unable to find any other occupation.

Every day there appear more and more freedom fighters full of noble ideas. They say we have not many things to lose, and they are ready to risk everything for freedom. Unfortunately their zeal lasts only until they find a comfortable apartment and a safe position in the chairs of the government.

One such freedom fighter is the former journalist Dainis Ivans, whose family—a wife and two kids—also live in a communal apartment, in a room almost as small as ours. As he himself describes it, his kids are sleeping in two-storey beds. Dainis Ivans, however, is willing to risk, to fight and to win. Our math teacher speaks about him a lot. Wherever she herself or somebody else mentions his name, there's always that gleam in her eyes and her cheeks turn red. I find it funny.

19. On the way home from school, I read thousands of ugly filthy graffiti against Latvians in tunnels and on the wall of the central train station. Russian teen gangs hang out at the twilight hours all over the streets of Riga.

Outwardly I am excited about all the events recently happening in the country and about the swift changes. Inwardly I am still so tangled up in my own problems that I am simply not able to care much about what is going on around me.

20. Samanta has dyed her hair and she is wearing make up even to school. Because of all the changes brought about by perestroika, we are allowed to wear to school whatever we want; there's another misery for me. All the girls, at least all the top girls, are wearing jeans and pullovers and make-up. Only me and Urzula are wearing these odious uniform skirts which do not have any style and usually are longer than knee length. I know I look disgusting in it. I burst into tears whenever I have to put it on, but my mother says, "The skirt is good enough for school." So that my misery may be complete, I am forced to wear also my mother's old, gray woolen jacket, which looks too big and too baggy on me. I hate my school bag, too. I have had it at least for five years, and even though my dad has repaired it, still it looks ugly.

When I remember the ugly remark Samanta once made about my bag, tears of anger and bitterness run into my eyes. She was standing outside the school with Svens and the whole bunch of top girls, when she saw me she said, "Look at her bag . . . my mother would be ashamed to use such a bag even for carrying the potatoes from the Central Market." The others started to laugh. I was too hurt to give her a decent reply.

21. I always knew one day I would show Samanta, and that day came sooner than I expected. We were in German class, when teacher without any warnings made us take a test. I know German better than anyone else in the class, and I know also that Samanta is one of the weakest students in German. I remember when teacher ordered each one of us to find a separate desk, Samanta sat down right in front of me. I knew I would not tell her anything if she asks me. When the teacher explained the test, I noticed Samanta nervously fidgeting in her chair. When the teacher turned away, Samanta turned around and looked pleadingly at me. I pretended that I was deep into my work and didn't notice anything. Samanta whispered something and passed me a note . . . I pretended that I didn't see the note, and, as if by accident (yet on purpose), threw it on the floor. Samanta's eyes flashed. The teacher had noticed something; she was coming straight to where we sat. She picked up the paper and looked at me for a while. I just shrugged and made an appearance that I didn't have the slightest idea of what she wanted from me. I guess she recognized Samanta's hand writing. She bent over to Samanta and ordered her to leave the classroom. Samanta looked at the teacher, and, even though she was scared, said to her, "Please let me continue my test. I won't do it anymore, I promise."

Samanta is the most spoiled child at school. All the teachers are trying to flatter her, even though her success in the classes isn't that remarkable. She always gets through somehow, while the others have to stay in the same class for one more year. I guess it's because her parents are active in the communist party; besides, their relatives from abroad send them all kinds of clothes and other valuable things, and they make a business selling it to our teachers who do not have relatives abroad. However, the German teacher apparently has not been bribed yet by Samanta's parents. She ordered Samanta to leave the classroom, and when Samanta repeated her pleas, the teacher looked at her indignantly and said, "Don't you understand what *no* means? You think if you have pretty looks and parents with bags of money, you can do whatever you please? Well you are deeply mistaken. Why should I throw others out of the classroom for cheating and spare you? In God's eyes we all are equal."

At the mentioning God's name the whole classroom gasped. Everyone was excited and ready for discussion. However, Samanta was sent out and the teacher ordered, "The rest of you get to your tests, please, and I do not want to see anyone turning around or especially turning towards..." and then she mentioned my name. Suddenly all eyes were on me. Some looks were full of jeers, some of respect.

After the class I saw Samanta standing in the hall surrounded by dozens of other girls. She was in tears. Svens was holding her hand and comforting her by promises that he was going to help her, for he is quite good at German. When Samanta saw me, she jerked away from his hold and screamed at the top of her voice, "You are to blame for everything." She attacked me, trying to hit me, but I pushed her away with so much strength that she fell on the floor.

She jumped up and seized me, but I pushed her away one more time. Unfortunately, exactly at that moment Mrs. Klavina appeared in the hall. I knew it meant trouble; however, I was too proud to run away. When she came closer, the rest of the girls all screamed, pointing at me. "She pushed Samanta; she pushed her on the floor."

Mrs. Klavina asked me and Samanta to come with her into her office. She questioned me: "Why did you push her?"

I said, "Because she was jeering at me and calling names, and she is hurting me all the time. I am just getting fed up with it."

"I was not!" Samanta exclaimed in a voice of an abused child.

For a while she didn't say anything, just looked at us both and then slowly began to speak. "Is fighting and calling names a proper way for the girls at the eighth grade to settle their affairs and misunderstandings?"

I said, "But Samanta attacked me. What was I supposed to do? Let her push me and hurt me?"

To this the teacher said, "Only savages in the jungle settle their affairs by pushing and fighting each other. We live in a civilized world. We live in the country where all people are free and equal, in the country where there are no wars anymore because the human race has reached its highest stage of development in the evolution. We are free and happy nation, and for this happiness to continue each one of us has a responsibility to be a good and faithful servant to our Soviet Union."

After such a monologue she refused any further questioning. All she said was, "You should be ashamed of yourselves!"

On the way out she grabbed my hand and said, "Your behavior will be unsatisfactory this semester." Of course my behavior will be unsatisfactory, and Samanta's won't. Where is there the equality the teacher was talking about? She didn't even try to go deeper into the matter, and it's all because Samanta's daddy has relatives abroad and is bringing to that particular teacher blouses and jackets, and my dad has a sick heart and has no relatives abroad and there's no way he could get nice clothes to bribe my teachers.

I bet if Samanta had pushed me, nobody would even pay a bit of attention to the matter, for who am I in comparison with Samanta? Equality? Then why are some people rich and some still poor, why do some people get the best apartments in Riga and some like my dad have to wait on lists forever? Why do some have the permission to use special shops and some don't?

I have come to the conclusion that all these talks about happiness and the great welfare of the Soviet Union is a lot of bullshits, for if it was true, why should our teachers be so eager to get foreign clothes from Samanta's dad? If we were so free and happy here, why should there be secret talks and underground meetings that prepare for rebellion against the Soviet government?

And concerning the highest stage of the development of the human race in our country, if our people really were that intelligent, why should they yell at each other and push each other in a row for bananas? I think monkeys are more polite to each other while sharing bananas.

But then monkeys have bananas all over the place, while Soviet people see them maybe once a year.

22. Sometimes Urzula asks me to come over to her place. I like these visits, even though she is also living in a communal apartment, and her living room, which is also used as a four-people bedroom, is not much bigger than mine. Urzula also doesn't have trendy clothes and she does have fat legs, but she does seem to be much more positive about life than I am. Maybe she has more self-confidence. Of course, she's got an older sister (with as fat legs as herself). It's amazing and unbelievable, but they are best friends. Besides, Karlis likes her; that's visible. It doesn't matter that he is the smallest and the tiniest boy in the whole class, it doesn't even matter that he is the worst student of all (although Urzula herself is one of the worst students of all the girls in the class). All that matters, in this case, is that he is a boy, and if you are liked by a boy, no matter how miserable looking that creature may be, you are definitely one step higher on the common evaluation system of looks and talents of each individual in the class than if you are not liked by anyone at all.

Urzula has the newest "Modern Talking" record. Even Mitja does not have that one yet.

On these happy times we listen to the music, eat cookies and chocolate candies and talk about the matters of life. The feeling that Cook possibly likes me has already faded away. Since that remarkable day we have met in the hall countless times, and he has never honored me with merely a look. Of course what a haughtiness of me to think that Cook could possibly like me!

The German teacher has gone away from our school. Either she left on her own, or maybe she was asked to leave because of throwing out Samanta and mentioning God in front of the pupils. Nobody knows.

23. I have started to grow long hair, and today for the first time I was wearing a short skirt to school. At least shorter than the knee length. Knee-length and longer is my most hated type of skirt. The very thought of putting on a skirt seemed terrifying to me. My legs are too skinny and too ugly for wearing a skirt; they have no shape at all. I think putting on a skirt this morning was a great act of courage. Of course I was preparing to be mocked and called sausage and beanpole and pine tree, but once and for all I was determined not to take these jeers close to heart. Some days ago I had decided that I was meant for solitude, and that's exactly what differs me from other people. Since that day I made a firm resolution that I will behave differently. I will be cold and unapproachable, and I will not let anyone close to me. I will act weird, I will write poetry about the things like dead birds and horse shits, and I will wear what I please, and if somebody tries to mock me, I will direct to him or to her a cold look of contempt and just walk away without saying anything. I won't show anybody that I am hurting. Such was my resolution, and I am determined to cling to it no matter what.

On my way to school I rehearsed all the possible expressions and looks of hatred and contempt meant for my mockers. When I opened the door to our classroom I was ready for the cold war. I suspected it would be a ruthless war. However, to my GREAT surprise no one laughed; no one even spat any of the sharp remarks I am so used to hear. I noticed the guys staring from aside. I am still not sure what was behind those stares; however, they didn't say anything aloud. Maybe my air of dignity and coldness kept them back. I do not know, but the day was a success. I didn't even need to put into practice any of my carefully rehearsed looks of contempt.

Still, this resolution probably wasn't the best option, for my grandma from dad's side always tells me that if deep down in your heart you harbor hatred and contempt for others, you can't get any far in life. Well, whatever. I am so tired of always being a source of amusement for others that I have to do something about it. If I came to school and people started to bully me and I just stood there and smiled like a ninny, would it help me? No! I won't let them hurt me any longer. I will show them what I am capable of. They and only they are to blame for my insecurity and hesitance concerning all matters of life. I have been too scared to try anything new. Since today I will do what my heart pleases.

I feel much better now since I had a courage enough to make the first step by putting on that short skirt. Today when I came home, I went even so far that I tried to put on a little bit of make-up: the lipstick (carrot red, the only one my mother has and then never uses) looked freaky. The eye liner, however, became me very well. Maybe I should start to wear a little bit of make-up, just a little bit. Such little that my mother, a woman strongly virtuous and therefore prejudiced, will not even notice.

And although I still have no waist, I think I am starting to get used to the size and the shape of my breasts.

24. A girl named Daina is my new friend now. She is a newcomer from some other school. She came to our school only because her dad got a higher position in the party and was given a brand new apartment in a freshly built house. Daina is a very beautiful and delicate creature, but to my amazement she's an outcast too. I guess because she acts weird at times and is exceedingly timid with boys. Since my resolution day, however, I have declared an open war with boys in our class, at least with the the ones who mock me.

I sometimes have fights with guys, such as pulling each other's hair, or trying to break each other's arms; however, in most cases whenever they try to provoke me, I give them a contemptuous grin, turn around and walk away showing them by my body language how much I really despise them. They have noticed that I have turned from a scared and insecure creature into a furious fighter. Inside I am the same scared girl, but I am trying to be brave, trying to show them that they cannot hurt me, and if they even try, they know what they get.

Once I slapped Svens for kicking my old bag. When he turned his surprised eyes on me I told him, "If you ever touch my bag with your shitty feet again you will regret it for the rest of your miserable life!" That was a horrible threat even though I am not even sure what I could do to make Svens to regret it for the rest of his life.

Daina admires me. She is scared of boys more than the devil himself. She cannot even talk to them. Sometimes when they bully her, I am the one who has to defend her. I have Daina's full admiration and respect. In my notebook, however, meant for my parents to inform them about my success at school, I have a line, "Behavior—unsatisfactory." I know my mother will die of shame when she finds out.

25. We three white crows—me, Urzula and Daina—stick together. I guess we are VERY different from the others in the class, white crows indeed in a crowd of black ones. Each one of us three has something that differs her from those so-called normal people. I differ with my ugliness,

Urzula with her thick legs (because the rest of her body is quite skinny), and Daina with her weird ways.

Daina is still wearing braids, like traditional Latvian girls, which is highly unacceptable in the society of Samanta and her friends. If you want to be Samanta's friend you have to dye your hair, you have to wear make-up, you have to have trendy clothes, and you have to be liked by at least one of the top boys. If you do not meet even one of these requirements, you are not eligible to enter her society. All the girls in class are obsessed just to be in Samanta's crew. They steal make-up from their mothers, cry days and nights to get from their parents jeans and pullovers with foreign words on them (they cannot guess how their parents could possibly get these things) and hang on all the top guys' necks just to be on top. It's probably quite a hard career which requires lots of effort, lots of tears and lots of gumption.

We three do not even strive, for we know we will never fit these standards, and since I have chosen the way of solitude I try to pretend that I am not a bit impressed by their good looks and their success with boys.

26. Sometimes I still hang out with fat Anda; however, I sense she considers me inferior, for she also uses make-up and goes to the discos and wears trendy clothes. She's got some relatives in Australia. The only reason she is not accepted in Samanta's crew is that she isn't being liked by a boy, because she is too fat. Even though once she bragged to me that she's been kissing with some boy after disco, I do not believe it. She is telling lies and making up stories to get her self-assurance and self-confidence.

I think much about kissing in the recent time. It must be something wonderful, or why else would people get so excited about it? I think I would like to try once, but nobody even wants to dance with me. How can I get to kissing without starting with a dance? A fast dance at first, and then a slow dance afterwards and then my imagination doesn't go that far.

I am very ignorant about these kissing matters. Sometimes in the movies I see naked people laying next to each other in bed and kissing and caressing each other. When I told it my mom, she hushed me and told me not to watch such dirty and nasty things. She said I should be ashamed to think of such things when I am so young.

I do feel ashamed really. I do not know exactly why I like watching such things. Maybe because I am growing up and changing. Samanta for sure has kissed with somebody. She's got so many boyfriends. She must be very experienced and I guess not only in the kissing area. I guess

Daina and Urzula are as ignorant as I am. I once asked Daina what she thinks about kissing and slow dancing. She turned all red and managed to stammer, "My mom doesn't let me do any such things; she tells me not to even think of such things."

I do not know why most people, especially our parents, are so scared that we get to know something of that kind. I do not understand what's wrong with it and why I should feel ashamed. I have never asked Urzula about these matters. I wonder if she ever thinks about kissing at all. She doesn't look like one who would.

27. There's definitely something wrong with this world, or maybe with this place, yet I can't put my finger on what it is.

My aunt Olga says it's the double-faced life people are forced to lead in this country. You can't show what you truly think or believe. Instead, you are supposed to think and act in accordance with the principles and standards set by the communists. You must swear that you are truly devoted to the party. If you do not do it, you do not get the bananas and red meat in the communist shops; instead, you are considered to be a rebel, a dangerous element, a threat to our precious wonderland, somebody who must be silenced immediately. People who are aware of the wrongs, misdeeds and injustices done to the population by the communist party are forced to swallow their anger in silence and pretend they are too dull and too dumb to notice anything. In such a way they are living in constant lies and deception, and by serving the communist party, they're contradicting their own consciences. Nobody who goes against his own conscience can feel comfortable or happy.

Yet there is a spark of hope in all this miserable grayness. All the recent demonstrations and speeches at the feet of the Monument of Freedom, the excitement and mixed emotions in the crowds of people. More and more people, even kids from our class, are wearing the badges resembling maroon-white-maroon flags. I wish I had one, too. I don't know where people get them, for you cannot buy them in the shops or anywhere.

My both aunts, even Zelma who used to be a passionate and devoted member of the communist party, now has turned her coat over and is running along with her younger sister to all the possible meetings and gatherings. I like to mock my aunt Zelma sometimes. I ask her, "How come you, a devoted-to-death communist, now are running to all the gatherings of the Popular Front?" To my sneers she just pushes out her lower lip and says in a hurt voice, "I did believe in them; they promised a bright and secure future for all of us, even though the beginning may be rough. However, it's been rough already at least for fifty years. I put all my trust in them. I gave them the best years of my youth and my physical strength, I gave them my votes and my very heart; yet all I have got now in my old days is a 25-rubli pension. If I had only known about their wicked schemes, about their deception! However, they concealed everything from us ordinary people."

Zelma is full of hurt pride and bitterness. I feel sorry when I hurt her even more with my foolish remarks about her party times and about her devotion to the Popular Front now. The Popular Front seems to be full of brave folks indeed. They are scared of nothing. They for sure have already been added to the black books of the KGB.

My parents are also considering joining the Popular Front. Maybe there is a chance for getting an apartment. We have heard that some of the Popular Front members have got new apartments, SEPARATE apartments.

28. It's not far until summer holidays. Everyone at school is excited. All the grown-ups, including my mom and dad, are fussing over political matters. It's kind of exciting to watch the huge demonstrations, to see the ever-growing crowds at the Monument of Freedom, to hear Latvian folk songs being sung by thousands and thousands of people. But I have come to the conclusion that even though people have fought for equality, it cannot be maintained in a human society for a long time. People are people, and there will always be some who will like to be superior, who like to determine things for others and put others under their rule. The same way there will always be the rich and the poor even in such a country as the Soviet Union. In my opinion, there are many other things which are far more important than political meetings and excited speeches. These other things are: the end of the school year, the last big party for all the eighth-graders, the possible dress I am going to wear.

And Cook. Even if he doesn't like me, I still think about him at times.

I am not sure that I am going to attend the party at all. I hate to sit in the corner like an old cake and watch others dancing. Urzula and Daina are trying to persuade me, but I don't know.

29. The party was gorgeous. They played the newest hits all the time. Most of the time, as I had expected, Urzula, Daina, and I sat in the corner observing others dancing and enjoying themselves. I kept on remembering the saying my grandma told me once: "Let the joy of others be yours." Oh, what stupid words these are! I think one should never watch the joy of others, for it will just make them more aware of their own misery and it will make them even more unhappy. Well, that's my life's philosophy.

Because I didn't even expect anything other than sitting in the corner, I was sad but not at all disappointed.

In the middle of the party I told Daina and Urzula that I needed to go to the bathroom. The truth, however, was that I was simply sick and tired of their silly chattering and wanted to be alone with myself. I was leaving the hall when Cook stopped me in the door. He leaned his face very close to mine, so close that I had to move back a little bit or our noses would touch, and said with a grin, "Will you dance with me?"

At first I couldn't believe my ears, but then a bitter realization came over me; he, the same as Uldis, has a bet with somebody that he will dance with me.

I asked him, "With whom did you bet about me?"

He gave me a weird look. "What do you mean?"

I repeated my question. "With whom did you bet that you will actually dance with me?"

"Oh, I see. No, I didn't bet with anyone. Why are you asking me such a question?"

"Because I know nobody would ever dance with me just for dancing's sake?"

"You are a silly girl," he said and grabbed my hand.

"But I don't even know how to dance." I tried to resist, but he pulled me towards the crowd of people. I was mortified, for it was a slow dance. I had never danced it before. I didn't even know what to do. Cook put his arms around my waist and pulled me close. I could feel the warmth of his chest. He was so strong. I felt dizzy. He was so wonderful. We didn't dance actually, we just stood there in the middle of a large crowd of people hugging each other. I wanted to pinch my ear lobe to make myself sure that it was real.

Suddenly among the many other faces in the crowd I noticed Sanita's face and a crooked grin directed to me and to Cook. As through the mist I remembered what Anda told me once: Sanita was supposed to be Cook's sweetheart. I noticed Cook grinning back at her maliciously.

I knew then he asked me to dance because he wanted to hurt Sanita, for what reasons only the devil knows. He grabbed me and pulled me into the crowd not because he liked me or because I was special in his eyes. I was simply close to hand—a total accident. I looked at him; he stared back. His eyes were dull and remote. Only then I noticed that he was drunk; his breath stank with alcohol. I freed myself from his grasp and ran into the hall, hot and bitter tears running down my cheeks. He had made a fool out of me. Tomorrow the whole school will talk that Cook was so drunk he couldn't even tell which girl he was dancing with. Tomorrow girls will walk around in pairs, and when they see me they will put their heads together and say, "Did you see yesterday Cook dancing with this sausage? He must have been really drunk. She will never get a boyfriend, for she is taller than any guy in school."

I will not go to school tomorrow. It's the last day of school, anyway.

30. It's already June, and I am glad school is over. This summer, to my great surprise, I am staying in Riga. My mother managed to find me a job in the most hated Sungarden, the botanical garden in Mezaparks. Every year the Sungarden organizes a summer job program for kids who have nothing to do during the summer months. They believe that kids should learn to love hard work and discipline at an early age.

Every day I have to get up at 7 o'clock and put on old, shabby clothes, which emphasize my natural ugliness. Then, in such horrible clothes, I have to go through the very center of the city to get to the tram stop, and even then my torture and humiliation do not end, for I have to get onto the tram No. 11, which is full of people, and get to Mezaparks.

My major task at Sungarden is to pull out the weeds in beet fields or take care of flowers. Such people as Samanta and Svens, of course, aren't working during the summer months. They are having great fun in their summer cottages in Jurmala. They can swim every day and sunbathe, and in the mornings, walk along the sea shore in the white sand, and breathe in the fresh air smelling like pines. They can watch sunsets and take boat rides and get plenty of ice cream. I get to Jurmala very seldom, since my mom is working the whole summer and my dad is sick. I am not allowed to go there with my friends, because my mother is very worried about me. I think she worries too much about stupid things.

However, about things she should really be concerned, she doesn't pay a heed to them. I tell her about my humiliation while wearing these shabby clothes throughout the center of the city. I ask her why she doesn't let me to wear some other clothes and take the shabby ones with me. I tell her I will run away from home. I really mean it, but she doesn't believe me. She just gives me that indignant look of hers and says, "Do not pretend to be a lady when you are not. I was never in my life ashamed to wear work clothes; instead I was proud of them."

Yeah, and when I complain about the work in Sungarden, she calls me a lazy bone and threatens to send me to grandma's. In such cases from the two evils—either staying with grandmother through the whole summer and laboring for her, or staying in Riga and working in Sungarden—I would choose the second one. At least then I have a chance of staying in Riga.

31. Today my both aunts were like on fire, for some kind of rebellious meeting was planned at the Monument of Freedom. They didn't let me and Dad alone. They wanted us both to come and watch. Despite my hearty protests and grumblings, I was dragged there, and I had to stand for hours in hot sun, listen to boring talks, and watch some weird people putting the flowers at the feet of the Freedom Monument. That was something unusual at least, for until today, nobody was allowed to put flowers at the Monument of Freedom. The group of people who put the flowers at the Monument is called Helsinki 86. I heard people talking that these are freedom and human rights fighters. For a couple of minutes the Latvian flag was displayed—not the flag of Soviet Latvia, but the maroon-white-maroon one, the one Latvia possessed during its time of independence after the First World War until the Second World War. After a while, however, the talks were disturbed by the noise of a motorcycle parade, which meant that any further talks were not possible, and we got to go home. People were exasperated. I heard the crowd saying, "Rubiks did it on purpose. He organized the parade to ruin the meeting." Rubiks is somebody in the government. The government didn't like the meeting or all the fuss about putting flowers at the monument. They saw it as a spark of rebellion against the existing political powers. Even though Gorbatschow has given the permission to think and feel free, the old communist system is stagnant, prejudiced and unchangable. The communist party is scared, because they do not know how far they can let people think and feel freely. They know one thing for sure: even though Gorbatschow has permitted them to think and feel freely, he did NOT intend them to ACT freely and ruin the whole communist system. I think Gorbatschow himself has realized what a huge mistake he has made.

32. I am having extremely exciting summer holidays. The most part of my days I spend bending my back in the beet fields under the scorching sun. My clothes, especially my slacks, are dirty and heavy with soil; the skin on my hands and palms is dry and scratched, my face is covered with dirt and stained with sweat. Oh, what a disgusting picture I make. I look like a street person.

I pray always that I will not meet any of my classmates or acquaintances on the way home, but of course what you fear the most, it eventually happens. Today I had just got off the tram. I was in good spirits. I thought, "I will be home soon, and then I will change my clothes." Usually I am so into my own world that I do not notice anything or anybody around me. I was already near my house when I suddenly heard "hello" from somewhere. The voice sounded strangely familiar. I looked over my shoulder, and to my great horror I noticed Cook standing next to the ice cream shop. He was staring at me and grinning, with an ice cream cone in his hand. He looked so strong and handsome and careless. I dashed into my house and didn't even look back.

All I wanted was to get into the apartment unnoticed by any of my neighbours, get into the bathroom, and change. Running up the stairs I prayed that Anastasia or Mitja wouldn't be at home. I carefully turned the key in the lock. Shit! There was light in hall. That was a bad sign; Anastasia was not only at home, she was in the kitchen washing dishes and her little girl Alesja was taking a bath. There was not even a possibility to wash my hands and face. OK, I decided I would have to wait. I wanted to sneak into my room and at least change my clothes without anyone noticing me. Then Mitja came into the hall. The hall is very narrow, and we had to pass each other. Mitja pushed me as if accidentally, but I knew it wasn't accidentally. I pushed him back. I heard him complaining in the kitchen to Anastasia. Anastasia was comforting him: "Do not take her close to your heart; what can you expect from a child who was born in this peasant and beggar family? She has no culture, no upbringing; Gaida, her mom, is yelling at her constantly; of course she is just savage. They do not have even money to take her to the theater or to movies."

How dare Anastasia talk about my family like that? Yes, my parents indeed come from peasant families, but they are intelligent and cultural, especially my dad. And about the theater, it wasn't true either. Last week we went to the theater and on Sunday to the movies too. Mom and I go to the movies every week. We have never been rich or extravagant, yet we are NOT beggars either. It's not our fault that we have been given this shitty train compartment room and that my dad's got a heart's disease. Besides, her Mitja is a skinny and weak creature, a real softie, always complaining about something, courageous only behind the backs of his friends. But Anastasia is so proud of him. I think Anastasia is very narrow minded too; actually she's just a Philistine. All she thinks about is how to get foreign clothes in the black market and how to boast about the food they are having. I find it dull.

Usually Anastasia spends summers with her family in Jurmala. They have a summer cottage there. We all await that moment with great anticipation. At least for some weeks we can use the bathroom and kitchen, which is a luxury we do not enjoy while Anastasia is at home. The other family is quiet and decent. They're Latvians, of course. Nevertheless, my mom has managed to create a war situation even with them, too.

I hate this apartment! There's no privacy possible. Not even in the hours of night. There are always drinking parties and loud laughter at nights. Little Alesja, disturbed by the loud and obnoxious voices of her parents and their nightly friends, is unable to sleep. So she crawls out of her bedroom (Anastasia's family have four rooms; each member of the family is entitled to his or her own room, even little Alesja) and is restlessly running back and forth in the hall. Nobody notices her but my mother. She wakes up from the noise, goes into the hall and yells at Alesja. Crying, Alesja flees to her parents' room, and the quarrels start.

Today it seems to me there's no hope of ever getting into the bathroom. Sometimes I wonder if Anastasia does it on purpose when she notices that others may need the bathroom too.

These summer evenings are long and boring for me. I can't wait till my work at Sungarden is over, but when I come home I don't know what to do with myself. I cannot find any other occupation than to spin sad thoughts.

33. Today as usual I was working in the Sungarden when I noticed nasty Uldis from our class also pulling weeds at the back of the rose garden. I could never imagine that anybody else but me was destined for such an exciting summer job. Anyway the sight of Uldis pulling weeds from the rose beds was quite hilarious. I hoped he wouldn't notice me, but of course if I had noticed him, he had noticed me, too. He went all red and stuck out his tongue at me. I did exactly the same thing. Deep down inside I thought, "You just try to touch me, and I will rip your head off." However, we both felt too embarrassed and too humiliated by the circumstances to start a fight. Besides Uldis was alone, and he is a coward when he is alone. He would not fight me, for he is scared of me. I am taller than he is, and he knows also that I can kick and bite and pinch and pull hair and scratch his face. He knows it very well, for he has experienced it on his own skin.

I don't know why boys are such cowards, for I am a girl and I always have to defend myself alone. I have chosen the way of solitude and isolation. Instead of being kicked out of the so-called normal society as an outcast, I'd rather go away myself. In such a way I will at least maintain my dignity. "Hey, I don't need anybody." These are the words I tell to myself every morning I wake up. This is inspiration for every day, and I think I am doing pretty good at it. If I was beautiful I could afford myself the luxury to be kind and loving, but since I am not, and since I am constantly attacked only because I am not beautiful (as if it was in my power to choose my own face and body and now everybody is blaming me for not choosing a better one), I have to defend myself somehow and I have to be tough.

And such I was with the nasty Uldis. I could sense Uldis observing me from the corner of his eye. I thought indignantly, "Why are you staring at me? Mind your own business. Your rose bed is full of weeds, while mine is almost done."

Suddenly he came a step closer to me and said, "You tell your friend, that fat cow, that she must stop calling me every night. I am sick and tired of it."

I just shrugged and said, "I have no idea whom are you talking about."

"So you hang out with the fat cow, and now you pretend you do not know anything?"

"Indeed I do not. Besides it's not my responsibility to tell anybody what to do or not to do. If you do not like her calls tell her yourself."

He moved even closer to me and asked, "Then tell me one thing. Why are you always so thorny?"

Thorny? That was the same thing my dad is telling me always.

I turned to Uldis and said, "I am thorny because that has become my life's necessity to defend myself against all kind of nerds and morons like . . ." I almost blurted out "you" but stopped in time.

"Like?"

"Like some guys in our class."

"You know what?"

"What?" I asked in a voice full of suspicion.

"You have changed drastically during this year."

"What do you mean?"

"You used to be timid and shy, but now you are hating everybody and fighting everybody. You do not let anyone get close to you."

"That's just my protection system. I do not want anybody to get close to me and then hurt me. I am being hurt every day, and trust me I have had enough. I know you all think that I am the ugliest and the nastiest and the lowest, but I tell you I do not give a shit about what you all think."

Uldis stared at me for a while and then said in a low and solemn voice, "You are not the ugliest. You are considered to be one of ugliest and weirdest, but you are not the ugliest."

"Thank you. That's a great comfort indeed and a great compliment too; however, there's no need for you to flatter me," I said sarcastically.

He was observing me. There was a deep frown on his forehead. "By the way, you are not that ugly after all. I think it's just a perception people have about you."

I looked at him sternly. "Uldis, tell me honestly what's under your skin. I know you hate me, and I do not get the point why are you trying to kiss my ass now."

Uldis pretended that he hadn't heard my remark. He asked me after a while, "Is it really true that the fat cow is after me?"

31

I said, "If you mean Anda, she's got a crush on Cook." As I mentioned Cook's name I bit my own tongue.

"Ha-ha," Uldis roared. "So Anda is having a crush on Cook? And what about you?"

His gaze was impertinent. I had a strong desire to slap him, not because he asked me that particular question, but I simply didn't like the way he stared at me. I blushed and said in a cold voice, "I do not have a crush on anybody. I hate all boys, and I know they hate me and after all it is none of your damned business to meddle into my affairs asking all kinds of silly questions."

"OK. I will tell you which girl I like from the class; but then you must tell me the truth about Anda."

"I do not care whom you like or whom you do not. I am not going to tell you anything and please stop being an old parcel of gossip."

He was trying to throw at me a piece of soil. I told him to go to hell. The lady who is responsible for our work appeared in the door. She looked at the rose bed. "Uldis," she exclaimed, "You should be ashamed! I have given you the easiest task today and you haven't accomplished anything. I am really disappointed."

She turned around and I saw Uldis making faces at her behind her back.

34. Today was the hottest day of the whole summer. I was lying next to the muddy duck pond, with my eyes closed and my mind floating in some unearthly dimension. I was unable to hear or see anything around me. Suddenly something touched my half naked breasts — my horrible breasts, I am so ashamed of them, for in the recent times they have grown so large, way too large for my age and my skinny body. I drowsily opened my eyes, and to my mortification there were two guys standing right next to me and staring down at me with weird grins on their tanned faces. One was touching my breasts with a twig. I jumped at my feet in an instant. I was too startled and too embarrassed to kick or punch them. One of them was actually my cousin Janis. He lives seven kilometers from here, but I haven't seen him for ages, and he looks quiet different now.

"Hey," he said and laughed heartily. "You have quite grown up since the time I last saw you."

"So have you."

"The point is, we came to invite you to the Ligo party."

Midsummer festivity has been prohibited for years, yet since dear Mr. Gorbatschow has permitted people to feel, and act and breathe more freely, Ligo is an officially acknowledged festivity now in Latvia. At the bonfires some people get drunk and then decide to jump over the bonfires. Disaster is inevitable, and every year many people are burned or injured during Ligo night. There is eating cheese and pastries and an endless beer drinking. There's also a tale about this festivity that mostly concerns young people—young couples actually. The young couples in the midsummer night have to go far way from all the other (drunk) folks in a search for some mysterious flower which is believed to blossom only during the midsummer night. It's funny, though, that the flower shows its blossoms only to the young people and only to the people of the opposite sex. But of course everyone, including the little kids, knows that all this flower thing is a lot of bullshits, and the search for a mysterious flower is actually an excuse for love-making... which must be something wonderful, although I don't quite know how it happens.

So on Saturday night I, with pounding heart and trembling knees, was preparing for the Ligo party. I always get nervous when I have to go to a party. I always have difficulty with finding what to wear. I have plenty of dresses and jackets and skirts, but none of them fits my crazy body the way it is supposed to. Anyway, I chose a light summer dress with big red flowers. I knew I looked freaky, but since I knew also that most of the party I would be leaning against the walls and watching others dancing, I didn't care much how I looked.

It was a warm and pleasant evening unusual for Ligo. It's always rainy and cold during Ligo nights. When I arrived at the party place, my cousin and a bunch of other guys were already there. Since it was a nice and pleasant evening, the party was held outside. All around the dancing spot were enormous tables covered with cheese and pastry plates. On each table were at least ten bottles with beer, and the men sitting at the tables were carefully hiding some other kind of bottles under the tables. In those bottles was something stronger than just beer, which was being saved for later.

The music was playing at its loudest, folk songs mainly, and also some sickly sweet love songs with a touch of sentiment borrowed from the Germans. These songs are mainly played for old people to help them to remember their youth and their first love and all that bullshit. I get sick of listening to such music. However, Janis promised that later when the old people got drunk and drowsy and deserted the dancing spot, there was going to be some disco music. I thought, "When the disco starts, I will quietly sneak away and go home." I am not afraid of darkness, and besides, the Ligo night is the shortest and the lightest night in the whole year. I like walking at nights in the full moon. I sneak around the house like a ghost. Or maybe I am just a lunatic.

Anyway, I was determined to leave before the disco started. Janis had noticed me. He was showing me to his friends from a distance. I was mortified. I thought he should be ashamed of such a cousin. He should have pretended that he didn't even know me, but—oh God!—they were all coming straight to me.

"Those are my friends, Peters, Marcis and Linards," he told me. "And this is my cousin."

The three guys grinned at me, yet I could sense they were as embarrassed as I was. It gave me courage. I grinned back, pretending that they hadn't made the slightest impression on me. Sometimes I am acting like a wild cat, always ready for attack, even though danger may not be even close.

One of the guys, Linards, asked me to come and sit at their table. I knew my dress with the large, vulgar flowers made my ugliiness even more obvious, and there were those huge blue circles under my eyes. I looked like the Phantom of the Opera. Yet I went with him anyway, and I tried my best to pretend that I was very confident about my appearance. I sat at table and tried to look conceited and spoiled. All the guys, including Janis, were jumping around me offering food and drinks.

"Ha," I thought to myself. "Those guys are country men; they haven't seen anything better. That's why they are jumping around me like bunch of fools."

One of them said, "I heard you are from Riga."

I looked at him and said, "Indeed I am." I am always proud of the fact that I am coming from a big city. The guy smiled and blushed. "So am I," he said in a shy voice. Well, I guess I was not the only person there from the city. We talked a lot about Riga, but we did not have any friends together, so we talked about places like Central Market and Mezaparks.

The time passed by swiftly. I hadn't even noticed that it was already midnight. For the first time in my whole entire life I was enjoying the party. Also for the first time I was drinking beer as much as I wanted. I thought happily to myself, "If my parents only could see me like this! They would swoon." Like all the other teens, I enjoy doing things that are bad in the eyes of the grown ups, and if they tell me to do one thing, they may be sure I'll do just the opposite.

I guess I was a little tipsy. But not drunk. Alcohol doesn't have any serious influence on me. I remember once I drank a half of my mother's wine bottle (she had bought it, she claimed, to improve her digestion) and absolutely nothing happened. I drank it because I wanted to know how it feels when you are drunk. When nothing happened, I was disappointed. Alcohol is of no use to me, and I honestly can't understand why people are so eager to drown their sorrows in a bottle of vodka, and why they are worried about the new government regulations. If vodka had magic power, I would drink as much as I wanted. Yet vodka would not take my ugliness away and might even increase it.

That night, however, I was drinking beer, and I was drinking as much as Janis and the other guys. I was almost as happy as on that day when Cook smiled at me in the dark school hall. I was watching the old people dancing and having fun. They looked odd, even ridiculous in their folk costumes, yet they seemed to enjoy the party a great deal. Some young couples were dancing too. I was watching them with that snobbish, mocking look in my eyes.

The folk dances were soon over, and the disco was about to start. I heard some old people saying to each other, "The show is over, and we have to free the stage for the young generation." I was about to disappear quickly and quietly. I took my jacket and got up to leave, when one of the guys named Marcis caught my hand.

"Where are you going?" he asked.

"Home," I said, and tried to free my hand from his grasp. He was so drunk, I suspected he hadn't been drinking the beer only.

"You can't go home. Who is going to dance with me?"

"I don't like to dance," I stammered. He jumped to his feet and started to drag me to the dance spot. I freed myself from his arms and started to walk away. He came after me.

"You cannot go away, you cannot go away alone in the middle of the night."

I said, "I am not afraid."

He grinned at me. "I will go with you for a little bit."

I shrugged. What could I say to him? He came right after me. I couldn't understand why he wanted to come with me. When the drunk voices died away, we were suddenly alone in a remote meadow. It was a full moon night. I could see our house from far away, the two chimneys and the white door. Marcis was right next to me, yet I avoided to look at him. His breath stank like alcohol. He took my hand into his. He was trying to look into my face, but I didn't want him to.

"You are nice, a very nice girl. And pretty too," he suddenly said.

"He is drunk. That's why he finds me nice and pretty," I thought to myself. "He cannot see very well now."

He sat down in the grass and pulled me down next to him. It was weird. He was looking at me, and I was staring back at him.

"When we were sitting at the table, I thought you were different," he said very quietly.

"What do you mean different?"

"I thought that you were a haughty city girl, yet you are shy."

Shy was the least I wanted to be. Of course everyone has noticed that I am shy and insecure.

"I am not shy," I said in a hurt voice.

"You are the white girl, aren't you?"

"What do you mean, white?" I questioned him.

"Well, you look so pure and so innocent."

"What is he talking about?" I wondered. "Innocent—you mean stupid, gullible, yes?" I questioned him.

He was smiling. "No, you are not stupid. You are—eh, it doesn't matter."

I stared at him, my eyes were asking for an explanation.

Suddenly he leaned his face close to mine. "Have you ever been with a guy?" he asked.

"Been where?" I asked. I couldn't get the head and the tail of what he was talking about.

He laughed. "I told you, you are innocent. What I mean is have you ever slept with a guy?"

"No. As far as I remember, I haven't even danced with anyone."

He laughed again.

"What is there so funny?" He was surely mocking me.

"You yourself are funny. I mean, you are such a child." His voice was caressing and tender.

I hate when somebody calls me a child. I may be a white crow and a failure, but I am definitely not a child anymore.

"I am not a child. I am quite grown up already," I said to him. "This fall I am going to be in the ninth grade already."

"How old are you actually?"

"I am already fourteen."

"Well then, I am sorry. I thought you were older." He laughed again and put his arm round my shoulders. He obviously had noticed that I was trembling.

It was pleasant to feel somebody's arm around me, even if it was an arm of a drunk person. After all, he was very nice.

"Are you still cold?" he asked me gently.

"Not anymore," I said, and leaned closer to him.

We were sitting there quite a while, wrapped in the full moon light and the aroma of the wild flowers around us. I think I fell asleep for while. I felt warm and comfortable. Then suddenly strange voices woke me up. I saw Janis and the other guys; they were yelling at Marcis.

Janis dragged me to my feet and ordered me to follow him. When we were far away from others, he turned to me and asked in a harsh voice, "Now tell me the truth, what did you do with Marcis?"

"Well, we walked and talked and then sat down."

"OK, spare me this romantic introduction. What did he do to you— honestly?"

"What did he do to me? What do you mean?"

"I mean, did he touch you?"

"Yes, he held my hand, and when we sat down, he put his arm around me, for I was cold."

"Do not pretend to be a bigger fool than you are."

"But I am not pretending."

"Well did he try to kiss you? Did he try to take your clothes off?"

"My clothes off? Why would he want to take my clothes off?"

"Are you really that stupid, or you are just making up? So how did he touch you? Tell me exactly where and how?"

"Well, okay, I will tell you everything in order. First he touched my hand, I think two, no, actually three times. Then he stared at me couple of times really heard, and then he sat down and pulled me down too."

"And?"

"And what?"

"Don't try my patience. What happened after that?"

"We were sitting and talking, and he told me that I was such a child. He told me that I was innocent and that I was pure. I just couldn't get the point. He asked me if I had ever slept with a guy, and of course I never have. I do not even know how it happens. In the movies they usually do not show how it actually works."

Suddenly Janis started to laugh. He put his arm around my waist and said, "Come! You are such a little freak, even though you are from the big city. Besides, you are drunk. I shouldn't have let you drink that much beer. Grandma will kill me, but one thing you must promise me, never, ever to follow the guys you do not know. Okay?"

"But I didn't follow him. He was actually following me. I just wanted to go home. I didn't want to stay for the disco, because I was afraid that . . . well, you know how ugly I am, and then I do not even know how to dance. I just never had a chance, for nobody ever asks me to dance."

My cousin was roaring with laughter. "Come, you are really drunk, and you need to have a good sleep before you appear at Grandma's. And do not tell anything to her, okay?"

"But why?"

"Let's go now. You are staying at our house for a while."

Only later I got to know what Janis had suspected. He thought that Marcis would rape me. Rape me? I have never feared that somebody could rape me. This is crazy. Mostly pretty women are raped. I was never afraid of being raped. Maybe Grandma is right that in all the bad

37

things one can find something good: I am so ugly, I will never have to fear to be raped.

Yet Marcis told me I was pretty. Well, he was drunk, and I have heard that for a drunk man every woman is beautiful.

Anyway, all that fuss brought at least some changes into my life and at least one drunkard has liked me. Isn't the life wonderful after all?

35.

My days at the Sungarden are coming to the end, and to my great horror just recently I got to know that for the rest of the summer I will be deported to my grandma's, which means I will be completely cut off from all the civilization. I will not see ice cream for weeks, and I will have to entertain myself playing with 6-7 year old kids. What exciting prospects!

Since it's the last week for us in Sungarden, a big party is planned at the end of the week with lots of food, music and performances. Urzula, as a very diligent worker, gets to lead a group of other students. Until this very day I can't get the point how Urzula can enjoy the work at the Sungarden so much. It is beyond my comprehension how somebody could find satisfaction in digging the soil like a bird looking for worms and getting all her clothes dirty and a sunburnt face. However, it's because she incapable of anything better than digging the soil. She's hopeless at school, even at the Latvian class. She hasn't got looks, like Samanta, to carry her through; besides, as I have noticed, she is kind-hearted but very simple-minded. I really do not want to be judgmental about my friend, but then I find a grim satisfaction in the fact that somebody is in a worse position than me. I guess I am very cruel and wicked if I can think this way and even find pleasure in such thoughts. At what way am I better than Urzula? Not at math, definitely. However, there's one thing I have found out about myself: I am not simple-minded.

I think a lot, and I analyze why things happen exactly this way and not the other way, why people act in certain ways in certain situations, why they say and do certain things. In such a way I have developed a sharp mind. Sometimes I can see people through. I can predict how they are going to act in a particular situation, because I have been observing them, and I know what to expect from them. I have been analyzing my own actions, and to my great surprise, even though I hoped to be unique in my ugliness and in the way I respond to the world and people around me, I have noticed that lots of people act the same way I do. They are as insecure and as uncertain of anything they say or do as I am.

Urzula, however, doesn't have a sharp mind about people or about anything. She seems to be happy in her little sunny, narrow world, and she doesn't long for anything else in her life. She's happy with her thick legs and her small and uncomfortable room. When I once asked her how she could tolerate living in such a small room, she just smiled and said, "I have plenty of flowers here and they make me happy." She is happy with the fact that Karlis, the teeny weeny freak in our class, likes her. She is happy digging the soil and getting dirty. She doesn't long for anything in her life. When I told about her to my grandma, my grandma just said, "That child knows how to be content with what God has given to her and that's a key to happiness in this life."

I do not understand her words! How can somebody be happy with a life like Urzula's? Yet she seems to be happy. She doesn't desire anything. She likes the way things are in her life. She even considers after the ninth grade to go and live in the country. The very thought seems repulsive to me: going to the country, being cut off from the whole civilization, living in the mud and stench, laboring for the collective milking their cows and pulling out weeds in the endless beet fields in the hottest sun, beet fields belonging not to you but to the collective, and getting only some copper money for all your labor. Always being shabbily dressed, always being away from the big and noisy Riga. No! If somebody would send me to live in the country, I would be dead after a year there. Not because of the work, however—because of boredom, because of the sorrow after a big and noisy place, because of unbearable longing for crowds of people around me. Country is nice, but not for me! I want . . . actually I do not know what exactly I want. Sometimes I feel as if I were a bird in a cage. I feel I could fly high and far, but I cannot even move my wings properly, for the top of the cage is half a foot above me. I seem to have so much inside me, so much to tell, that sometimes I feel as if all that stuff inside me is going to strangle me. I think I am longing for some other kind of life, everything around seems so colorless. Everybody around me is having a sullen face. All the world seems to be wrapped into a cover of sadness.

36. There was another demonstration a few days ago at the Monument of Freedom, but the government gave an order to the police to scatter the demonstrators. The poor policemen were utterly at a loss seeing the enormous crowds of people gathering at the Monument. They had no idea how to stop them. Then somebody made a suggestion to call the fire department and ask them to help out. The firemen indeed came and hosed the demonstrators with water.

This is the only time I regret not attending the demonstration. I was sent to the country to visit my grandmother, luckily only for a few days. I am supposed to be back for the party at the Sungarden, where I am assigned to be a witch at our play. I missed the demonstration, which must have been pretty exciting with the police and the firemen and water.

Aunt Olga is very glad she had a chance to be there, for now the demonstration is already a matter of history, something that will remain in all Latvians' memories for years. Young people who were there will be able to tell their children and grandchildren how they had been soaked with water fighting for the separation of their country from the Soviet Union.

Aunt Olga is in raptures, even though she is not married and she's already in her fifties, so her chances of getting grandchildren to tell the great events to are as well as impossible. She seems to be happy even without having children and grandchildren. She's also a member of the Popular Front, just like her older sister, and this new occupation takes all her time and energy. She is positively ecstatic about some freak, a freedom fighter named A, which is not his real name after all. He was very active at the recent demonstration. People consider him not to be all there; however, that doesn't stop him from fiercely attacking the ruling governmental forces, like the very Mister Rubiks, who ruined the Helsinki 86 gathering by ordering the motorcycles to ride around the Monument of Freedom and pretend they were having their parade exactly at the same time when Helsinki people were trying to speak. A is brave and aggressive, but a little foolish with his eagerness. He has a nasty habit of meddling into other people's affairs. He's been leading some opera chorus or something and has had some performances at the Monument of Freedom. He's been also active in the work of the Popular Front. However, most people refuse to take him seriously. Besides there is a gossip spreading around that he is gay and seducing little teenage boys. But maybe this gossip is being spread by KGB.

37. My aunt Olga is secretly attending some other meetings held in some park called Arkadija. People have been gathering there already more than a year and a half. She doesn't want to talk about it either to my dad or her other sister. She is scared they may freak out, for it must be a risky thing to go there every Sunday. She doesn't know, however, that my dad is very well informed about her secret goings on; he just pretends not to know anything about it. The meetings at Arkadija are organized by some Environmental Protection Club, but their name is one big disguise. They pretend they are coming together to discuss the environmental matters, for the pollution of the Baltic Sea and the Latvian rivers is a big issue currently. The truth is, as aunt Olga knows, their environmental concerns are just a mask. Once she told a funny story to me. One Sunday there was a meeting as usually. The weather was just perfect: warm and sunny. Leaves fill the branches of the huge maple trees, which are the pride of the park. The speeches were more passionate and more provoking that day. People looked cheerful. There was excitement and anticipation in the crowd. Suddenly some people noticed that amidst the freedom fighters there was also one small black figure with a video camera. The man—short and shabbily dressed, his nose bluish red from the chilly wind, and his eyes small like a pig's—was nervously searching through the crowd. People standing near him had noticed his odd behaviour and the camera, too. Somebody exclaimed, "It's a spy; get him out of here."

Some teenage boy yelled at the top of his voice, "Let's better beat him up!"

People started to push the poor creature, who was already so scared that probably he was wetting his pants. Of course, he was sent there to spy for KGB or maybe some party, so the hottest freedom fighters and speech givers could be entered into their black books and could receive a proper punishment, "for their insolent mouths have to be shut; after all, they are criticizing the sacredness and blamelessness of our communist party." That's how the communists think about our patriots and freedom fighters.

The little coward, suffering pushes and cursings, was desperately trying to find his way out of the infuriated crowd. Everyone was amused at the incident. The little man put his camera, which was nearly damaged, under his arm and changed his pace into the run. Maybe he belonged to the International Front that the communists and the Russians together have established in response to the Popular Front. The very title is stupid and inaccurate, for their so-called front has nothing to do with internationalism. However, Russians (who feel undermined and abused in Latvia) as well as Latvian communists like Rubiks (who proudly and obstinately have refused to turn over their coats and join the Popular Front) think that the name is perfect. By naming their organization an International Front, they are hoping to get recognized at an international level.

38. August is the last month of summer holiday, the last month of careless freedom. Of course, as I already expected, I am spending my last month of freedom cut off from civilization in a remote place in the country. While other people are enjoying the hot summer days somewhere near the sea in Jurmala, I am stuck in a remote and deserted place 300 kilometers away from Riga. Absolutely nothing is going on here. The days are hot, lazy and monotonous. Yesterday I was spending the day swimming in a muddy duck pond and riding my bike. While sitting in my grandma's potato and beet fields pulling the weeds, I have plenty of time to develop my philosophies. When I try to talk about my miseries to my grandmother, she says I am blowing things out of proportion. In her eyes I am just a grumbler and a rebel, and, as she warns me often, "such people are not pleasant to God." Well, whatever God may think about me, I will never see how a person can be content and happy spending the whole summer in beet fields either at the Sungarden or at the Grandma's. How can a person be happy, being aware of so many unpleasant about herself, which are TRUE?

39. My grandma often cannot sleep at nights, so she keeps on telling me stories about her life before the Second World War, when our country was an independent and sovereign land. She tells me how she was working for rich people as a servant. She was working in fields and also as a maid for spoiled young ladies. She tells about the parties and about her countless suitors. Grandma likes to remember all sorts of weird things from the old times, "the good old times" as she assures me. She liked the independent Latvia, even if she had to work for others. Those years seemed to be the golden times for our land. The large farms in the country were blossoming. The farmers were not only able to sell their products (like milk, butter, cheese, cottage cheese, beef and pork) in the inland, they were even exporting them to countries like Germany and Denmark. People living in big cities like Riga were mostly wealthy people, whose ancestors had come from the German gentry that used to rule in Latvia for more that 700 years. The majority of them were the owners of large factories, stores, pharmacies and hospitals. Grandma never forgets to mention the sentence, "Our capital, Riga, used to be rich and beautiful back then. But look at it now. They have turned it into a large, noisy, dirty Russian village."

Those memories always bring tears to my grandmother's eyes. I do not understand why my grandma likes those times so much. We are being taught at school those were the worst times of all. The poor people were treated like to slaves and were mercilessly exploited by those who were wealthier and more powerful. The poor had to work for others often for food only, and they had to submit to all the demands of their "employers" for anything; otherwise they might be thrown out on the street with nothing to take with them. When I mention that to my grandma, the large frown brings her bushy brows together and she says in a grumpy voice, "You, child, keep your mouth shut concerning the things you know nothing about. It's all a pure nonsense they are teaching you at school. They have deceived us and robbed us and . . . eh, there's no sense talking about that. Such talks just make me bitter."

My grandmother assures me that the people she was working for were good and kind people. They paid her a good wage and took care of her when she was sick. I usually do not argue with her much . . . after all, she is right: I know nothing about the life back then. Besides, I like to listen to these stories which introduce me to a completely different world. She never gets tired of describing the weekly balls and Christmas parties where servants were officially allowed to participate and even were treated as equal. My grandma was considered one of the most beautiful girls in the whole district, and in order to dance with her, the boys had to fight several tough fights. I usually listen to these party stories with a secret envy. Of course, I like to hear that my grandma was beautiful, but now there's very little left over from her beauty: her face is wrinkled like a wet rug, her hair is thin and gray now, and her much admired slender body has become plump and heavy . . . only her thin legs and her tiny feet are still the same. Now they look ludicrous in proportion with the rest of her body. How could she have so many suitors? How did she manage it? When I ask her directly, she just shrugs and rolls her eyes in that funny way: "In fact, I never knew all those womanly secrets on how to attract men," she says; "nevertheless, they were sticking to me like the glue. I simply couldn't help it. I swear I didn't do anything on purpose to attract them."

Her other stories, however, are not at all that exciting or pleasant. To some of them I listen with horror and disgust. Those are the stories about the war and about the deportation of the rich farmers to Siberia. From all those stories, one seems to be especially vivid and tragic to me. One day my grandma was visiting some of her relatives in Riga. She, of course, was completely uninformed and completely unaware about any kind of deportations going on in the country. At the train station she was surprised at the enormously large crowds of people everywhere; however, these seemed not to be the ordinary passengers. There was something desperate and horrifying about those crowds. People were grabbing at things which were falling out of their hands into the mud and were left there. Some were crying hysterically; some were searching through the crowds with an odd lost look in their eyes. They were too stunned and too terrified to be able to see anything. Some were hugging and holding each other close. The women were being separated from their husbands. Some parents had been taken away and kids knew nothing about it. There were families of which one part was ordered to get into the cattle carriages; not even the pregnant women were spared. The other parts were left alone. The platform was covered with notes, which were floating out of the small windows of the carriages like a cloud of enormous snowflakes. People were writing those notes hoping against the hope that their relatives and friends would find them.

Grandma was trying to pinch her hand to make sure she wasn't dreaming, to make sure it wasn't a bad nightmare where her mind was playing tricks on her.

Suddenly, among the many strangers in the crowd, she noticed her cousin. She was in her sixth month of pregnancy. She was very pale, trying to hold back the inevitable hysteria that would follow being separated from her husband. They were kissing each other, and maybe for the last time. Her older kid was not to be seen anywhere. Her mother was there, too, handing her a bag with some food. The daughter took it and accidentally dropped it into the mud. She didn't have enough energy or desire to pick it up later. She was too numbed by the unbearable pain of losing her husband and her other kid to be able to care for food, even though she might need it really bad on the long way. Grandma was trying to squeeze through the desperate crowd, but her cousin gave her a warning sign not to come too close. She was fearing that my grandma could be taken too, and Grandma was also having two little kids at home—my mom and my mom's sister.

Grandma waved to her cousin a desperate good bye, and since then she has not heard of her cousin. My grandma remembers also picking up the notes with following texts:

"Marijs, please take a good care of my flowers!"

"Peter and Anna, do not forget to feed the dog and the cat!"

"Henrij, no matter what, remember I love you!"

It's difficult for me to imagine what torture and cruelty those people have gone through. However, there's one question which doesn't give me peace. Who did it? Weren't those people who made the decisions about who was going to be deported and who wasn't the members of our beloved party, the same ones who speak of love and peace and a better future? After all, the communists were the ones who declared all people should be equal and should have equal properties. They simply couldn't stand that somebody could have more than they themselves, somebody who had earned it all working hard with his own two hands. After taking away the rich farmers' properties and deporting them to Siberia where they were welcomed by hard and fruitless work, starvation and death, the communists robbed their houses. They took all the good clothes, stole the jewelry and furniture, seized their land, and established those horrible collectives where people were forced to work for some copper money. Now, being wolves in the clothes of the sheep, they are making noble and heart-moving speeches about peace and love and a better future in our common land called the Soviet Union.

40. Grandma has told me also about the early collective farms, how she'd been milking cows, pulling weeds and picking potatoes on cold autumn days with bare hands only. Working for the cooperatives had ruined her health and had taken away her beauty and her good posture. It made her the way she is now: crooked, wrinkled and lame. However, my grandma has always been an optimist, and I greatly admire her for that. She has that weird saying: "In all the miseries and disasters, one can always find a little seed of happiness." I don't know what happiness I can possibly find in the fact that I am an ugly duckling. When I told her that, she just smiled. She cannot understand my sufferings, having been a beauty queen in her youth. "The ugly ducking may turn into a beautiful swan one day, but then you are not that ugly after all."

I know very well it's all a bullshits, and she is just trying to comfort me. Whatever. I won't shed tears about my ugliness anymore, for they're not helpful at all.

41. Today, I am sure, will be always mentioned in the history of our country, and in the history of all Baltic States. Already a month ago one could hear rumors that freedom fighters from all the Baltic States have in mind to organize a so-called Baltic chain. People would go out in the streets holding hands. Millions of people would hold hands and the chain would stretch throughout Estonia, Latvia, and Lithuania. The chain would symbolize the unity of the Baltic peoples in their common fight for independence. Baltic peoples do not have the guns or tanks to defend themselves. Being next to each other and holding hands, neighbour to neighbour, nation to nation, is the only way for us to demonstrate our unity and our mental, ethical and spiritual strength.

Most people considered the idea effective and unique, yet some, as always, were skeptical. They were simply scared that such a performances could bring Russian tanks into the capitals. Despite the oppositions and the conflicting opinions, the Baltic chain was actually made real today. People went out on Brivibas Street, Freedom Street—oh, how appropriate!—the old and the young, including toddlers and infants. Also people in wheelchairs, even the blind and the deaf. People went right in the middle of the driveway and took each other's hands. They were so many that they had to stand in three, four rows holding hands. Old people were supported by their relatives and friends, daddies were holding their kids on their necks. There were thousands and thousands of people at the sidewalks as well. And foreign tourists, who now are partly permitted to enter the Soviet Republics, and American Latvians who are visiting their new-found relatives in their newly reclaimed home town, Riga.

A mixture of excitement, joy and anguish filled the air. People were full of hope yet scared and desperate. The future is unknown and uncertain. We all know that Russia can easily wipe us out if they want to, for they have an enormous army, guns, tanks and bombs. And if they do, the rest of the world will not know anything about it. For them the Baltic States are just another part of Russia, and who cares if Russia decides to fight against its own parts?

If I am sometimes not interested in all these freedom fights, it's because I have too many other things to think and to worry about, which in my opinion are more important and more tragic. Yet the Baltic chain, the crowds of people standing in the warm dusky August evening holding hands—all this scene somehow strangely touched my heart. Suddenly I realized that it's our future we are fighting for, our common future, and my own future as well, for I am a part of this very nation. Intellectually I have known all my life that I belong to the nation called Latvians, yet this particular evening for the first time I felt it deep within myself. I lived it through. I understood it not only with my mind but with my heart and soul as well. It was a revelation to me.

42. It's the first of September, which means that a new school year has begun. This very first day is like a messenger of all the sufferings in store for the students and of countless teachings, preachings, and rebukings coming from the teachers. I watch all kinds of pupils passing me by. The little ones, the first graders, are so touching. Their little faces seem to be more pale than usual, yet they are glowing with excitement and anticipation. Some of them are still holding tight to their mom's or daddy's hand, yet they are trying to be brave, trying to look grown up and sophisticated. Some kids are so tiny and frail that their enormous backpacks seem to be as heavy as stones on their backs. Well, that's part of the burden they are to carry, starting with this day, and throughout the rest of their school years. The older kids—the third, fourth and fifth graders—seem to be more confident and self-assured. They are excited all over to see each other again. They already know what the school life means and what its advantages and disadvantages are. They are already accustomed to their heavy backpacks, early mornings, boring homeworks and furious teachers. These kids have already experienced the good times and the rough times at school.

Yet this day, even though the beginning of all kinds of troubles and sufferings, is a day of celebration. The kids, starting with the smallest one to the twelfth-graders, are all dressed up: girls in black skirts and white blouses, and boys in black slacks and white shirts. The air is thick with smells of flowers and women's perfumes. Soon the solemn speeches will start, the most annoying part of the whole affair. The teachers will talk, sing praises to each other and to our government. Our country is NUMBER ONE, and the fact that I, a small, ugly teenager, sometimes dare to disagree with it does not change the opinion of others. The teachers will also express their hopes concerning their pupils. All the kids, even the smallest ones, will be forced to listen to all that three-hour-long bullshits. Kids are forced to stand still while the teachers are talking, or they may get themselves into a serious trouble by daring to disturb the sacred speeches. So the kids stand, bored and tired. There are even cases when some smaller ones faint. Their fainting is a protest against the long and tiresome speeches, which, by the way, are exactly the same each and every year, so the older students like twelfth-graders probably get stomach aches at being forced to listen to the same bullshits so many times.

After the speeches the kids who had brought some flowers with them (and majority of them have) rush to the dizzy and blushing teachers and give the flowers to their enlighteners and the path-showers. Some teachers are so trapped in the heaps of flowers that they have to call for help to carry them away. After all this fuss is over, the kids are permitted to go to their classrooms and sit down.

Today I am watching my classmates with curiosity and a secret envy as always. They all have changed so much during the summer. In our school, and I guess in all the other schools as well, it's a sort of unwritten law that during the summer holiday one has to change upside down and inside out. Like the way you look and the way you dress. If you don't, you aren't being respected anymore.

Of course at the end of each school year I have an iron hard resolution to change so that nobody would recognize the white crow anymore. I want so very much to become a respectable bird. Isn't this a pretty humble request?

Usually at the end of August I am in a deep despair, for I have frantically tried to do something radical with my hair style (if my hair has any style at all) or with the way I dress. Yet instead of making me look better and prettier, these changes just make me look more ridiculous. And what radical changes can I perform if my mother doesn't let me to dye my hair or use any kind of make-up? And concerning my clothes, all my clothes look old fashioned and worn out. When I put them on, they seem to emphasize my clumsiness and ugliness. Since I do not have any relatives abroad, I have to bury my dream of ever getting a pair of REAL jeans. And if you do not have real jeans, you are not a normal human being. At least not in our class.

No matter how desperately I try, I am still that same at the beginning of every school year, and this year is not an exception. I secretly cast some stares at Samanta. She has dyed her hair again; besides she has also changed her make-up. Her eyes, in some mysterious way, seem to have grown even bigger and even more expressive. Her best friend, or let us better say her right hand, Evija, has changed too, especially her hair. In my opinion Evija is even more beautiful than Samanta, and I have heard rumours that most guys (except for Svens of course, who is totally blinded by Samanta's charms) have admitted that, too. Yet Samanta still has more authority than Evija. Maybe because Evija is a nicer and kinder person and not so bossy as Samanta. Evija is nice even to me. Samanta is simply more popular, and there's nothing anyone can do about it.

43. It's another boring math class. I cannot concentrate on what the teacher is trying to say, because Samanta is giggling behind my back. She is writing her silly letters to somebody again. Last week she had a large quarrel with Evija. They do not sit together anymore. Now Amanda has become Samanta's right hand. Amanda is another top girl in our class. Concerning the beauty of the face, Amanda could probably even surpass Samanta. Unfortunately, Amanda has got skinny and bowed legs, and she has no tits at all.

They are talking about guys. They mention several names, including Cook's name. Does Amanda have anything to do with Cook?

The teacher gets up from her chair and she clears her throat. She looks freaky, with her enormous glasses, a huge badge with artificial pearls on her chest, and mud brown, old-fashioned slacks. She has noticed Samanta rocking in her chair, which is strictly forbidden, for rocking is considered a vandalism towards the precious school inventory consisting of some old desks covered with filthy graffiti and some chairs with shaky legs. But maybe the shaky legs are the reason for such a prohibition.

"Samanta," the teacher's voice is sharp and unpleasant, "I would like to hear the answer of the exercise four." I turn around, for I hear the moans of horror behind me.

Samanta gets up. She is very pale. Her hands are shaking. Amanda is pale too.

"Samanta, I am waiting. . . ." The teacher stops abruptly. Samanta's odd appearance has scared her too.

"Samanta are you not feeling well?"

"Yes, teacher . . . if you please excuse me. . . ." Samanta takes her backpack and rushes out.

After the class there are rumors all around. The kids are surrounding Amanda.

"Well I do not know how it all happened. . . I just saw this thing disappearing in her mouth."

"How did she manage to swallow it?" Kids are pushing each other and yelling excitedly past each other. I cannot tell what they are talking about.

Later, however, I learn that the teacher had caught Samanta rocking in her chair and she had scared Samanta, who had a pen in her mouth and accidentally swallowed the pen's cap. The cap, which is about four centimeters long, did not go straight down into her stomach; unfortunately it stuck somewhere in Samanta's chest. Samanta was taken to the hospital immediately. I think now she's okay already, but still a little traumatized by the shock.

When the rumors calm down a little bit, we are sent back to the classes. During the Latvian class, the teacher asks us to write a composition with a title "If I were. . . ." We have to fill the empty space with our own ideas. Lots of my classmates choose "If I were a president, a politician, a leader of the Popular Front," even such silly things as "if I were a princess, or a spaceman." The desire of becoming a space man was especially popular some years ago, for in the Soviet Union it is considered to be the noblest occupation of all. Unfortunately, since the wind of change has stared to blow, young kids' choices concerning their future occupation have also started to change.

I am trying to think of some extraordinary idea. In the end I write, "If I were a black crow. . . ." I write a four-page composition, a very abstract one by the way, about what the difference between the white crow and the black crow is. I think the teacher will be furious having to read such a nonsense. However, later she tells me that she enjoyed my composition a lot, for to her it seemed to be very original.

44. The new year has turned out to be a tragic year for our country and for our sister countries Lithuania and Estonia as well. In the end of February and the beginning of March one of our governors asked OMON soldiers to come from Moscow to Riga and surround the TV and radio to make all possible communication and connections impossible. In his opinion, the new Latvian political powers (the members and supporters of the Popular Front) have become too rebellious and too impudent. Their mouths have to be shut before the whole world knows what is actually going on in the Baltic States—and neither Moscow nor our local communists would want the world to know it.

Work in the press house, where most newspapers are being printed, has ceased, and the Russian army has surrounded the building. There have been also several attempts at taking the TV studio and the radio station.

Bad news came from our neigbour country Lithuania. Many people had gone out in streets unarmed, to protest the Russian army. The army received the command to quiet the rebels, so Russian tanks started to drive right into the crowds. Thirteen people were killed. The TV studio in Vilnius was already surrounded by OMON, but operators from Kaunas TV were announcing events as they took place. The people in the studio were panic-stricken, for they already could hear the steps of the OMON soldiers marching downstairs. Suddenly all connections were disrupted, and all we saw on our television sets was the gray and white stripes. So we knew that the Russians had taken the Kaunas TV studio as well.

In Riga one can see the Russian tanks, like large ugly monsters, prowling around the narrow streets of the old city and also along Brivibas Street. There is nothing on TV or radio except news and reports of the latest events on the streets of Riga and in the Baltic States in general. My family is in despair, especially Dad. Since he has this horrible heart disease, he gets sick if he worries, yet he does worry for it's impossible not to. Being sick, he sees all the things in a more tragic light than they actually are. I am miserable, too. Because of the tragic events in the country, school has been canceled, and for the first time in my life I do not feel happy about it. I spend my days sitting on a couch curled under a warm blanket. Even though it's quite warm in the room, I feel strangely cold. All kinds of fears in a colour of mist are creeping all over the place. I am scared and depressed. I try to listen to some music, but it doesn't help at all. I look up at my dad's face, and he looks old and sad. I am seriously scared that he might get sick from all this tension and die.

It's already the third day like this. I am tired of sitting at home. I have no idea how to kill the time. Anastasia's family has mysteriously disappeared somewhere. Are they frightened too, even though they are Russians? Or have they received advanced warning of some coming invasion? No one is at home besides Dad and me. Mom is still working. I walk back and forth in the long dark hall. The apartment is so frighteningly quiet since little whimpy Alesja is away. Olga and Zelma call often and talk for a long time with my dad. He thinks we will be wiped out by the Russians in a few days. I will be dead along with everybody else. I do NOT want to be dead.

My aunts sound frightened too, yet they are not so pessimistic as Dad. They think we will get through it with a safe skin.

One of the Popular Front leaders is asking all the Latvian people to come and meet at the coast of the Daugava. My dad also wants to go, even though he is not feeling well. People are in a strange mood. Nobody really knows what will happen after the meeting at the coast. Russian tanks are all over the streets; one can see also the OMON people in their odd uniforms crowding next to the Lattelecom building.

45. It is cold and gray outside, so cold that it hurts, and there is no snow. Somebody on the radio said that all of us who are able to walk should go to the churches, which are now open, and pray. I guess it's all we have left. After the prayer, the radio said, we go to the Daugava coast, and what happens, that happens. So crowds of people were rushing to the churches, the old and the young, parents dragging their kids along with them. I felt like the day we were all united in the Baltic Chain. Danger and distress is what makes us one again. The churches were crowded, people praying with tears in their eyes. When all the hope is gone, there is nothing left but God.

Stuck in the middle of the crowd of sobbing people I thought to myself, "God must see and know how we feel. After all there must be some justice in this world."

Again I am thinking about God, after a long interval. I always remember Him when the times are rough, but then God is there to help. Sometimes I talk to Him about anything and about everything. I don't pray; I am simply telling Him how things are in my life. When everybody is so scared, we cling to Him for help and comfort. Deep in my own thoughts, I heard the preacher only at intervals. "Let all those who died in Lithuania rest in peace. Help us to guard and protect our land, strengthen us in the spirit." All people were taking the holy bread and drinking from the cup which is supposed to be Jesus' blood. The Lord's Supper was a completely new experience to me. I didn't understand much about the mystery of Jesus's blood, I only knew that if people are talking about blood and taking the Lord's Supper, it must be serious. I have seen in movies and read in books that the Lord's Supper is usually offered to those who are about to depart from this world.

After the church, everyone was supposed to leave for the Daugava coast, and nobody knew if they will still be alive this very night.

46. Now in Riga everybody is talking about barricades and the necessity of having them on the streets. All day long there are people coming to Riga from all over the Latvia. The cooperatives have given them the cars and lorries which normally are used for service only. People have left their children and their old relatives at home and have come to Riga, not sure if they will ever come back. Everybody, big and small, is carrying lumber and all kinds of construction materials, like panels and sand, to block the main streets. Some have brought even fishing nets. In their opinion the fishing nets are a very good remedy for hindering the tanks. Old people who have nothing to give for barricades are giving away their wood, which they had bought for an expensive price.

The barricades are constantly guarded by people from all the districts and far away villages of Latvia. Some are armed with no weapons other than the knives normally used to butcher the pigs, and some have only sticks. Almost all the traffic is stopped. There are bonfires at the each barricade. The people who are guarding the barricades pretend to be happy and carefree. They are telling jokes and singing the Latvian folk songs, trying to fight against the demons of fear. Yet everybody can feel the unpleasant tension in the air. Time after time the OMON soldiers are passing by, staring insolently at the frozen barricade guards.

Some crazy and adventurous teens have run away from their homes to Riga to take part in all the great events happening here. There are countless announcements on the radio from their parents, who are worried to death about their beloved ones. The rest of us who are not guarding the barricades support and cheer up our heroes. The only thing we can do is to bring them food and something hot to drink. So most of women, including my two aunts, are constantly baking pastries and filling up mugs with hot tea or coffee. Even my mother has managed to bake some muffins.

The doctors and everyone else who has some medical practice or some experience have hidden themselves in empty churches in case the fighting really starts and there is any need for medical help. The OMON people have already been provoked by our tireless singing and by the posters people have put at the top of the barricades as mocks to the communist government.

People guard the barricades 24 hours a day, despite the cold and the threatening stares of OMON troops, despite the sounds of the monstrous tanks driving back and forth right on the next street. We do not leave because we do not have any other choice: either the Russians will wipe us all out and we will be dead, or if we give in they will enslave us again. It's better to be dead than to live under Russian control.

47. All the horrible fuss is over, but not without a tragedy. Dad and I were watching the news on TV when suddenly we heard real gunshots coming straight from Bastejkalns Park near our house. The OMON troops were firing at the TV operators, who were filming there. One of them was shot dead, one was seriously injured, and the third victim—by pure accident—was a teenage boy, just a by-passer. Fortunately the OMON people hadn't noticed the other television cameras, and some foreign television reporters as well, who were hiding themselves behind the massive walls of the Freedom Monument. The information was immediately delivered to the TV and radio stations abroad, and in an instant the whole world got to know what was actually going on in the Baltics. For many of people I am sure it was the first time of hearing about Baltic States. At least if we die, we will not die forgotten by the rest of the world.

48. For a couple of weeks everything is quiet on the streets of Riga. Nothing has been solved, but at least we are not dead. I can worry about my school again, and about my own life.

I am a high school student now, which is equal to being grown up. I so very very much want to be grown up. My new school was established only a year ago. It is called The Grammar School of Nordic Languages. It think it sounds great. Aunt Olga persuaded me to come to this school, since I have a gift for learning foreign languages fast. Who knows? Maybe I wasn't born in vain after all. I will study languages and I will be something in the future.

If it wasn't for my aunt, I would have never even given a thought of coming to this school. I would have never dared to appear in such a new and modern school. However, I was simply dragged there and introduced to the school director and the teaching staff. They all were observing me, a pale girl in an old pink pullover and black skirt, below the knee length, of course. My mother said that to appear before the director I had to look decent. Her understanding of decent is a skirt below the knee length. I think at first they were quite skeptical, even displeased with such a girl daring to appear in their offices, yet when I showed them my marks, they looked on me with much kinder eyes.

The very next week they invited me to take an entrance exam in German, since German is my strong side. I passed the exam, not at all hoping to pass it, and now I am here. The system has decided that this will be my school and my life. I have new classmates too. They are also from different schools. They treat me a little better than the ones in the old school.

I had a firm resolution not to show my new classmates what an ugly duckling and a failure I am, yet on the very first day I already showed them how inferior I am, and they of course took advantage of it. One of the guys asked me something about the timetable. I looked at him with eyes full of fear and confusion, blushed and mumbled something incoherent. He gave me a weird smile and left. When I realized what a great impression I had made about myself, bitter tears were already burning behind my eyelids. No matter how I try, I never succeed. However, I didn't let them roll down my cheeks; I looked into the restroom mirror and smiled at my miserable reflection. The picture in the mirror looked so funny and queer that I had to laugh. Well, I blushed only because he was a guy and because I feel awkward in front of any male. The girls, my new classmates, are not any better than Samanta and her crew. They are as conceited and spoiled by the guys' attention as Samanta was.

Now when I am more aware of growing into a woman, I have noticed that I am more attracted to boys than I was in the old school. Unfortunately I am scared that they may find out about it, and then hate me, so I try to avoid them. Nobody is attacking me or mocking me anymore, yet I know my new classmates think that I am odd. When I try to talk to them, I try to tell a joke. They just stare at me in surprise. I know I am not welcome in their company.

49. In the recent times I have noticed my appearance is not so hideous anymore. I have grown up a little bit, and along with it, my body has changed. I am not anymore like a monkey, with long and skinny legs which have no form at all, and with enormously big tits, completely out of proportion to the rest of my body. I am not so skinny anymore, and not so clumsy either. When I put on a little bit of make up, just for lashes, I look almost pretty. People have told me that, yet so far nobody has shown any liking for me. Except for Atis, a fat and clumsy guy who is sitting right opposite me. He is staring at me all the time in the Swedish classes. Now that I am in the Grammar School of Nordic Languages, I am supposed to learn at least one Nordic language. When we have to talk in pairs, Atis always wants to be in a pair with me. He is so funny at times. He's got horrible difficulties with learning English. When the teacher asks him something he gets red as a tomato and rolls his eyes and starts moaning and grumbling in such a funny way that everybody else can't help laughing.

English is my favourite language to learn. I like our teacher too. The German teacher seems to be too obsessed with the German language. Sometimes I think she doesn't have any other interests in her life. All she cares for is German. Boring, boring, boring. There are so many other things to care about in this life.

The Swedish teacher is a freak. She is a real Swede and comes from the high society. Maybe that's why she puts her nose in clouds and thinks she is the very center of the world and that's why all other matters should be subordinated to her. Unfortunately that is just her very personal point of view. Most of the school staff have already found out she's a freak, and of course they do not take her brags or her threats close to the heart.

Since she is a spinster, they have given her a cozy apartment right at the top floor of the school. There she lives in three rooms alone with her cat, Bagira, which is dearer to her than her own soul.

Sometimes I watch her and wonder, "Will I be as odd as she is at her age?" There is no doubt that I will be a spinster. I have reconciled to that fact.

Even though I have come to a new school where nobody knows anything about my past, I guess they have noticed my clumsiness. I have stopped going to the parties and discos, for what good they are to me if the whole evening I sit like an old mushroom in a corner and watch others dancing?

Instead of going to parties, I sit at home and write poems. I have a whole notebook full of them, and the title is "Misunderstood." Of course it's my fault. When somebody tries to talk to me, I scare them away with the icy look in my eyes. Even Atis has stopped staring at me now. He likes Aira, a beautiful girl who cannot tolerate his presence anywhere near to her.

I can't talk to my parents about this because they are deep into their own concerns. The company where my mother works is about to go bankrupt, and my dad's health is getting worse. They do not have time to go into my problems. All they are interested in is my success at school. I have good marks, only Swedish could be better, but otherwise I am doing pretty well.

Yeah, I have good marks and good parents. They give me money and buy me all kinds of things, forgetting about their own needs and necessities. They make sure that I eat at least three times a day and that I wear a hat and warm mittens during the winter cold. I am just selfish, always feeling sorry for myself.

Sometimes I remember God and I talk to Him. I pray to Him for help. I do not know if He hears my prayers or not, yet I think He maybe is my only hope. I have heard people saying that everything is possible for God because He is almighty. Then it means He can change me too.

50.

Yesterday was 25th of March, a mourning day for the relatives of the deported people back in the forties. Now it is officially allowed to mourn, even in public. Yesterday it was even allowed to hang out the maroon-white-maroon flags. The day was gray and rainy. The low dirty gray clouds, torn by the icy wind, looked as if they had sucked up all the tears and moans of the deported and their families.

In the morning, despite the cold and nasty weather, there was a large meeting at the Monument of Freedom. Crowds of people trembling in the cold, holding their umbrellas, which were almost torn into pieces by the wind, were standing again at the feet of the Monument of Freedom. In recent years, the Monument has become our mother. We come here to share our joy and to shed our tears.

Later a pilgrimage to the cemetery was planned. In The Brothers Cemetery are laying the soldiers who gave their lives for our country. Our country is just an insignificant little spot on the world map, yet it is precious and dear to us as a nation, a nation to which no other is similar in this world.

All the people who were willing to take part in the pilgrimage were meeting at the Dom Square, the heart of the city. My mother and my other relatives, who had come from distant towns, all wanted to participate. Only my dad was sent home, for they feared it might affect his health. So we all went. It was a long walk, maybe ten kilometers, yet there was a strange excitement among the people. They never stopped out of exhaustion. They kept on walking despite the cold and the rain, warming themselves by singing songs. Some TV operator from a helicopter was watching the people walking. Later in the evening news, he told all he had seen were thousands of umbrellas, black and colourful, moving ahead steadily. On that evening I couldn't stop wondering if God was also seeing the thousands of umbrellas moving ahead steadily.

We are living in times of changes. We all know that there is no way back in our fight, yet nobody is sure what the future will bring. Every Sunday endless prayers are held in the newly reopened churches. People are so desperate that they have even turned to God Himself for help. Where else one can turn in an hour of despair and anticipation? We are scared even to hope that we will ever be able to get rid from Russia's iron grip.

Despite my depression, I like going to school. I like to study, especially languages. Maybe that's really my vocation. Laura, one of the top girls in our class, is jealous of me. She likes to be the first, not only concerning the looks and guys, but also concerning the marks. Unfortunately she is very absent-minded during the classes. That's why I always get better marks than she, and along with it I get the praises from teachers. Laura cannot stand that; she is telling others that my marks are so good because I am a bookworm, and that I am doing nothing else but sitting at home and studying. Well, she is right about sitting at home, but I don't think I am studying that much. In fact, I am pretty careless concerning my homeworks. I procrastinate until the very last moment. However, in tests and compositions I get pretty good marks. I am secretly observing Laura the same way I was observing Samanta. Laura is not so beautiful as Samanta, yet she knows how to show herself off. And she is so damned self-assured.

51. Since last week we have to take swimming lessons once a week. It is mandatory. I hate swimming, first of all because I cannot swim very well, and then I feel embarrassed to appear in a swimsuit in front of my classmates. This feeling of embarrassment appeared only last year. I think it's because I am kind of grown up now, and I am so shy. I am spending my days in a constant torment thinking of how I look. Somebody told me not to concentrate on that and simply relax, yet I cannot relax. During the day thousands of times I run to the mirror and stare at my reflection. Sometimes I still take my clothes off and observe my naked body. Some time ago I did it with interest because of the slight changes in my body. However, now I look at my naked picture with more critical eyes. I think my breasts are ugly, and I have no waistline, and my legs look funny. They still do not have any form. Oh, my gosh! I put my new swimming suit on, and it makes my waistline even worse. I wish I was sick, sick for the whole year, so that I didn't have to attend swimming classes.

But since I am not sick in any possible way, I am forced to attend these damned classes. Today we had to swim ten strokes. I was half dead after the class, and what's really painful, I do not swim a bit better. I think learning to swim is as impossible for me as turning into a dark crow. If one could only imagine what pain and embarrassment I have to go through during these classes. The coach thinks I am not trying hard enough. Of course she looks at me from her height, and cannot understand and appreciate my desperate attempts and my humiliation at failing. I try to swim time after time, putting my head into the stinky water, but it only hurts my eyes and makes me run out of breath. When I try to swim with my head out of the water, I look even more ludicrous, and of course that my misery may be complete the damned swim suit keeps on falling off and showing parts of my body, without me even noticing it.

I do not understand why I cannot swim. I am not physically weak. I can run long distances without stopping, and I can lift weights, and I can jump far away and easily catch the ball while playing basketball. Yet when it comes to swimming I am hopeless. This class is torture for me, especially now, since the handsome blonde guy from twelfth grade is coming to swim at the same time. We always happen to be in the same track. When I first saw him, I tried to change the track, but the coach ordered me to get back to where I started. Whenever we meet at either end of the pool he smiles at me compassionately, and I have no other choice than being a ninny and smiling back at him.

52. Today I do not even want to entrust my diary with this story, but maybe after some years when I will be reading it, it may seem hilarious.

I always get in trouble when it comes to guys. Today it had to happen with that handsome blondee from the twelfth grade. Of course I was the last one swimming laps; that meant I was also the last one who crawled out of the pool. All the girls had already gone to shower; only the guys from the twelfth grade were hanging around. I am painfully aware of the faults of my body, so I wanted to pass them with cold dignity. They were fooling around the pool, pushing each other on the slippery floor. I wanted to sneak through them, yet they blocked the way, and one of them accidentally pushed me. I slipped and fell, in a very ugly way of course. I had hurt my back. I was near to tears because my back hurt so badly and because it was so humiliating to lie there not be able to get up in an instant to run away and hide. The blondee guy came up to me and stretched out his hand. Again there was that compassionate smile on his face; obviously he wanted to help. But I angrily pushed away his hand and stumbled up somehow. I hate him! I hate him for his compassionate smile, which is nothing else than irony after all.

I hate them all, for even though they were showing tragic faces, I saw how they were trying to smother the chuckles. I guess it's some people's mission to serve others as a laughing stock.

I came home miserable, hoping against the hope that Anastasia would be somewhere out and that my dad will be gone to someplace like Central Market, which is his favorite place to be. He enjoys the fuss and the crowds of people and the enormous tables with vegetables and fruits from our sister republics, mostly southern. The bananas are still kind of a luxury in our country, though. Yeah, my dad likes the Central Market. He says there is that special feeling in the air, the yells and the smells and the drunkards with bluish noses secretly offering vodka and cigarettes. It's an exotic place for Riga.

Of course Anastasia was at home. She was in one of her wicked moods, banging the jars and the pans in the kitchen, nervously running back and forth in the hall. Dad says she reminds him of a rat. She looks kind of ratish. I think it's her eyes. They are very unpleasant looking, little and brown with a wicked stare in them. Her hair is thin and dyed at spots like the leopard's skin, and when she moves around in the kitchen I get nervous and uneasy merely observing her. Anastasia has always hated my mother; now she detests her even more, for my mother offended her beloved sonny Mitja by ordering him to get his ass out of the hall when she was cleaning there.

My dad was at home, too, so I didn't get the chance to lock the door of my room and to bawl in a loud voice. Sometimes I cannot stop regretting the day when I was born, but then nobody asked me if I wanted to be born.

53.
Today I was writing a topic in German. We had to write our point of view about what happens after we die. I do not know exactly. I haven't been dead yet. It would be interesting to find out; maybe life on the other side is much better than here. They must have liquidated the communal apartments there, so you do not have to live in constant observance by your neighbours. I guess over there they do not pay a heed about the looks either, and maybe you do not even have to know how to swim. What I am saying is nonsense, but seriously, this question of life after death bothers me a great deal. It cannot be true that I was born into this world to live and to suffer through all this and then simply perish. Then why I was born at all? OK, my body dies, but where do all my thoughts and reflections and feelings go? Do they die along with my flesh? Do they turn into a different material? Where, after all, is that thing called the soul?

Yesterday I wrote a letter to God. I wrote Him about all things in my life which are not the way they are supposed to be. It's really strange, but for the first time in my life I felt it was something real, as though I was writing to somebody real, somebody who is able to receive my letter and read it and even answer it. I guess I must be getting crazy. I feel so strange in the recent time. At school we have a religion class. The teacher is a weird woman, as all religious people are. She talks about Jesus, eternal life and sacrifices and self-denial. She is very thin and looks very pale; besides she's got that unearthly gaze.

Most people in the class, especially the boys, simply ignore her. When she tries to talk to them, they just turn away as if she wasn't even there and keep on talking to each other. She doesn't get mad or anything, just gives them a sad smile, a smile of a person who seems to feel and know more than people normally do. She gets especially upset when the boys play cards during her class, for in her opinion it's a horrible sin to play cards (our boys usually play for money). She thinks that if they do not repent in time, their souls will be doomed. I don't know why it's so, but in a strange way she attracts me. I like to listen to her, even though I have to disagree with many things she says. Maybe she attracts me because she talks of God as of a solution to all the difficulties and miseries. I wish I could believe her.

When I think about it, I would not want to have the life she has. It's too painful and too sad. Her facial expression is the one of a martyr. I get the impression that she likes to torture herself. She simply does it on purpose. She likes to deny herself all the pleasures of the world. If even such a little thing as playing cards is considered to be sinful, then I doubt I will ever become a Christian. Nevertheless, I do think about God, and I think about Him a lot. One thing I really do not understand is why He demands so many sacrifices from mortals. This is one reason which keeps me back from trusting in Him completely. Sometimes I wish I could see him or talk to Him in person. God, however, demands a blind trust, and that is what scares me. Maybe I am very wrong saying such a thing, and I know for sure it would upset our religion teacher, but I really would like to be a Christian just without having to go through all these painful sacrifices and self-denials. Maybe God Himself is mad at me for hearing me talk like this.

These are just my reflections about religion. I reflect about anything and everything and God must already know how crooked my life's philosophy is. I think about God because I have nothing else to think about. I am bored with the school and I am scared of people who want to get close to me. I do not want them to see who I really am, and I am not shrewd enough to play a comedy, pretending to be someone I am not.

Sometimes I think I am in a gray swamp. I am trying to get out yet my feet sink deeper and deeper into the soft soil of permanent depression and fear. I cannot define what I am so afraid of, or so depressed about. It's not only my ugliness anymore. I have grown to understand that even ugly people are accepted, if they are able to prove what they are capable of. There are a couple of other ugly girls in my class. One of them I dare say is even uglier than me, yet they feel good about themselves. The ugliest one has even caught a guy. Ha! That's a comfort for me that even ugly girls have got a chance.

54. I cannot say the tragic events in January left me unimpressed as they would have a couple of years ago. Sometimes late at nights not being able to fall asleep because of Dad's snoring, I think what would happen to us Latvians if Russians will invade us and enslave us again. Their army is strong, and if they wanted they could easily wipe us off this earth. We hope that the Central European countries or United States would defend us. However, this is a vain hope. The West is not at all concerned about a little shitty country called Latvia. And why should they care? They have security and freedom and wealth. They have everything a human being can desire. Pampered by their good fortune, they are unable to comprehend our desperate, even ridiculous fight for survival as a nation with its own language and cultural values. We are the same as other people in this world. We have two eyes, two arms and two legs. At least most of us do. We have a heart, too. We want to live in a free and civilized country pursuing our own economic and cultural goals. We want our kids to speak our language and sing our songs. We want to see them grow up free, happy and safe. Is that asking too much?

However, people who have never walked in our shoes are unable to imagine our situation in all the details, nor are they able to comprehend how we really feel. Maybe somebody is sick or some of his relatives have died. Maybe somebody is hurting in the middle of the crowds on the streets. Well, who cares, for we've got an excellent excuse: "Everyone has got his own cross to carry." For the world, somebody's sufferings or pain is a minor thing, like a drop of rain in a stormy ocean. Yet for the person who is suffering, it's a tragedy. His world has all crumbled down.

I can relate to this person's feelings. It's just like we Latvians are feeling right now, and so are the Lithuanians and Estonians, for they are as small and insignificant in the big world's eyes as we are. I think my anxiety is partly my dad's fault. He is absolutely unable to see anything positive about our situation. He is an incurable pessimist. I think, to some degree, I have inherited it from him. Sometimes merely listening to him can lead me into a depression. My depressions are like the late autumn mist: gray and heavy, hanging over the tree tops and totally concealing the sunshine and the blue of the skies above. Grim and freaky faces hide behind every tree stump. Sometimes it seems to me that the gray mist will suffocate me. In such moments I want to scream aloud to break the dreadful spell and scare all the grim and freaky faces away. Sometimes I can see the mist clear a little bit so that I am able to see little blue spots of the skies. But then I look at my dad's face, and the heavy mist is there again darker and more threatening than ever before.

I do NOT want to be a pessimist. I want to look positively and optimistically at the world. Yet I am scared to hope for anything good: the situations around discourage me completely: the current events in the country, the uncertainty, the anxiety. Nobody is able to tell what the future will bring to all of us. Then there is my dad's slowly declining health. When I realize he may die, I wander around the dark house terrified, not able to find peace anywhere. Dad looks so old and sad and so tired of life.

And so that my misery may be complete there is still this communal apartment! I am fifteen now, and privacy is important to me. Maybe I am a very evil and ungrateful person to say so, but I confess that my parents get on my nerves quite often. I long so very much for my own room where I could be alone with my thoughts for a while, where I'd be able to spend time with myself contemplating. Just some place where I could sometimes invite my few friends for a cup of tea. Whenever they ask if they could come and visit me, I have to refuse. I cannot tell them that I am so deeply ashamed of my train compartment room with drying underwear hanging all over the place. We do not even have a decent furniture. Although we could have afforded to buy it, we have no place to put it.

I dream about a cozy place of my own, with posters on the walls and my own tape player which I could play to my heart's content, and I would have a writing table all by myself with drawers where I could hide all my secrets, my diary, some poems, a secretly taken picture of Cook, some imagined interpretations of love letters (yeah, I have already written a love letter to somebody; I do not know, though, where he may be, yet I so very much want to love somebody with all my heart), a little silver chain with a silver heart, and—yeah—also some letters to God. These are all my cherished treasures and I could put them in the drawers where my parents couldn't find them. I feel really embarrassed when they accidentally find either my letters or my silly poems and read them. I bet even they think I'm a freak. I really want a place of my own where nobody would disturb me or my thoughts.

55. I should feel happy now. I am home all by myself. Anastasia's family—including herself, her always growling and roaring husband, who, thanks God, is at home very seldom, and her cranky and whimpy kids—have left for some family celebration at Anastasia's mother's place. Her mother is a fat, loud and vain woman who knows nothing else in this world but to brag about their summer cottage and about the two Zhigulji they possess thanks to her husband, who is a war veteran... and a devout communist of course. To this very day he is faithfully bringing flowers to the Lenin monument.

So they're away for this evening and I can breathe with relief. The other family is a single mother with two teenage kids; compared to Anastasia's family they're quiet and decent people. They have left for the theater. Even my parents are down at my grandmother's. For tonight I have the apartment all to myself. I feel rather bewildered being left alone in the large apartment. I carefully investigate the dark hall. I go to the bathroom and, for a while, carefully examine my face and my body in the wall mirror. I think I am starting to look better. I go to the kitchen and make some tea. Finally I have no other idea except to go to our room, snuggle under a warm blanket and think. Everything is so quiet. The silence freaks me out a little bit. It's odd not to hear quarrelsome voices in the kitchen, running children in the hallway... even the phone doesn't ring. If I had a boyfriend I could call him and invite him to come over. In the teenage magazines kids always try to snatch the rare opportunities when their parents are out to practice kissing and love making. But whom could I possibly invite to my room with shabby furniture and a half broken sofa? And what concerns kissing...?

Yesterday I had a conversation with Aira, one of the top girls. We had a free class, and Aira asked me to come over to her place. She lives very close to the school. At first I was so scared of Aira, I thought she would definitely notice what a cake I am. However, yesterday when she asked me to come over to her place, it was as if we already have known each other for a long time. It was a wonderful visit. We ate chocolate candies and talked about boys in our class and outside our class and about the big life ahead of us. It wasn't at all like a talk with thick-legged Urzula, timid and freaky Daina, or fat and deceptively self-confident Anda. Even though they try to act and feel superior to me, we all are from the same bag . . . all of us are white crows in the crowd of black, outcasts trying to raise our self-esteems by encouraging each other with silly compliments. Aira, however, is a top girl who's got the coolest guy at school. She knows all about kissing and has already slept with a guy. Well, she has all my admiration and respect for that, and Aira has something of what we call life's wisdom. I even went so far that I told her how I feel about living in this world. She listened to me carefully, nodding understandingly, and when I had finished, she smiled at me and said, "You know, I used to feel like that same ugly ducking: sullen, miserable, depressed and insecure. One day, however, I realized that I was so fed up with my ugly duckling's image that I decided to change my image. And I did! First I changed the style of my clothes. Instead of the knee-length skirts and colorless sweaters, I started to wear mini skirts, trendy jackets and tight jeans. I bought a new lipstick and dyed my hair. I started to run in the mornings and attend aerobics classes. I tried to look positive and smile at people, and it did help me."

"Yeah, that all sounds great. But I do not even know with what to start."

"First of all, quit thinking that you are ugly and a failure, because you are not. You look pretty, only you should change your clothing style. And what if we dyed your hair?"

"Are you crazy . . . my mom would throw me out of the house."

"All right, then," Aira said, examining me with an eye of a professional. "Let's try all the lipsticks on you. Yeah, I think this one looks perfect on you and now. Let's put some make-up on your eyes. Wow, you look gorgeous! And now put on my jacket and my skirt. . . ."

When I was all made up and smelling like a perfume factory, Aira dragged me to the large mirror to hear my own opinion. For a while I starred at my reflection in the mirror dazed and confused. Aira told me to smile. Who was that girl in the mirror smiling at me so strangely? She definitely didn't look ugly. For the first time of my life, I looked trendy and pretty.

Aira was beaming. Later she even told me how it feels to kiss and described me in all details what happens exactly when you sleep with a guy. Until now I didn't really have a clear picture about it. I was too embarrassed to ask somebody, and since I have never had anything to do with a guy not even so much as a slow dance ... and since at home such literature is a taboo, where could I have possibly found out about it? So even if I will never get to the practical side of this matter, at least I know the theory in all its details, for Aira tried her best to depict it as brightly for me as possible.

Well, Aira is a lucky devil! How could she manage to crawl out of her ugly duckling's skin into what she is now, and how could she manage already so much in her age, when other girls haven't even had boyfriends yet? We decided to go to the disco next Friday to see what will happen. I am all excited about this prospect and a little scared, too. Today is only Wednesday! Suddenly it struck me that I have no clothes to wear! I rushed to our wardrobe full of my clothes, as well as my mom's and dad's clothes, and I pulled it open. The wardrobe is always stuffed. My father always jokes about it, calling our wardrobe a cut belly with all the guts falling out. I began frantically to go through the available clothes: a couple of skirts, knee-length, of course! I threw them on the floor. My examination of sweaters and blouses bore better results. I found a pink, almost decent looking blouse (decent looking for a disco party) with short sleeves. That was even better. Since it's the winter outside, I could put one of my ordinary pullovers over it, so my mom wouldn't even notice that I had borrowed her blouse for an important occasion. Mom, always morbidly cautious, is constantly warning me. If Aira only knew how strict my mother is and how ridiculously preoccupied she is about all kinds of possible disasters happening to me at a school party or disco, I would be a fresh laughing stock for everyone. On Friday, however, I have to get out of the house no matter what. If I will need to lie, I will. I will make up something very real.

So the blouse will be an option for the top, but what else could I wear? No suitable skirts, not even a decent pair of jeans. Only the ones my mother's colleague brought from Poland for me. They all go to Poland frequently to get some cheap clothes made after the models of the originals, bring them here and sell, and lots of people buy them, for never in their lives have they had a chance to see and touch the original ones. I know my jeans are not the originals, for we have a girl in our class who is an expert. She also has got some relatives abroad. Since the day she told me that my jeans were fake ones, I have never worn them to school. Of course I can't wear them to the disco either, even though there may be a lot of people in fake jeans from Poland. The very feeling that I am wearing shit may affect my self-confidence.

Maybe I should ask Liene, my neigbour, the girl from the quiet family. Even though Liene is two years younger than me, she has got experience concerning parties and discos, and of course she could advise me what to wear and what kind of a make-up better to put on. Yeah, I can do that! For now I had to dress in as much as I had and try to imagine the rest of the picture.

I quickly put on the blouse, and one of the despicable knee-length skirts, only I folded it shorter and pretended it was a mini skirt. I also put on my mom's high-heeled shoes and colored my lips bloody red. I dashed out of the room to the bathroom where the mirror was larger than the miniature mirror in our train compartment. I had to see the whole picture of me. Everything was so quiet in the apartment. The hall seemed dark and scary. "Come on," I told myself; "you are fifteen. You should stop believing in fairy tales about ghosts!" I ran through the long dark hall straight to the bathroom and jerked the door open. "Aiiii!" I yelled at the top of my voice, and slammed the door and like a mad person dashed back to my room. There was someone in the bathroom. I heard the steps in the hall. Somebody knocked at my door. "Who is it?" I tried to sound grumpy, but my voice trembled, and that's why I sounded so funny that the person behind the door burst into laughter. Shit! That was Ivo, Liene's brother. Apparently he had been at home sleeping or something. He sleeps a great deal.

"Oh, I am sorry!" I said, too ashamed to open the door. "I thought nobody was at home; that's why I freaked out."

"It's okay!" said Ivo through the closed door. A few moments later, I heard him entering his room.

Then I looked at myself carefully in the bathroom mirror. I do not think I am beautiful like Aira, but I think I will look good enough for the disco.

56.

It's Saturday and I cannot believe last night! I went to the disco with Aira. Not to some shitty, boring school party, but to a real night club. I told my mother that Aira was having her birthday party at her grandmother's, and I was invited to come. Since it's quite far from my home I would probably have to stay at her place overnight. Luckily Aira's grandmother doesn't have a phone at home, so Mom couldn't call and check if I was actually there or not. Dad didn't say anything, for in our family mother is the only authority. Without her approval, nothing can be done. Dad only looked at me with those sad eyes of his, and suddenly I felt ashamed for lying to my parents. Without lying, however, I couldn't have gotten out of the house. I even successfully managed to borrow my mother's pink blouse while she was in the kitchen preparing supper and calling names at Anastasia. I had no other choice as to wear my fake jeans MADE IN POLAND, for Lienea's jeans also turned out to be made in Poland.

Well, the disco was quite an adventure. When I arrived at Laima clock to meet her, Aira was already waiting for me. She was smiling excitedly, and her cheeks were slightly flushed. She was hiding something under her arm. I couldn't figure out what exactly it was.

"We will wait for Renars, and then we all will go," she explained.

I sighed silently. Renars was her boyfriend, which meant that they will have a good time while I will be the fifth wheel, supporting the walls for the rest of the night. But Aira, as if she had guessed my thoughts, said suddenly, "Yeah, and Renars will bring a friend with him . . . for you."

I looked at her, a little nervous. A real disco was something, but a disco with a boy. . . . I was not sure.

Then Renars had approached us without us noticing it. He dumped snow right on Aira's head. Aira, having the reaction of the leopard, turned around and pushed him into the large and dirty snow heap. Renars threatened to kill her. He pulled her close, and they started to kiss. I felt a little uncomfortable . . . so did the other guy. I noticed he was observing me carefully from the corner of his eye. Then he approached me with an uneasy smile on his face. "It's cold tonight isn't it?" he asked.

"Yeah," was all I could answer. I was blushing, trying to be brave, and staring right into his eyes. It was one of Aira's lessons to me. "Always look straight into the guy's eyes and smile. Eye contact is very important. Never cast your eyes down, for then the guy may get the impression that you lack self-confidence."

I must have looked silly staring at him so persistently, for after a while he turned away. "I have disgusted him with my staring," I thought; "Maybe he doesn't like me already." I was near to tears, but another one of Aira's lessons was, "Never let the guy see you cry." Then he shyly took my hand into his. I was happy. We were slowly following Aira and Renars. I didn't know what to say or do, and neither did the guy. But I was walking next to a guy, and he was holding my mittened hand in his. I was so excited and confused and frightened that I couldn't feel anything, only my own pumping heart.

Only at the entrance we told each other our names. His name was Raivis. I could not decide if he was good looking or not. I don't really know what criteria girls at my age have for handsomeness. To me he looked all right, and that's all that is important. He was a guy, and he was holding my hand.

Renars had a friend working in the club, so we got in for free. From somewhere there was coming a loud dance music. We took off our coats, and I dashed to the mirror to check if my hair and my lipstick was still all right. Aira pinched my arm. "Smile! Leave that scared child's face behind the door," she whispered.

I put all the effort and managed a crooked smile.

Aira giggled, "You're so funny! You would be a perfect tragic character in a comedy." Renars and Raivis were already waiting for us. The big moment had come. We were at the entrance of the dance hall.

I was dazed by the loud music and extraordinary lights, which gave the hall and the dancing people a slight touch of unreality. Aira and Renars went to the bar to buy some drinks. They said they needed to warm up a little before the actual dancing. I heard Raivis shouting right into my ear, "Do you want something to drink?" Gosh! What was I supposed to answer?

"Do you . . . ?"

"Yes," I said, looking aside.

"What do you want to drink?"

Shit! I knew I was to order some kind of alcoholic drink, yet I am completely ignorant concerning the alcoholic drinks being sold at the disco bars. I had never been to one before, and I had never had anyone to buy them for me.

"I will have the drink as you," I said.

"Are you going to drink vodka with Coke?" He looked at me as if I had said I would fly to the moon tonight.

I nodded, looking aside again. I didn't want him to see my face turn red. I should have consulted Aira before; however, when I thought about discos, drinks were the last to enter my mind. Of course I knew that one must have a certain degree of drunkenness to be able to dance better, yet thinking of discos, all that came into my mind was my lack of competence concerning the very dancing procedure and the whole big life that teenagers at my age are so fond of, but which goes past me.

Well, Raivis came back with two glasses of vodka mixed with Coke. I could see Aira and Renars already dancing at the other end of the dance hall. I couldn't stop admiring Aira for the way she was dancing. In her new leather mini skirt and her transparent blouse, she looked stylish and sexy. I noticed other guys were staring at her, too, and drooling over her. However, they had not the slightest chance to compete with Renars, for Renars had looks and posture and the way with girls.

Raivis handed me the glass and I murmured a husky thank you. He took me by the hand and pulled me in the direction of remote table in one of the corners. I sighed with relief. We would probably sit for a while and talk before dancing. I have been to many school parties at my old school and to some at the new one as well, although recently I stopped going to the parties because I can't stand to sit all night long in some remote corner and and stare at other people dancing.

I have been watching people dancing at parties. It does not seem difficult at all. Sometimes I try at home myself. I wish I had a bigger mirror, so that I could see myself moving. Yet when I was faced with the reality of the disco, I was scared. We sat down. I didn't dare to touch the drink Raivis had put in front of me. Raivis was sucking his drink and observing me as if with half closed eyes. "What does he think of me?" I wondered. I was dying to know, yet he didn't say anything, just stared. Gosh, that was embarrassing! I started to hate his gaze.

"Why don't you drink?" he suddenly asked.

I took the glass and obediently put it to my lips. It tasted good—a little too strong for me, but I was not going to show it to Raivis. I wanted him to think that drinking vodka with Coke and coming to discos was a casual thing to me. The music had become slow and romantic. Raivis got up and extended his hand. Oh, no—I had never slow danced before, yet I couldn't refuse.

I was following Raivis, my hand in his. I could feel his palm was sticky with sweat, but then my palms were no better. I always get sticky palms when I worry. I was nearly paralyzed. We stopped. Suddenly I couldn't remember where I was supposed to put my hands. I had seen people doing it so many times. I thought I knew it. The girls are supposed to put them around the guy's neck. My brain still seemed to work, but my body felt as paralyzed. Raivis smiled at me. His face was so unusually close to mine. He embraced me gently and pulled me close to him. I could feel his warmth and the muscles of his chest and thighs. He started to move. I looked at him with such fear in my eyes. "What is it?" he asked softly.

"I don't know how to slow dance. I have never actually danced."

He looked at me, his eyes so dark and so close to mine that they seemed blurry to me. He was smiling mockingly, I thought.

"I do not know how to dance either," he whispered. His lips slightly touched my forehead. Oh that felt good! I somehow managed to put my arms round his neck. His grip tightened. It was good to feel someone so close. I felt dizzy from the drink and from his closeness. It was all unreal. After all, we were moving somehow and even managed to keep up with the rhythm. I thought Raivis was lying to me about not being able to dance.

When the dance was over, Raivis was still holding me close. I felt happy and scared at the same time. I didn't want him to notice what a cake I actually am. I was scared that if he hadn't found it out yet, in the course of the night he most definitely would.

The fast dances were being played again. Raivis released me. I was slightly trembling, not from the cold, but from some strange inner excitement. I didn't quite know what it was. We were dancing, and with each dance I began to feel better and better. I wasn't sure if I was dancing up to the newest standards, but at least I managed to keep up with the rhythm. When Raivis looked at me, I grinned at him. I must have looked very silly, but I thought it was better than just staring back without moving any part of my face. In the middle of a dance Raivis suddenly grasped my hand and dragged me back to the table. I didn't say anything, just looked at him surprised.

"Let's have a little rest," he said. "Do you want anything more to drink?" I was thirsty, so I asked if he could bring me some juice. He nodded and brought me a glass apparently with orange juice, yet when I tasted the drink I realized that it wasn't the orange juice only. Instead it was as strong a drink as the previous one, maybe even stronger. But I was determined not to show Raivis that I had noticed anything. I drank it as if it was a juice, and with each gulp I began to feel more and more comfortable. I smiled at Raivis, and this time I didn't care if it was a silly grin or not. I felt so happy that I wanted to laugh aloud. Raivis looked at me at first surprised. Then he grinned back understandingly.

It was a slow dance again. I do not remember how we got to the dance floor, yet we were dancing, and this time I wasn't afraid anymore to put my arms round his neck. Without being aware of it, I was caressing his neck slowly. I felt his hands were sliding down my back into the direction of my butt.

"He is not going to touch that!" I thought to myself. I was embarrassed, yet excited. He was going to touch my butt, and he was also going to caress it. My embarrassment faded at his touch. Instead I got an odd feeling at the pit of my stomach. It was pleasant, yet somehow tormenting. I was waiting. I didn't know what exactly I was waiting for, but I was waiting for something to happen to release that strange feeling at the pit of my stomach. It didn't cease, though. Raivis was holding me so tight it almost hurt. Yet I didn't want him to free me from his grip either.

Raivis was breathing fast. Our bellies and thighs were touching each other. Suddenly I noticed something hard was touching me exactly at the pit of my belly. Could it be that he had a hard on? Aira was telling me about that, yet I couldn't believe that somebody could get a hard on dancing with ME. When the dance was over, Raivis put his arm around me and dragged me through the dancing crowds out of the hall. On our way out I noticed some people were kissing. "Maybe Raivis will kiss me," I thought. My stomach quivered at this thought. When we were outside, Raivis leaned close to me and whispered, "Are you coming to my place tonight?"

I stared back at him, not knowing what to answer. Aira had warned me that if the guy is asking you to come to his place he wants to have sex with you then. Who would ever get an idea to have sex with me? I was very scared. It was too much in one night: holding hands, slow dancing, all these strange excitements.

Raivis was waiting for my answer, that queer look in his eyes. What was it? I didn't understand it. However, it excited me a great deal.

"What for?"

Raivis laughed. "You know it as well as I do," he said.

"But I came with Aira. I cannot go anywhere."

"Hey, don't worry about Aira. They have already left."

"Left?" I think he saw the horror in my eyes. He was confused.

"What the hell! You are not coming with me? But Renars told me. . . ."

"Renars told you what?" I questioned him.

"Oh never mind. Nothing."

"Did you want to have sex with me?" I asked. I think I was totally drunk; otherwise wouldn't have been able to utter this sentence.

"Yeah. Renars told me that there is going to be a girl. . . ." Raivis suddenly blushed. I didn't know that guys were blushing too.

"But I have never had sex actually," I told him, looking aside.

"Neither have I," Raivis said, "but I wanted to try tonight, and Renars promised me."

I slowly started to realize how things worked. So that was actually how all the parties ended. People got drunk, danced a little bit, and then went home to have sex with whoever they managed to catch during the evening. I didn't know what to do. I was scared to have sex. I don't know why. I think I will never be able to have sex. That must be very embarrassing.

Raivis was examining the graffiti on the walls. I did not know what to do or say. Then I heard somebody sobbing, hiding behind the dressing table. I was curious to see who it was. I turned my neck to see better. It was Aira! I rushed to her, but she didn't even look at me.

"What's the matter?" I asked.

"I hate him. I hate him!" she yelled hysterically.

"Who?"

Aira didn't answer my question, just cried as if somebody had beaten her up and she was suffering great pain.

I took her limp hand into mine sympathetically. "Do you want to go home?"

"Yes. Please take me away from here. Please!"

I got Aira's coat and mine, too. I thanked God that Raivis had disappeared somewhere. Maybe he had gone to the bathroom to puke. Well, the hell with him. Aira and I slid out unnoticed from the disco. We took a night tram home. Aira had calmed down a little bit and was able to tell me what had happened. Renars had danced with her all the fast dances, yet when the slow ones came he had deserted her and had gone and danced with some other girl. She was a tennis player. Aira knew her. Renars is also a tennis player, and a good one. When Aira got him alone, she demanded an explanation. All he told her was, "I can do whatever I want, and I can dance with whomever I want. Don't you imagine too much. Even if we have had sex, it doesn't mean that I belong to you forever."

"Yeah," Aira sighed; "I had been naive enough to hope that if Renars slept with me it meant he loved me."

I thought to myself, "Aira, who seemed to be so experienced and wise concerning the big life, Aira the coolest girl in the whole school, now had to suffer such humiliation. It turns out that the beautiful girls also must be losers some times." That is incomprehensible to me.

I am very glad I went to disco. It was a good lesson in the big life for me. It was embarrassing, the situation with drinks and then the slow dancing and then the thing Raivis offered and the conversation with Aira, but all learning is hard at first. If I manage to get through this, it means I am one step closer to the big life now.

57. It's an unusual February day. I can sense the first messengers of spring in the air, that particular smell, the soft breeze of the wind, the fluffy little clouds in the skies. At such moments my heart starts to beat faster as if in anticipation of something I cannot exactly identify.

I am slowly starting to feel better about myself; after all, Raivis wanted me. Yeah, in the recent time there's some good news that I could tell to my diary. First, we are going to get an apartment of our own. Because of all the changes in our country, an owner to our house has appeared. He wants his house back, and of course he will liquidate all the communal apartments. This is very great news! At last we will have an apartment of our own, which means I will be able to use the bathroom as long as I want. I will be able to lie in the hot soapy water and dream. And I will be able to take showers, as many as I want. In our communal bathroom, the shower head broke a long time ago, and of course no one is eager enough to fix it. People in our apartment simply got used to doing without the

71

shower. One can wash very well with a basin and a towel, and once every two weeks you were even permitted to take a bath, which meant you were allowed to spend the whole entire hour in the bathroom, but only ONCE in two weeks, not more.

In our new apartment we will have also the kitchen all to ourselves, and I will be able to make scrambled eggs, my favourite dish, without feeling Anastasia's piercing gaze on my back. There won't be any more Mitjas lurking at me in the corners of the dark hall, and I will be able to talk on the phone and nobody will be able to overhear my personal conversations.

Personal conversations, ha! The only conversations which are personal are conversations with boys. But anyway, I will be able to shout and yell and sing aloud in my apartment, and I will be able even to take off my clothes and walk completely naked in my own apartment if I please. I won't have to bother about how I look, for there will be nobody to stare at me. The main thing, however, is that I will have a room of my own. That will be the beginning of a whole different life. I can't wait till we move in.

As far as I know, we will be moving in only in April. Until then, I will still have to tolerate Anastasia's insolent stares. Her small rat-like eyes seem to follow my every step in the apartment. Sometimes I see her eyes in my dreams. I feel these eyes are trying to trap me, and I feel I can't escape their terrifying gaze. It is very tormenting. Happily I always wake up from this dream, and hearing my father's snores in the room usually calms me down.

Mom thinks Anastasia is a person full of evil, and she is capable of putting a curse on somebody. I don't believe in all that nonsense about curses and bewitching, yet I must admit Anastasia's constant staring is utterly unpleasant. My mom thinks that Anastasia is envious of me, for I am fourteen centimeters taller than Mitja. I wish I could trade my tall body with Mitja's. I wouldn't be sorry at all, for I have suffered so much from being a tall, flat sausage. In fact my body looks very much like a boy's. The only thing that indicates my sex is my unnaturally big tits. I feel so deeply ashamed of them. Well, there isn't anything in my body that would be worth missing. I would certainly trade my height for Mitja's if I could get a little more girl-like body in exchange.

58. In the recent time we are submitted to suffer another inconvenience, thanks God only until April. Since Mitja is already nineteen, it is natural that there are girls and boys coming frequently to our apartment to visit him, and they are making horrible noise in the hall at night so that the other inhabitants of the apartment are unable to fall asleep. My mother, unable to put up with it, runs in the hall, furious, in her nightgown, her hair a mess, and yells at them. I feel deeply ashamed of her. She succeeds in nothing but making herself ridiculous. They are making fun of her and of me too if I happen to run into them while they are gathering in the hall. I am so sick and tired of those furtive trips to bathroom, praying to myself, "Please, Lord, do not let me to run into any of them."

Not that I am exactly afraid of them. I just hate to see them. They make me feel like an animal in zoo, thrown in a cage with twenty hungry tigers. I am tired of not being able to feel free and relaxed, even at home.

The other news is that I've got a new occupation, so to say. One of the girls at school offered me to go and sign up for some theater course, where they teach you how to speak and act and present yourself in front of a large group of people. They teach you also how to walk and move properly. At first I was skeptical, because I didn't know the girl very well. She is not in my class, and we meet only during Swedish lessons. Also, I do not wish to make a fool of myself in front of other people. However, Maija was so insistent that I didn't know how to get rid of her. I wanted to go and watch it for myself and then tell her that all this bullshit is not for me. Yet when I went there one evening I became quite interested. The kids there were supposed to play several funny skits based on a situation given by the teacher. It was quite hilarious. I liked the teacher, too, at the first sight. She is an older lady, but very skinny with a lot of vivid make-up on her wrinkled face. Oddly, it didn't look vulgar on her. She's so damn funny. She noticed me, too, the very first time. I wanted just to sit there and watch undisturbed, but she didn't leave me alone. She came up to me and was quite eager to get to know me closer. She told me that I should definitely sign up for the course. When I rolled my eyes at her, she just patted my shoulder energetically and said in her low pleasant voice, "But of course not using such a body and face for something great would be a great waste." Hearing that from a professional means that I am slowly turning from an ugly ducking into a—no! not into a swan, but at least into a very decent duck, quite acceptable for the society of the other ducks.

Yeah, when I sum up all the recent situations the picture is not so sad anymore. Raivis wanted me, Aira also thinks that I am cool and wants to be my friend. A top girl and my friend! Then the theater course teacher is telling me that I have a good body and good face too. And my mom's colleague—she thinks I have grown into a very pretty girl. Anyway, I really do not regret that I have signed up for the class. I am having a lot of fun there, and people there like me. The teacher thinks I am a talent. She thinks I could even be an actress when I grow up. In her opinion, I am a very interesting personality, and that's my strongest attraction. I think she's just crazy, but I am happy to hear it because this course gives me more self-confidence.

59. The spring has started pretty early this year. It's the end of March, and most of the snow and dirt is gone already. The first spring flowers have fought their way through the icy surface and are presenting their little faces to the sun. The evenings grow longer, and the nights seem to be slightly shorter. What do I enjoy most of all about these spring evenings? The color of the fading light, the magic of the twilight wrapping the world in a sliver-gray and slightly pinkish dust. I cannot really explain why, but I enjoy the evenings enormously. The long walks in the central park and in Bastejkalns completely on my own, watching the buds ready to pop out in blossoms, and contemplating, and inhaling the magical fragrance.

These evenings seem to fill me with a weird type of sadness, something between happiness and sorrow. Since pain and all kinds of sorrow have always been a part of my life, I have grown to find some queer satisfaction in being sad. I have figured out that sadness is simply another kind of happiness for me. Besides, I honestly cannot remember any moment of my life where my happiness has been without that little element of sadness in it. I cannot imagine how one can do without pain in his life. I think it's sort of a necessary thing. That is probably why these warm spring evenings filled with the magic of that happy sadness are so comforting for the inner state of my being.

My life as a white crow has given me plenty of time for observation, contemplation, analysis, comparison. These have helped me to develop some sort of an extraordinary point of view about the world and the things in it. Maybe some parts of so-called my life's philosophy and some of my opinions are crooked and unacceptable to the majority of the black crows, but they're mine, and I have learned to be proud of them. It's just me, and if some black crow refuses to accept me with all my white feathers, I am not going to jump out of my skin to please the dumb bird.

60. It is spring in Riga, but the atmosphere is full of dreadful premonition concerning the destiny of the Baltic States. The air is heavy with the horrors of the past months and fears and anxiety of the future. People keep on hoping and fighting, each one showing his patriotism and his love for his nation in a different way. Some write poignant and sarcastic articles in the newspapers and magazines, criticizing and condemning the cowards and betrayers in the government. Some shout aloud in the streets; some cover all the possible walls and house corners with patriotic graffiti; some go to the church and pray the Lord. Praying is not only allowed now, it's even strongly recommended. People believe that if we ever break free from Russia's grip it will be nothing but a miracle performed by God Himself on our behalf.

My faith in God has grown, too. There have been times when I have been mad at Him. I have felt hurt and disappointed, yet God has been loyal to me. He has listened to my tearful teenage prayers, and He has already started to change me. He has also granted me an apartment, and we are moving in maybe next week already. At last we will be free and independent from Anastasia and from all her evil stares and spells. If such impossible things can happen in my personal life, then it gives me also faith that one day we will be able to break free from the big brother's iron grip. My faith can contribute very little, yet it can do at least something, for I am not alone with that desperate desire. There are so many other people believing, hoping against the hope, fighting off the fears and overwhelming depression. All we have is that blind, stubborn faith in a miracle. It's the only real weapon we've got against Russian tanks and guns.

61. The crab apple trees on Brivibas Street are in full blossoms now, and the flower stands are full of spring flowers, and along with it comes incredible joy in our people's hearts. In some miraculous way, after countless congresses and negotiations with Moscow, we have gained our freedom back. On the 4th of May, 1992, our independence was declared officially.

Of course it didn't come without a fight. Russians came openly against Latvians gathering at the Dom Square, barehanded, with that wild glow in their eyes, so full of hatred and contempt. The both sides were ready to fight. Aggressive faces, yells, curses everywhere, and the police in the midst of everything, trying to straighten things out. But we knew in our hearts we had won already, and this knowledge written on our faces is what made Russians green with rage. When the declaration was being read, people went wild. Through laughter and tears they were hugging and shouting all sorts of greetings to each other. The emotions were too overwhelming to be kept inside.

The day when our independence was declared officially was a big day for everyone in our country. Everyone was celebrating and getting drunk. My Aunt Zelma is working at the hospital for people with tuberculosis. She is sort of a nurse there. Sometimes she is asked to perform the duties of a janitor as well. As far as I know, this is a small dirty and stinky hospital somewhere in the middle of the nowhere, merely some remote spot almost at the Estonian border. Yet even the sick people there stuck in that desolated spot, deathly ill, were living it all through, and not less intensely than the the ones at the Dom Square. Even the most seriously sick were glued to the blue TV screens and didn't submit to any of the desperate attempts of the nurses to get them back in their wards. They were watching the fight at the Dom Square when suddenly one of the nurses fell on her knees and all the patients followed her. They all were saying "Our Lord in Heaven...." An old meager woman, death sentence already plainly written on her exhausted features, was screaming at the top of her voice, "Lord! Oh, Lord, have mercy on us!" Some people joined her. Others were staring at them in horror, thinking they had gone mad from anticipation and despair. That was a moment when all the Latvians who couldn't come to Riga to be at the Dom Square were glued to their TV screens, praying and hoping for the impossible. They swore they would be ready to eat dry bread and gulp it down with tap water if that was the cost of freedom.

Nobody knows what our future will be like now. I know we will have to go through some rough transitions. Transition to what? Nobody even knows. Some people think we will not have fuel for heat or food to eat in the winter. Yet we do not care. Everybody is too happy at the moment to be able to think about the challenges and difficulties awaiting us in the future, to be able to realize their seriousness. At the moment dazed by the incredible turn of events, most people are not in the mood to face the harsh reality. They are taking their time to adjust to the fact that we are going to have a government and a president of our own. We will not be submitted to the regulations and decisions of Moscow ever again. After all those years of thinking and making decisions with the big brother's brain, we will be permitted to think and decide on our own now.

Yet the Russians are furious, and of course they cannot reconcile themselves to the fact that we have got our freedom back. They are walking around roaring like tigers ready to attack and tear us into pieces. At best, they hope we will fail and come crawling back like the worms to be part of Russia again. At the worst, they plan their invasions, looking for an excuse. But we will surprise them.

62. It is the 15th of May and the Russians were already trying to get into the Saeimas. Everyone freaked out again. I didn't have the slightest idea of what was going on when I came to see one of my very old relatives who had gone blind during this time. When I came into her room, she was sitting curled up on a couch and weeping. I didn't know what to say to comfort her. Despite her sudden blindness, she never grumbled or complained or shed tears about her evil destiny, but she looked so scared, like a little child.

"There, there, Auntie," I said. "Do not cry, please!" I softly patted her limp hand. "What is the matter by the way?"

All I could get out of her was, "Russians are invading us again. They are in our government house, tying to kill our new governors. Russians are mighty strong. They will get us under their shoe again. You will see."

"Russians invading the government house?" My mouth dropped open as I was staring at her searching, for confirmation of those horrible words in her blind eyes. Yet her eyes were distant and unmoved, similar to the ones of a dead person staring into some invisible distance past me. There was something terrifying about her appearance and her incredible words.

When I turned the TV on, I saw Latvians coming against Russian crowds, holding hands and singing our national songs. There was that same hatred and contempt in the eyes of the Russians. They were itching to smash us for daring to come so openly against them, singing the songs in a language they loathed the most. The crowds were wild. A serious fight was about to start. The OMON were given an order to push the eager Latvian fighters back, not caring if they got trampled over and smashed in the mad crowds. Suddenly the OMON people started to hit everyone with special sticks they used for fighting. They were hitting people's shoulders and backs. There was a lot of anger and confusion in the air, yet no one dared to go against OMON. They were armed after all. The crowds were shattered without breaking out in a fight.

63. Today it's the 16th of May, and I am mentioning the date because it's a remarkable day for me and my family. Today at last we moved into our new apartment. It didn't work out in April as we were hoping, yet even though it's a month later, we are in our new apartment now, which means we are completely on our own, free to live however we want and free to do whatever we want. Free from Anastasia's snorts and grins and her contemptuous remarks. Isn't it amazing that shortly after our country got back its independence we also got our new apartment? Our tenth-floor apartment in a Soviet block house in the suburbs of Riga was originally meant for some poor Russian family coming to Riga in search of some kind of work in the large factories. Our block was meant for the workers of the robot factory. Apparently there wasn't much demand for the factory's products, so they closed the factory. The apartments remained uninhabited. Now the centre of the city is being rapidly renovated by owners. People who owned the houses from 1918 until 1940, or their relatives, are entitled to ask their properties back and liquidate the communal apartments. So countless people inhabiting the center houses are sent to apartments in the block houses somewhere in the suburbs.

So all dreams are slowly coming true. The old owners, who lost their property, get their big flats back. And we who lived in communal apartments get flats of our own. It's an odd feeling to be so far away from the center, and whenever I want to get to the center I will need to take the bus or the trolley. Otherwise I am pretty happy about our new apartment especially about the fact that our windows are not east but west, which means I can see the setting sun and the woods and planes landing and taking off. From my window I can see even the church towers and the roofs of the old city. It's a marvelous view. If our windows happened to be east, we would see nothing else but other houses like ours, all alike each other with not even a slight distinguishing marks, all looking very Soviet. I still cannot believe that I now have a room completely on my own.

I can hear my parents talking in the other room. All our new neighbours have come to introduce themselves. There's laughter and loud voices in the hall and the big room.

"It looks quite crappy, especially if you come from the centre, but otherwise living here is quite nice and comfortable. Not so many cars, more fresh air," one lady says.

Dad cannot keep his superstitions to himself. "Everything seems fine; just our apartment number. It's 78." The guests all fall silent; they do not understand.

"Do not be ridiculous!" Mom says. She's embarrassed and immediately changes the topic. "But the view is simply wonderful! It's more than we could ask for!"

I know very well what dad meant with 78. In 1978 the doctors discovered his heart disease. Mom said it was a horrible time for her. I was one year old and my dad was very ill. He was in hospital and the doctors assured mother he would not live more than a year. Despite the doctors' threats, my dad refused to have a surgery, for almost all the people died during those surgeries. Dad was really, really ill. He could barely walk, and my mom was so desperate. Even with all the bad prognoses, Dad somehow survived, and almost seventeen years have passed since then. Now Dad thinks that the apartment 78 is sort of a premonition of his death. Dad may be weird at times.

The voices are getting louder. It's the vodka's influence. My parents are not drunkards, yet they are never stingy with drinks on big occasions. One of my mom's friends is making a speech. Everyone thinks she's got a gift for it. I do not listen to her until my ears catch "and we really hope that one day we will have your daughter's wedding celebration at this apartment as well." My mother is giggling oddly. Her friend goes on: "She is so pretty, your daughter. Where is she, by the way? Sitting in her new room?"

They are calling for me. I say, "I will come in a minute." In fact I am not at all excited to enter the big room and have everyone, including our new neighbours, staring at me. I am more shy now than some years ago. It seems I have become hypersensitive.

Someone sounding completely drunk is shouting, "Where is your daughter? We want to see your pretty daughter!" I have no thought of going and meeting my new neighbours. I am feeling very comfortable in my new room.

The neighbours are leaving one after another. Soon we will be alone in our new apartment. For the first time of my life I will sleep separately from my parents. I look around at our furniture, the old shabby chair which is being pulled out and used as a bed. My desk with the scratched glass. A couple of drawers with broken doors. A book-shelf with bending back. My joy is slowly fading. Yes, we have a new apartment, yet looking at these miserable pieces of furniture we possess I cannot keep the sad thoughts from creeping in my mind again. I still won't be able to ask any of my classmates or friends to come over for a chat and a cup of tea. I cannot let them see all this. In the Soviet times we had some money. The furniture was quite cheap too, yet we didn't have a space in our train compartment room for any kind of decent furniture. Our only furniture was my desk and our three old pull-out chairs. Now we have an apartment, but we do not have any money to buy anything new. We still have to pay the men who helped us to bring our furniture in here. Then my dad needs new medicine, and my mother is about to lose her accountant job, for the factory will be sold to some private company and all the old people will be fired. My mom is considered old. She is 56 already, although honestly, anybody over 30 is considered too old to adjust to modern enterprises. The times of good changes are through for our family. Only troubles lie ahead of us.

Mom is calling me. "Come have a cup of coffee with us. It's our first evening in the new apartment." I cast a glance through the window. It's a warm and beautiful May evening. The sun is setting. The warm breeze is coming in through the open balcony door. The warm breeze stirs up some strange feelings within me. I think it feels like being in love.

"Where are you? The pancakes are getting cold!" My mom's voice carries a slight note of annoyance. Reluctantly I turn away from the window and the beautiful sunset.

The kitchen seems to be so small in comparison with our kitchen in the communal apartment, but then it was a communal kitchen for common use, and this one seems to be much cozier anyway. Only the walls are ugly brown.

"We should redo the walls somehow," I mention sipping my cup of herbal tea.

"Well, if you have enough money, go ahead," my mother snaps at me. No, she isn't actually angry. She is bitter and sad. Bitter because of our obvious poverty. And then she is scared of what happens after she loses her job. My dad tries to smile at me. He is so gentle and supportive. He never snaps at me or yells at me. I turn my head and look aside. I am old enough to understand that my tears will upset my parents even more. My dad looks very very old. I am sorry. I am sorry, Daddy.

"Eat some more pancakes." Through my mother's harsh voice I can hear concern. Obediently I take two more. There's a large lump blocking my throat. I cannot swallow anything.

I am left alone in the kitchen with ugly brown walls and an old gas stove. My parents are watching news. They are worried about the Russians taking over our new government. I do not feel like joining them. When I am sad or depressed, I like being left alone, and for the first time I can afford myself this luxury. I go to my room. It's a good room. I haven't decided yet how to arrange it. I feel tired and a little bit sore, for the elevator is not working, and we had to carry all our things by ourselves to the tenth floor. I bury my head in the pillow. I like to hug my pillow, laying in my bed and dreaming with open eyes. I am glad tomorrow is Sunday. I will have one more free day to adjust. Monday I will have a long way to school, which means I will have to get up very early to be at school on time.

Then it strikes me. Monday is the spring Swedish exam, one of two each year, just like at the university. I get goose bumps and an odd quiver in my stomach when I think about Swedish. Of course the old witch will want us to go up to her apartment and take the exam there, or—what's even worse—she will want each of us to go and talk to her individually. One guy in our class seems to have found a way to win her heart. All you have to do is pet Bagira and compliment his beauty and grace. The old freak seems to melt when she hears somebody complimenting her cat. Sometimes I think I also will become so freaky when I am her age.

64. It's the end of another school year again. Tomorrow night is the graduation party for the twelfth grade. We are also invited. I do not feel like going anyway.

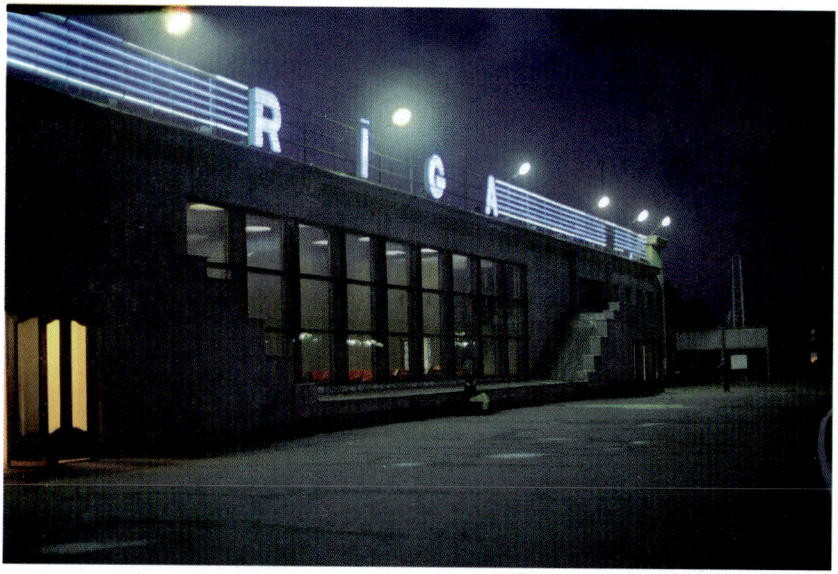
RĪGA

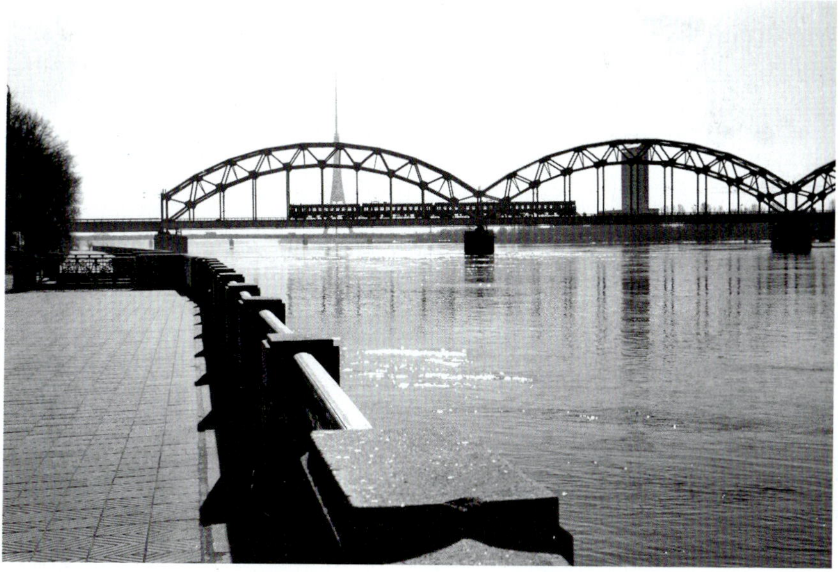

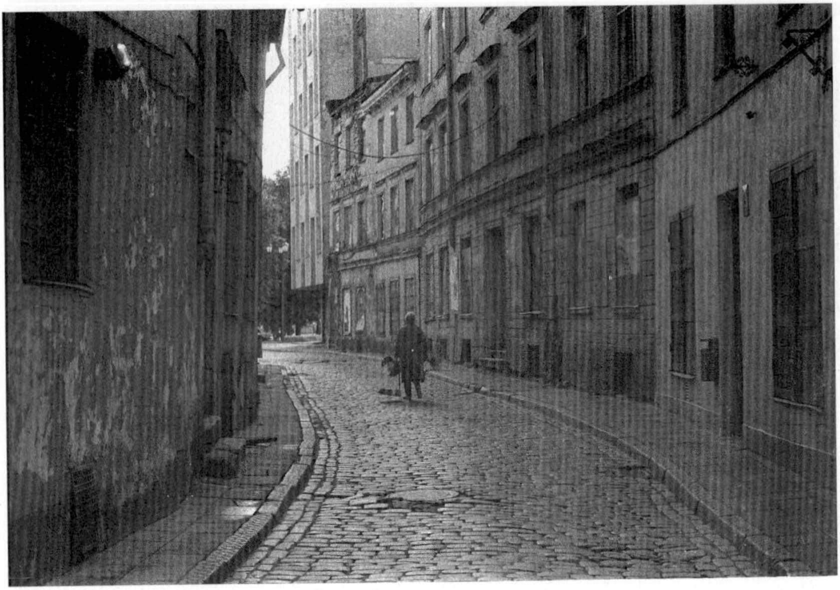

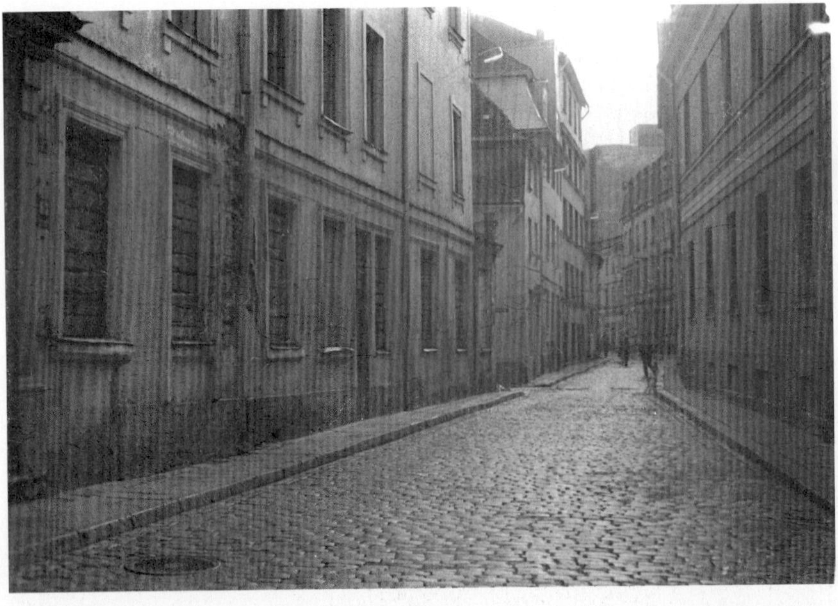

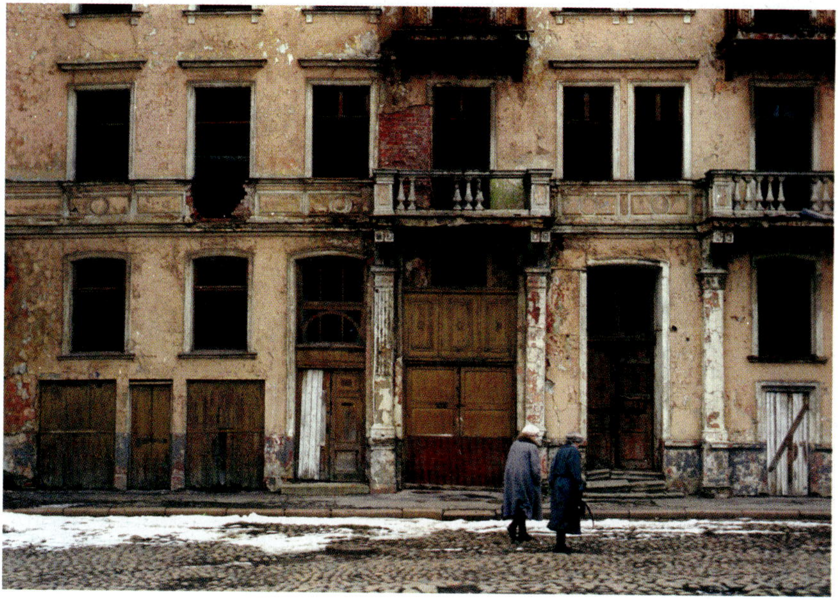

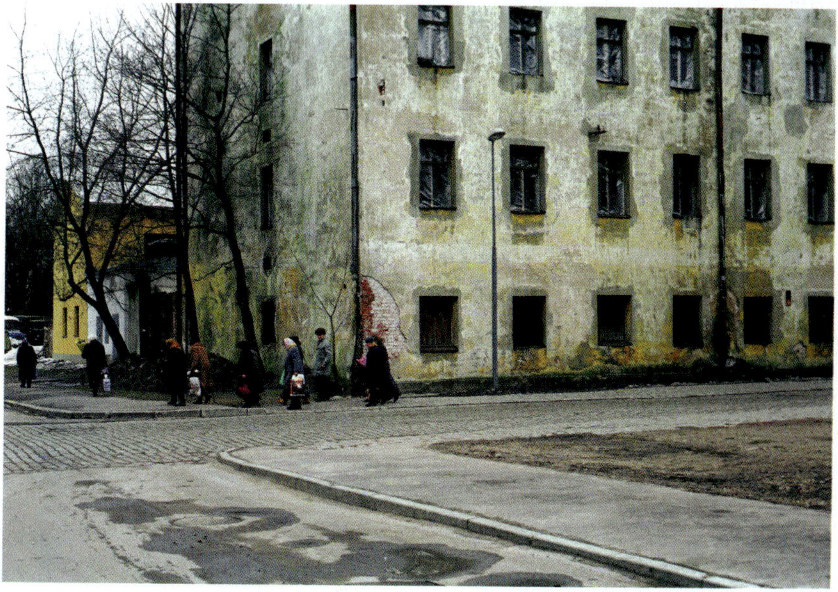

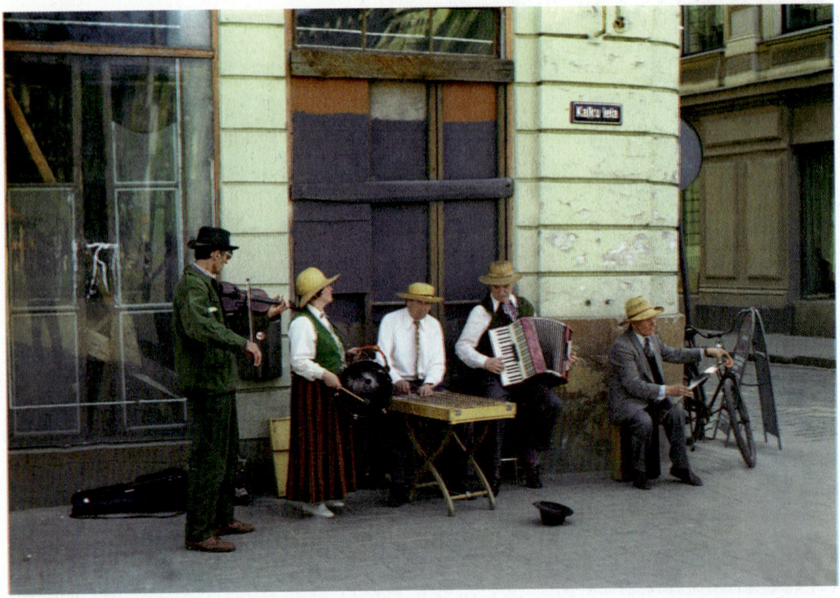
Kalku iela

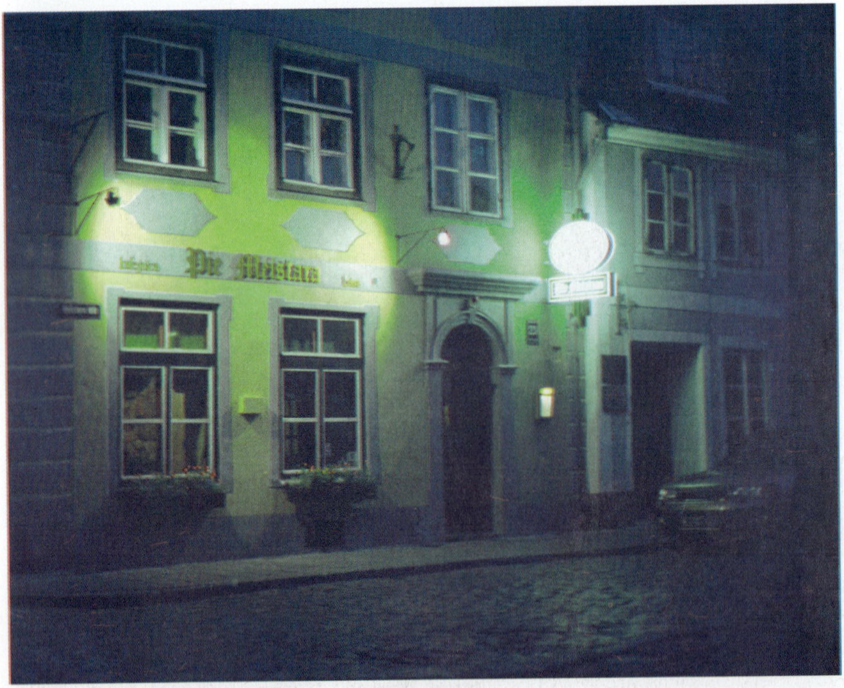
Pie Meistara

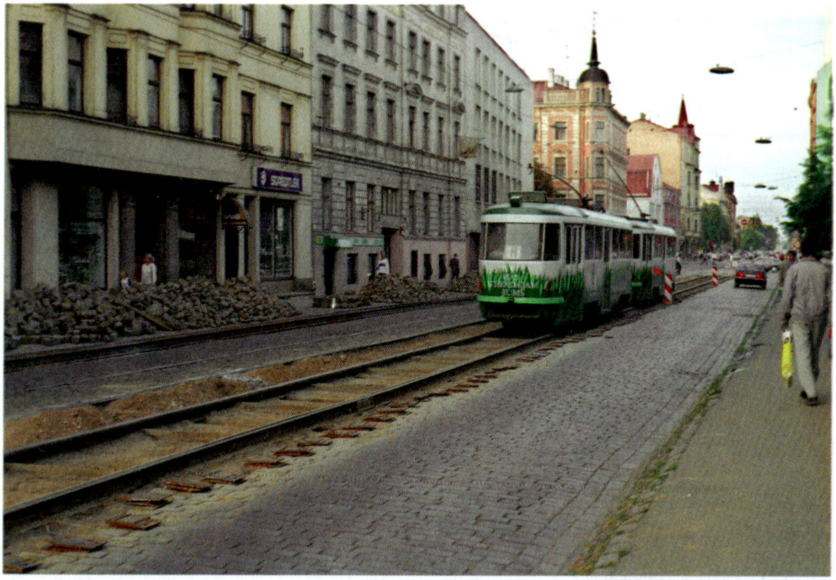

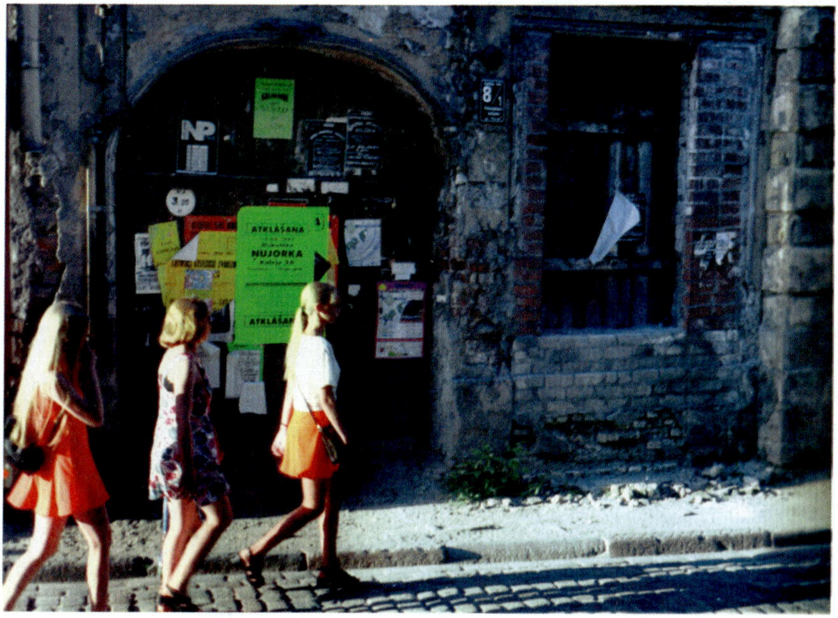
NP
8/1
ATKLĀŠANA
NUJORKA

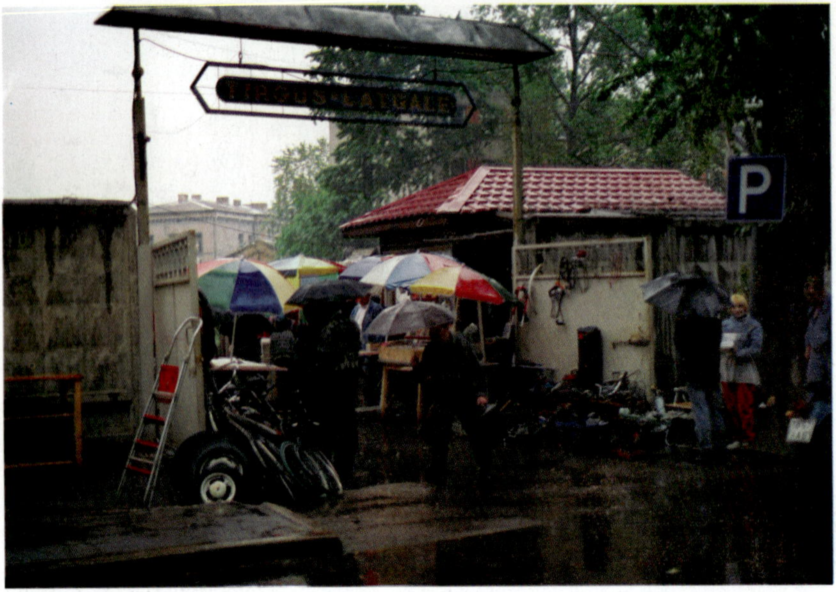
P

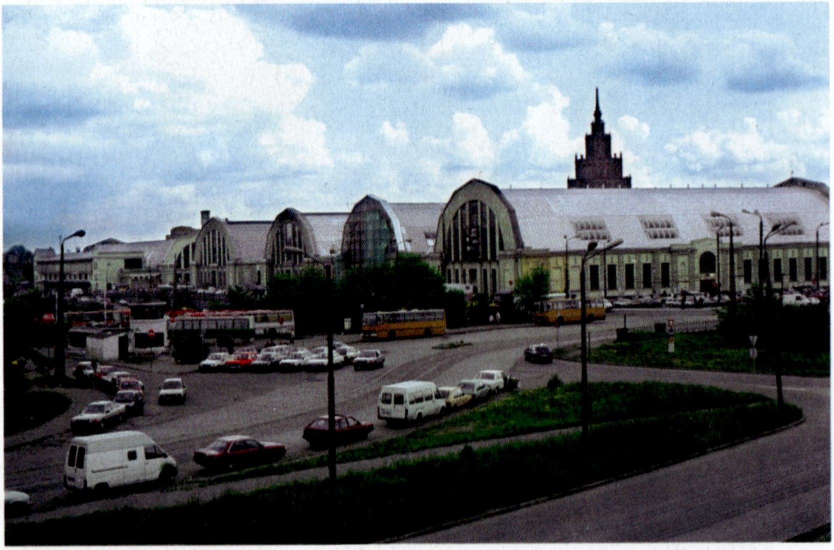

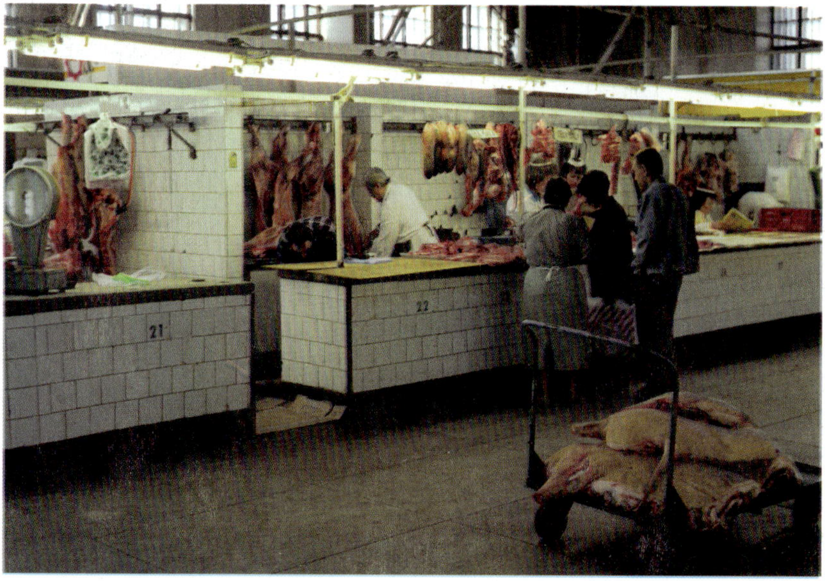
21
22

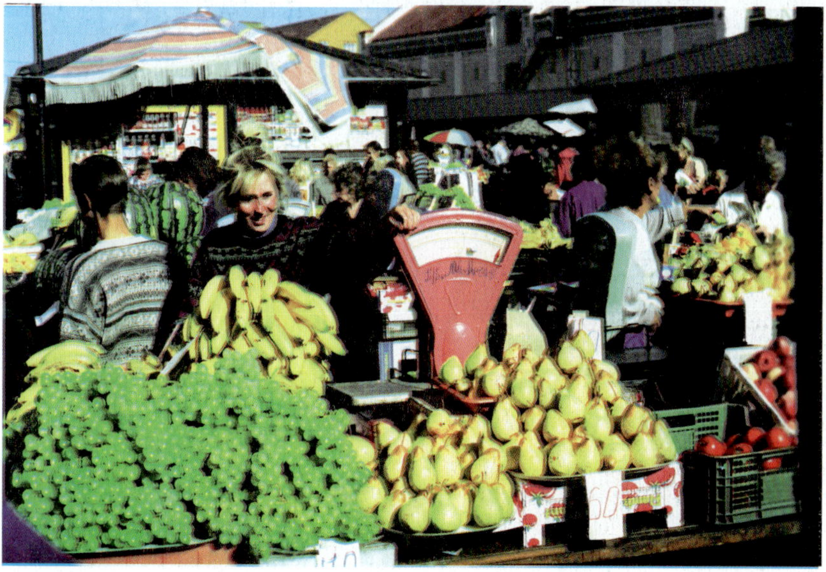
60

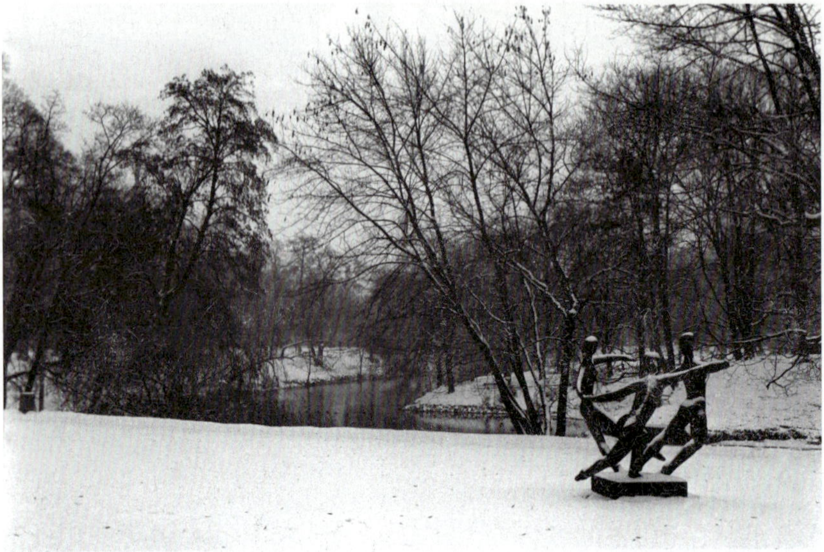

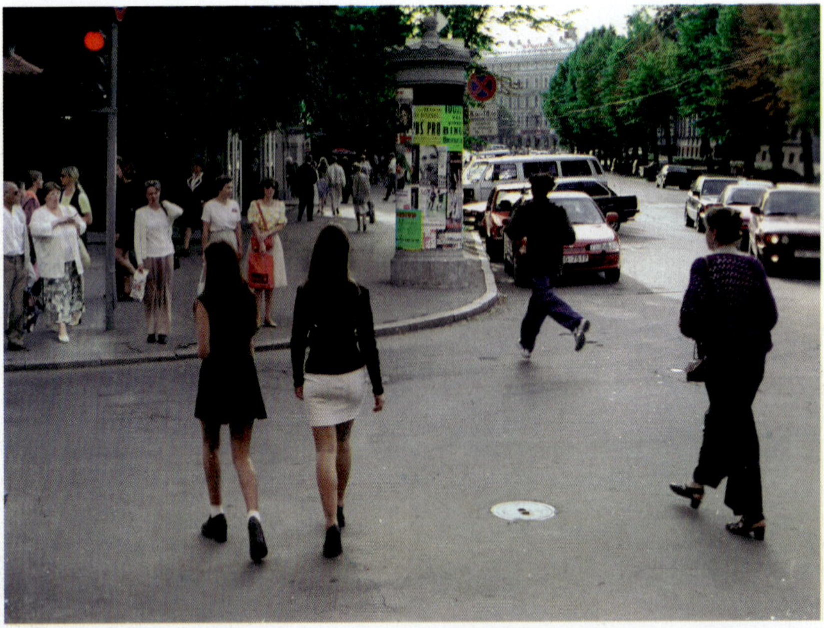

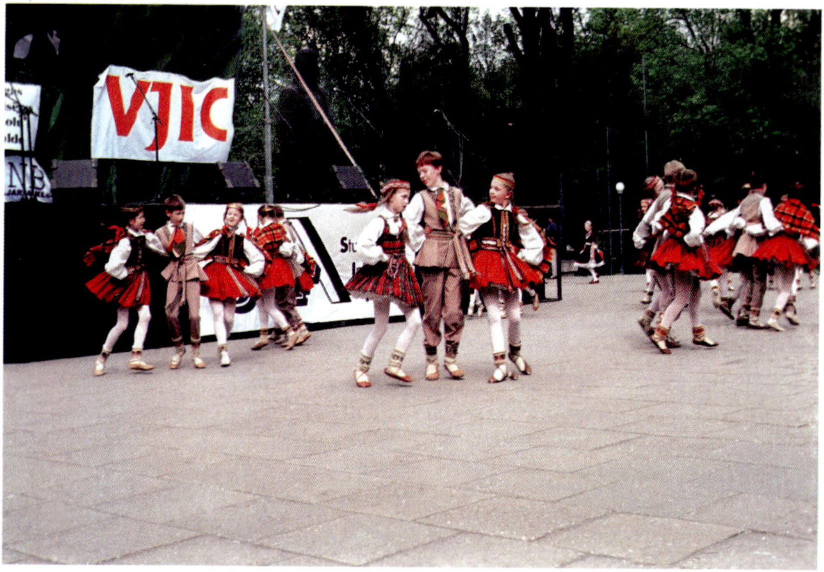
VJIC

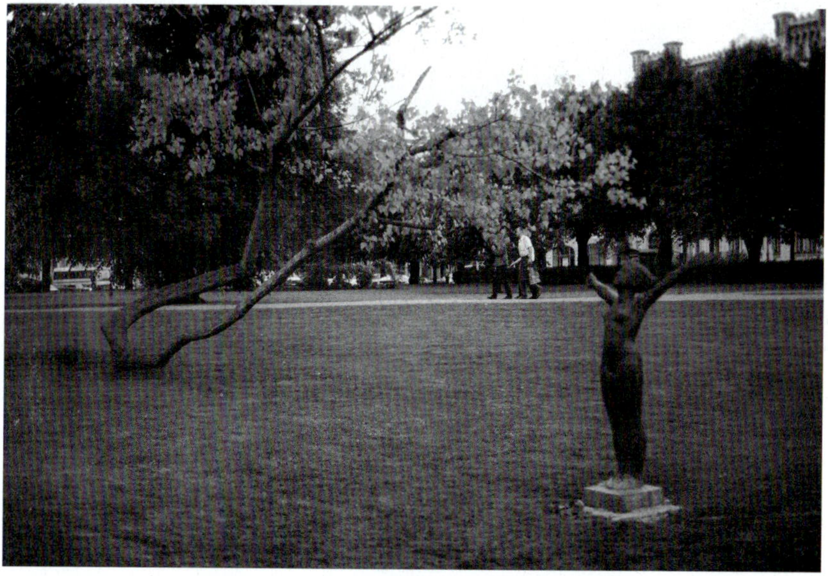

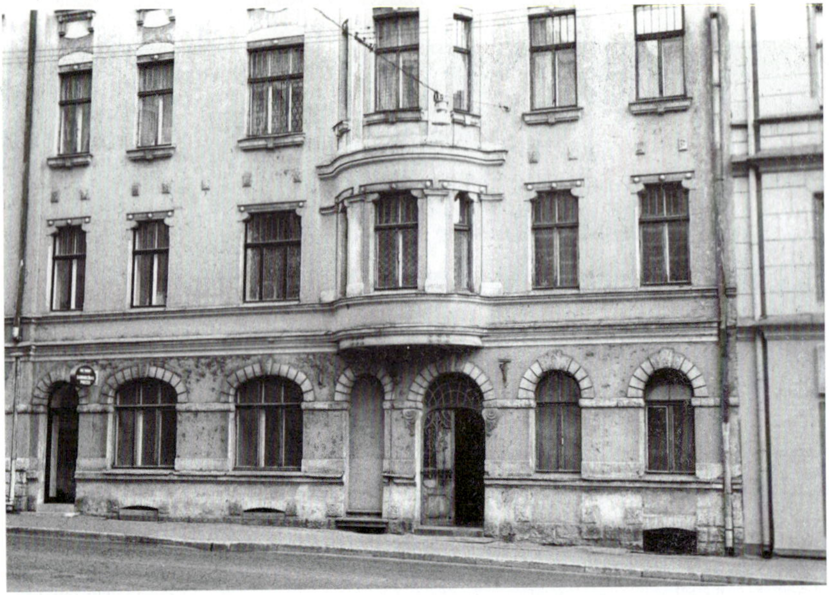

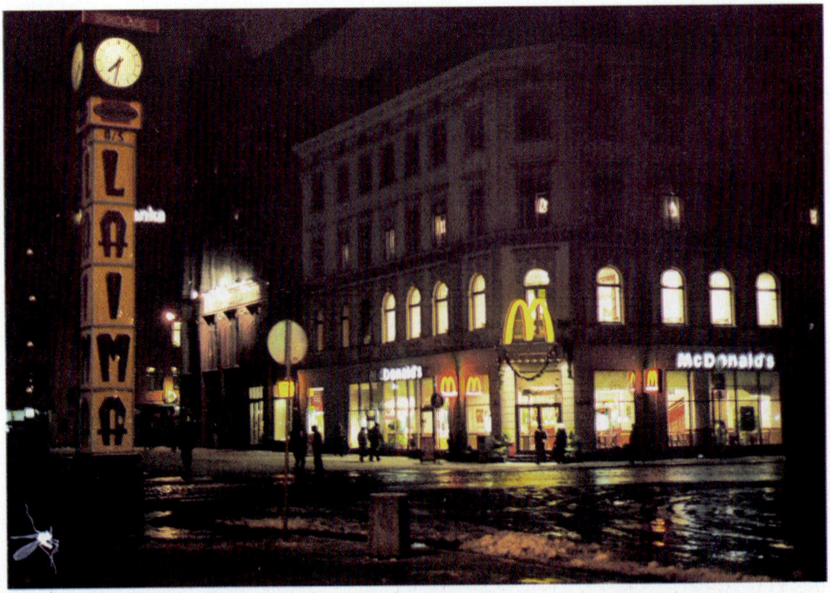
LAIMA
Donald's
McDonald's

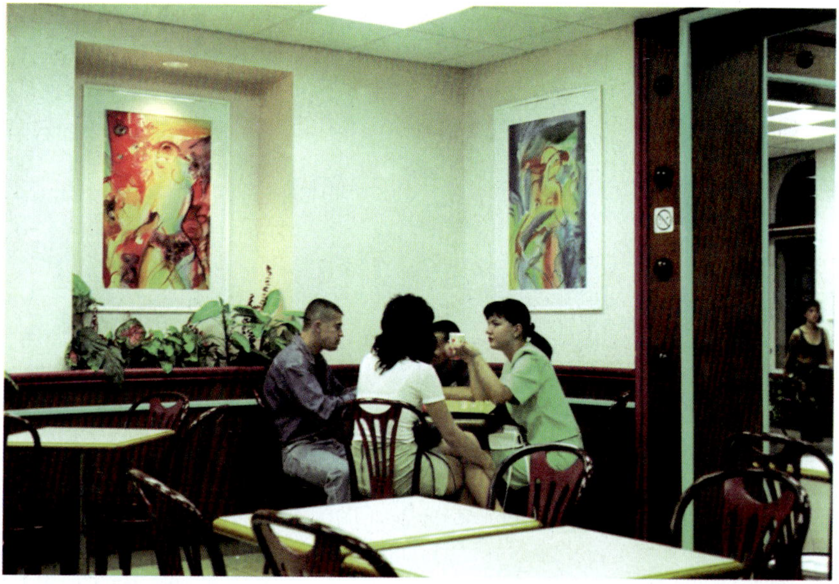

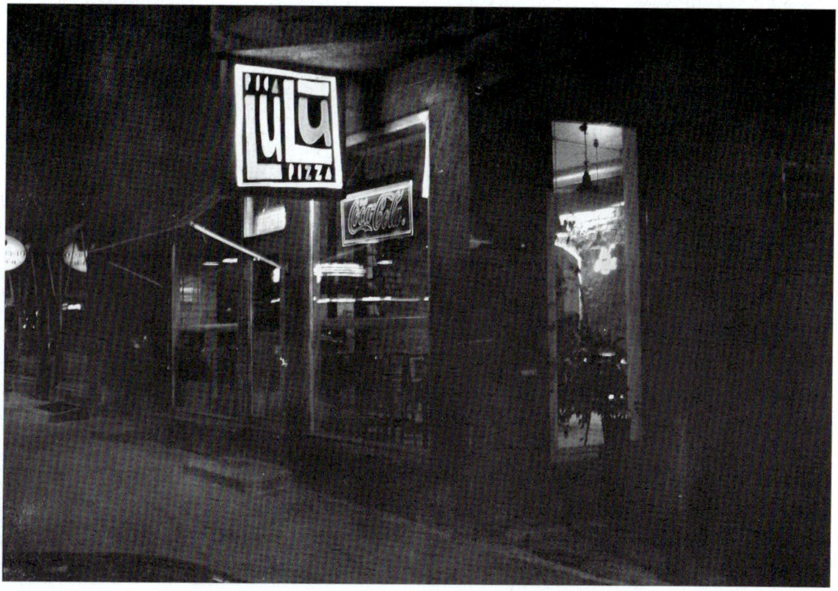
PICA
LULU
PIZZA
Coca-Cola.

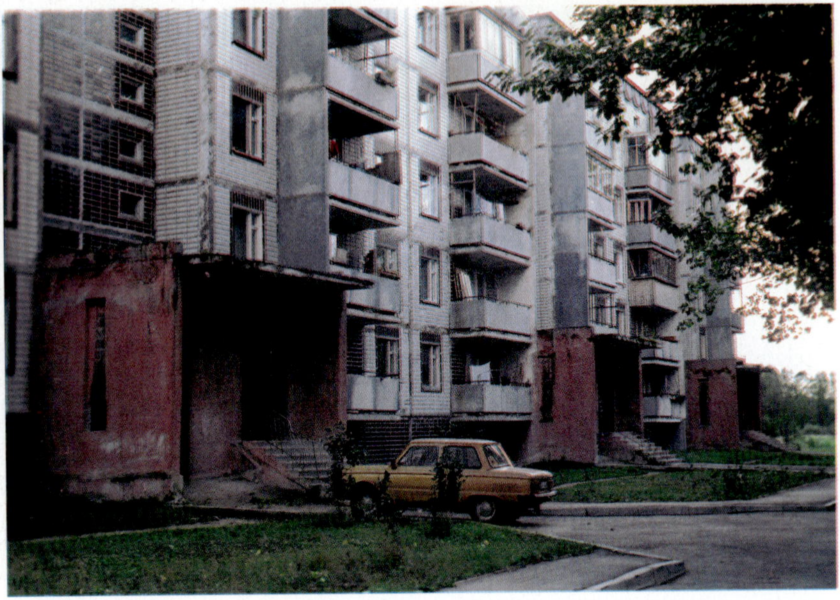

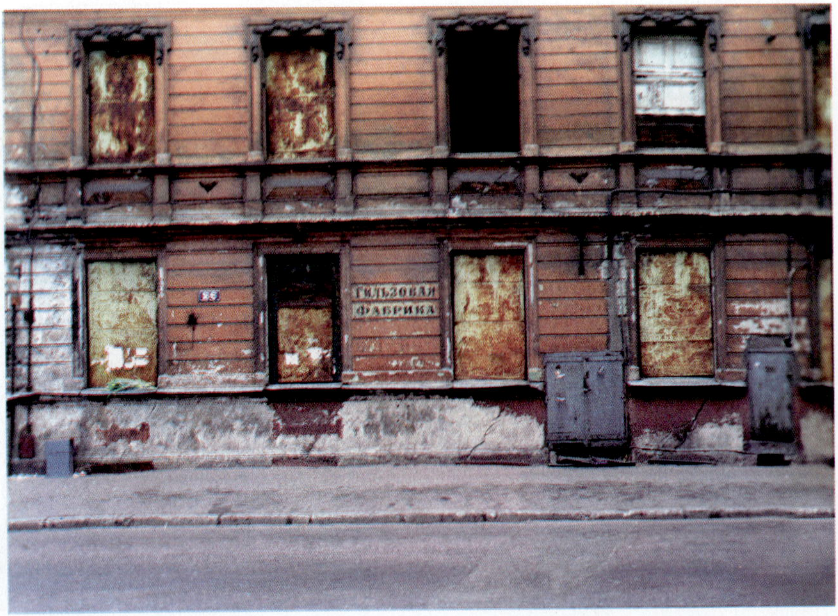
ГИЛЬЗОВАЯ
ФАБРИКА

The summer is coming and my classmates keep on asking, "What are your plans for the summer?" My plans for the summer? I do not like this question. I cannot imagine any other plans besides the work in the beet fields or taking care of withering flowers in the Sungarden. I must not let my mother sign me up for it. If she does I will go there myself and cross out my name.

It's very hot these recent days. The air is sticky from the heat and the fragrance of blossoming trees and flowers in the parks and gardens.

I enjoy living in my new apartment a lot. Especially I like the evenings when I can sit outside on my balcony and view the scenery, feeling the last caresses of the setting sun.

I was still lingering in the cool school hall today resting after the dreaded Swedish exam. I passed it somehow. At least I got a tolerable mark without even complimenting the blood-thirsty Bagira. Ingo—the guy from the other tenth grade, famous for his extremely good English pronunciation and his Swedish knowledge—was sweeping the floors. I was observing him curiously. In fact he is quite good looking, yet I do not know why most girls try to avoid him. Maybe because he is an odd fellow. I have noticed that he is a white crow, too, and a very outstanding one by the way. In the recent time I have come to a realization that there are more white crows in this world than I thought there were. Sometimes I think there should be a special club for the white crows, a White Crow's Club, a place where the white crows could come together and feel united in their isolation from the back crows' world. It would be a sort of a sect. Maybe white crows should stick together only with each other and shouldn't mess with the black ones at all. A white crow should have sense enough to realize that he will never be totally accepted in the back crows' world. Even if he tries to paint his feathers black, little white spots will stick out and betray his origins. Aira was trying to persuade me that everything is changeable, and the theater courses helped a little too, yet you cannot completely hide your true origins.

When I was watching Ingo, I almost felt some sort of a kinship with him. He threw a couple of glances at me too. I was waiting until the wet floor would dry enough to walk on it.

"Hey, what are you doing in here?" he asked, looking suspicious.

"I am waiting for the floors to dry." It's strange, but I never freak out or blush speaking with guys like Ingo. Maybe it's because we are the same kind.

"How did you do on the Swedish exam?" I asked him, painfully aware that he did splendidly.

"I got only 6."

My brows went up in a genuine surprise. "What the hell was the matter with you? You and only 6? Everyone knows that her feelings for you are equal to the feelings she's got for her pet. Everyone cannot cease wondering how you managed to win over her heart."

"She was sort of pissed off at me."

"Why?"

"I stepped on Baggira's tail accidentally."

I burst into a laughter. "Why, that's bullshit. What did you do to her?"

"Actually"—he looked so funny twisting the broom clumsily, that half funny, half tragic look on his face—"actually I told her I didn't like the way her Swedish cookies tasted."

"What did they taste like?"

"They reminded me of a fresh vomit. When she offered them to me I couldn't help that look of disgust on my face. She looked concerned. She asked me if I was worried about the exam questions. She swore she was not going to ask anything serious. I told her, 'It's not that; it's just the way the cookies taste. They make my stomach turn over.' "

"That's a lie; she didn't even offer you any cookies."

"Oh, yes she did. She always does, since I have more privilege with her than any of you."

"Why do you have such privileges with her?"

"I will tell you something if you promise to keep your mouth shut."

"Tell me what?"

"Well, sometimes I cannot help the thought that she likes me—likes me . . . as a man. You know?"

"The old freak's got a crush on you!"

"I suspect so. She actually wanted me to go to Sweden and study there. She promised to pay for my education, but I refused her offer, for I've got other plans for the future."

"She offered you to study in Sweden?"

"Yeah. She thinks I'm a smartie. But I feel ill at ease with her, and I definitely do not want to accept anything from her. When I told her that, she got pissed off. She's a mean old stick. Now she's mad, and I have lost my privileges forever, but I do not care for that language anyway. Next year I will switch to Norwegian. That will piss her off even more."

"I wish I could switch, too. I hate her picking on me all the time. In the recent time, however, she has found out that Janina is even more dumb and empty-headed than me, so she keeps on nagging her. Sometimes she brings her to tears."

"Janina." I noticed he blushed a little when I mentioned her name.

"What about her?"

"Nothing. I was just trying to recall what she looked like." He finished his little lie with a triumphant smile, hoping that his explanation was convincing.

"Why are you turning red?" I asked. It was the first time in my life I dared to challenge a boy, but then Ingo cannot be considered a real boy; he's just a freak like me.

He stared at me, lifting up his brows. "I am not blushing. I am flushing from working hard in this heat. Can't you see I am brooming the floor?"

"I see." I smiled at him, my eyes mockingly searching his. "He is cute—at least the way he looks," I thought to myself, but most girls avoid him because he's got a label on his forehead "a white crow."

"Hey, I have got a question for you. The old freak [he meant the Swedish teacher] asked me once if I could organize a group of students willing to go to Sweden for fourteen days and improve their Swedish. I have got already seven people. I maybe need three more. I was going to ask if you would like to go with us. Yes, the old freak said we won't have to pay for the trip."

My mouth dropped open. I? Sweden? I couldn't have been more surprised if he asked me to go to Mars. I do not have any plans for the summer.

"I don't know," I answered. "I will think about it."

"Think about it, and then I will ask you tomorrow, and . . ." He was turning red again.

"Yes?"

"Ask Janina if she too would like to come."

"Sure I will," I said, feeling a slight pang of jealousy in my chest. Even though Janina is not very popular at school and she is always cheating in English classes, guys seem to like her. Even though her waist is even worse than mine. But then Janina is not a white crow.

"You are turning red again. Is it really from the heat?"

He smiled at me. "Yes."

"I must go now," I said feeling sorry for having to leave.

"See you tomorrow."

"See you."

65.

Yesterday night after long weeping and wailing, my parents—which actually means my mother, for what concerns the decision making, most times she represents my dad as well—gave me permission for the Sweden trip. Dad actually didn't say anything, either positive or negative, just as usual looked at me with those sad, reproachful eyes. Dad does not like it when I go on long trips or excursions. He always thinks something horrible is going to happen. Sometimes it irritates me unbearably. How can one live all his life in constant fear and anticipation of some mysterious disaster? We are going to Sweden by ferry and my dad is convinced that the ferry is going to sink. My mom says he used not to be like this when he was younger. She thinks he has become like this due to his disease. There's something wrong with his heart nerves.

Anyway, I got the permission and I am in raptures about it! I could never imagine, not even in one of my craziest and most daring dreams, that I, a poor girl from the former Soviet Republic named Latvia, would ever go anywhere further than Estonia or Lithuania. Could any of us ever dream of such possibilities? For being in the Soviet Union prohibited us any trips to any country out of the Soviet Union. Along with gaining back the independence, there are so many unexpected changes going on in our country now.

When I met Ingo, I told him I was going and that Janina was going too. When I talked to him I noticed he had strange eyes. You cannot tell if they are dark green or brown, and then. . . . . Well, what's the matter with me? I am not going to start sweating him.

Later today I met him in the cafeteria again. Janina was by my side. Ingo smiled at me; however, when he noticed Janina he slightly turned away to hide his blush. I, as usual, smiled at him mockingly. It must be very embarrassing for a guy to blush all the time. Blushing is considered a girl thing. The ones who blush are usually the most shy and insecure creatures. I don't know why his blushing in front of Janina irritates me. Maybe I am jealous. Nonsense. I DON'T like him, not at all. Besides, Janina will never go out with him anyway; she is hopelessly in love with Renars, Aira's ex-boyfriend, the cutest guy at school, and one of the best junior tennis players in Latvia. Of course Renars pees on girls like Janina, who has no waistline and is dumb, and on white crows like me.

66. The big day has arrived. Our trip to Sweden starts tonight. To my great horror I just got to know that instead of the young Swedish trainee guy who was supposed to accompany us on the trip, the old freak herself is going to be all the way through with us. I am pretty pissed off with Janina, too. She is only my friend when she needs something from me. All the past week she was telling me that she wants to be in a room with me on the ferry and that she also wants us to stay with the same host family in Sweden. Yesterday, however, when we had to decide who will be in a room with whom, some girl from the other class asked Janina if she would like to be in one room with her, and Janina of course said yes without even thinking, because Everita is one of the cool ones, and me . . . well I do not want to think about it. I will always be just a substitute, somebody who is good when there is nobody else around, like an old doll who can be thrown into a corner and forgotten when a new one comes. I do not know yet who will be my roommate. Well, I don't care.

67. We are on the ferry after a long and exhausting trip to Tallinn, because there's no ferry from Riga to Sweden. Everyone is tired and most people have fallen asleep. I do not want to sleep, even though I feel tired too. I am too excited to fall asleep. Besides, I happen to be in a room with a girl from the other class called the Crazy Ines because of her carrot red hair and her crazy ways. According to the beauty standards of teens she could be one of the top girls. Skinny, large-eyed, elite clothes, dyed hair, CARROT red—a stylish one definitely. Yet the kids do not like her very much because she is very impudent and outspoken, and her loud and obnoxious laughter makes everyone around shudder in horror. I think I couldn't dream of a worse roommate. In fact there is one more free bed in our room; however, I doubt that anyone would want to spend the night in a room with a white crow and with Crazy Ines. I am pretending to be all into my diary. Ines is frantically digging through one of her numerous bags of clothes and make-up. Suddenly the door opens—that's Ingo. Is he lost here?

"I am afraid I will be your other roommate."

My heart starts to beat faster. Crazy Ines is making faces in a fake disgust. "Who told you to come to this room?" she asks grumpily.

"The teacher." There is a flame of triumph in his eyes.

"The old hen! Why didn't she take you into her own room? How am I going to change into my night gown?"

"OK, when you decide to do it, I will cover my head with three blankets."

"It's so embarrassing."

"Since when you have become so modest? As far as I know. . . ."

"Keep your shitty mouth shut, OK." I can hear real distress in Ines's voice.

"I remember the graduation party. . . ."

Ines seizes one of her high-heeled shoes and throws it at Ingo. "If you don't shut up, I will tell something about you, too."

"Go on, sweetheart." Ingo is grinning maliciously.

"In the graduation party, remember how Janina turned you down? Even though she is a plain and silly chick, she can get a far better guy than you."

Ingo turns purple from embarrassment and anger. "You are just a. . . ." He is about to slap Ines when the door opens again and the teacher comes in. Ines and Ingo freeze where they are. She looks at all three of us through her funny glasses.

"We are doing fine in here," Ingo says in Swedish, trying to cover his embarrassment with a bright smile. The teacher fixes her eyes suspiciously on Ines. Ines stares straight back at her. The old freak does not like Ines; in fact she does not like any of us, because she is Swedish. In her eyes we are just a bunch of thick-headed kids, dull, undisciplined, undeveloped as one should expect people from the former Soviet Union to be. She thinks if we cannot speak Swedish fluently after half a year of studying it, we are worth nothing. The old freak, however, has developed a special loathing for Ines because Ines does not tolerate her bullying us. Ines is never afraid to say what she thinks or feels, and the old freak is not used to any kind of resistance. Usually all the kids are scared of her. She would never have agreed for Ines to come on this trip, but since Ines is a Swedish student and her Swedish is better than mine, the old freak had no right to forbid her to come.

My fears and anxiety turned out to be futile. Ines, even though considered crazy, is very nice to me. She chats with me all the time and shows me her dresses and her numerous lipsticks. Since the ferry has a disco bar, Ines has made up her mind to go. Poor Ingo is completely ignored for a couple of hours already, but it seems he doesn't feel at all bothered about it. Ines is trying her best to persuade me to come with her. I feel scared and uneasy, yet I want to go: since it's maybe the first and last time I am on a ferry I should seize the chance.

68.
When we arrived, the disco was filled with all kinds of people. I could see my classmates and some of the kids from the other class, too; they were all dancing in a crowd. I hate dancing in a crowd! Ines was immediately asked to dance by some Russian guy, so I was left by myself again. The music was from the '80s, and people seemed to be in a dancing mood. I liked this disco bar better than any other place I have ever been to dance (but then there haven't been many such places).

They went from the fast dances to the slow ones. I felt sleepy. I asked one of my classmates who was accidentally passing me by where Janina was. The girl said, "She already went to bed." I was considering that idea too.

Suddenly I felt somebody was touching me by my shoulder. It was a man about twenty-eight at least. "May I ask you for a dance?" he asked in English.

"Gosh!" I thought to myself. I blushed and muttered, "Yes." Why, I cannot dance and I cannot speak English either.

We danced for a while. I was mortified by my ineptitude. Besides, I noticed all my classmates and the kids from the other class as well all were staring at me, their mouths dropped open.

"This is a bummer," I thought to myself.

The guy was squeezing me tight. I could feel his breath on my cheek.

"Where are you from?" he asked me, his lips almost touching my ear.

"Latvia," I whispered so quietly I almost couldn't hear myself. But he had heard me.

"I am from England," he said.

"Oh," was all I could say. "I am making a complete cake out of myself," I thought, feeling that pain of a tear coming soon in my nose.

The guy asked me if I wanted something to drink. I remembered my experience with Raivis at the disco and shook my head.

He smiled and said, "You are nice. What's your name?"

I told him my name; he said it sounded pretty to his ears. I blushed again and didn't have gumption to ask his name.

"How old are you?"

"Fifteen and a half."

He smiled again. "Now he is making fun of me." I thought he was looking at me curiously.

"You are very pretty for a fifteen-year-old," he said.

I didn't know what to say. The DJ announced it was four in the morning, which meant the party was over.

I smiled at my dance partner for the first time. I don't know if he sensed it, but that was a smile of relief. "Well I don't care what he thinks about me," I thought. "Hopefully I see him for the first and the last time in my life."

"Thank you," he said and bowed in front of me.

"Thank you."

He carefully took a lock of hair on my forehead into his fingers and played with it. "Yeah, you are certainly a very pretty lady."

He turned around to go, then stared over his shoulder one more time at me.

I stood for a while pressing my palms against my burning cheeks. A bunch of my classmates where still hanging out on the stairs. When I passed them, Laura (one of the top girl in my class) asked me, "Who was he?"

"Somebody from England."

"Wow! You're a lucky hen, eh?" Laura sighed.

I didn't want to talk to her, so I rushed down the stairs to my room. It was locked. I knew we had only two keys. One was with Ines, and the other I had given to Ingo. For a while I looked around for Ines, but she wasn't visible anywhere. I felt uneasy about going back to the bar and looking for her there. Instead I started to look for Ingo. I went down the narrow hall where the casinos were. Of course Ingo was there playing. I approached him. He looked weird. I could smell the alcohol on his breath. I asked him for the key. He looked at me as if I had asked him for the moon.

"The key? What key?"
"The key to our room."
"The key to our room?"
"Yes, exactly, the key to our room, you fool!"
"Oh, yeah; here it is. In fact, could you wait for me? I am coming soon. I have lost most of my money."

I observed drastic changes in his usually so tranquil behaviour, apparently due to alcohol. He seemed to be excited and somehow absent-minded.

"Let's go back to the room," I said quietly.
"Yeah, let's go."

He couldn't get the key into the hole for a long time. I was beginning to lose my patience.

"Let me try."
"I can . . . I can . . . I can do it myself."

At last he managed to open the door and to crawl in.
"What's the matter with you?" I asked him when we were inside and had locked the door.

"Nothing, really nothing."
"Now come on, I don't believe you. Have you been drinking?"
"No, not even a bit."
"Then why are you acting so weird?"
"I am not acting weird; I am just tired."
"Why did you go there? Why didn't you come with us?"
"I don't know."
"For sure you have been drinking! You stink!"

He looked embarrassed. "I drank just a little bit. I had never tried it before."

I wanted to laugh, to mock him, yet something stopped me.
"Are you all right?" I asked softly instead.
"Yeah, just feeling a little sick."
"If the old freak finds that out, we are in mess." He was really concerned.

"She won't."
"Where's Ines, by the way?" he asked suddenly.

"I don't know. I think she is still with that Russian guy."
"What Russian guy?"
"The one she was dancing with."
"Really? And she went away with him?"
"I guess so. The disco is over. But maybe they went for a walk or something."

Ingo looked pale and had dark circles under his eyes. "You are very naive."

"Why?"

"They didn't go for walk. You don't know Ines. She's a. . . ."

"She is a what?"

"She does one-night stands."

"Does that mean that she . . . ?" My eyes widened.

"Yes. She does not only kiss those guys, she sleeps with them."

"But she doesn't know them at all!"

"It doesn't matter to her. I think I am feeling real sick. I will go out for awhile. Will you come with me?"

I shrugged. "If you want me to."

We found the stairs and went on the deck. Everything was covered in a deep mist. The water looked black and threatening. I shivered. Ingo looked at me, his eyes attentive, anxious.

"Is he going to throw up now?" I wondered.

Instead he put his arm round me and pulled me close.

Suddenly I realized why I was jealous of Janina. I liked Ingo. I liked him but didn't want to admit it, not even to myself. He gave me a quick kiss on the top of my nose. "You are cold. Let's get back. I feel better now."

Then I had no doubt I liked him.

69.

I am in Sweden. For the first time in my life I am somewhere far out of Latvia. It is INCREDIBLE that fate could be so gracious to me. To all of us!

My host family seem to be nice people. The mother is a skinny blondee and awfully wrinkled, too; one can immediately tell that she is the one who holds the reins of the household completely and entirely in her hands. The father is a good-natured beer belly, who is unable to object to any of his wife's whims. There are two kids: a girl about sixteen, called Emma, plain and freckled; in fact her appearance seems to be even worse than mine, and I must admit that it makes me quite happy (there—my wicked heart reveals itself); and a five-year-old boy, Kalle, who is probably the loudest family member. Oh yeah, I forgot the two dogs: one big and skinny with large and incredibly sad eyes, as if she had the responsibility to bear all the sorrow of the world; the other small and fat and quite satisfied with life with a body set on four ridiculously short and chunky legs.

Here I am having a room of my own which I enjoy a great deal, mainly because I have not until recently had the luxury of having a room all for myself for twenty-four hours, and also because I am so shy and so clumsy that I rather spend my time in the room than hanging out with the family and submitting myself to embarrassments like spilling the apple juice all over the table or dropping a piece of baked fish on my lap after a desperate attempt to get it to my mouth with the help of a fork and knife. So I sit in my room and listen to an old Status Quo tape. Sometimes Emma comes into my room and we chat for a while. Sometimes we speak English, although we are supposed to chat only in Swedish. After all, that was the main purpose of this trip. Yet I do not feel at all confident about my Swedish; besides (I am scared to admit it even to myself) I do not like this language. Why do I learn it then? Well, I guess people make a lot of unwise choices during their lifetimes. Emma is not very sociable either. Maybe she is shy, too; maybe also she feels ugly and unworthy.

The evenings are usually filled with all sorts of activities. We go out to the movies and cafes and basketball games. Often I see Ingo from far away; he is always with his host brothers. I wish I could say hello to him. Laura lives with a host family about five minutes away from Emma, so I get to hang out with her a lot, which would never have happened under normal conditions, because she is one of the top girls. Laura has to be polite to me because of her host sister and because of Emma. Of course Laura's presence gives me a lot of tension; otherwise I enjoy these hang-outs a great deal. Especially the long rides in the car at night at a considerable speed. I cannot believe that Emma at the age of sixteen has got her own car and is even able to drive it.

70. Last night was the good-bye party and now it is back home again. Emma lent me her jeans for the party, and her jacket too. The party was fun. Emma's jeans were too short and too wide in the waist, but I had no guts to tell her that. She thought they look gorgeous on me. The jacket was a better deal. It emphasized my shoulders and my breasts; besides it looked kinda cute with the jeans. Laura had tight jeans and a black sexy top she bought just yesterday in one of the local shops. Did she look gorgeous! Anything she puts on looks gorgeous. There was a whole cloud of perfume round her. I felt stupid and so ugly again. I swallowed the familiar lump in my throat and smiled at her.

"Hey, how are you?"

She smiled back viciously. The hell with her. I got into the car and slammed the door. Laura has a crush on some Swedish guy called Waimar. He is a cutie, but concerning Laura he displays nothing but utter indifference. It irritates her a great deal, and of course it amazes me a great deal, too. Can't such people like Laura get anything their heart desires?

The party hall was nothing but a huge sports hall full of high school students. Coke cans all over the floor. Emma grabbed me by the hand and dragged me to some sort of girls' secret room. There was a label on the door in English: "Girls just wanna have fun!" I heard laughter and crazy squeaks inside. As we entered the room, every face turned to us. Emma tried to explain something in her own language. It sounded funny; besides she was blushing. I found myself smiling, a silly smile I guess. I was trying so hard to conceal my ignorance and my embarrassment. "Why didn't Emma explain to me what it is all about?" I wondered. We were all sitting in a circle. Somebody was patting my hand, somebody was passing me a bowl of chips. I noticed among the girls there was also the crazy Ines. I uttered a sigh of relief. Soon I settled down next to her. We were eating chips, drinking Coke and chatting. There was still plenty of time until the dance party started. I felt better then. I wished I didn't have to go to the dance party at all.

Then the dances started. The hall was crowded and full of the smell of rubber and human sweat. The funniest thing was that most girls were dancing with girls and most guys with guys. That was weird, but at least it gave me some sort of security. I did not have to be a wallflower. I always envied of people dancing while I just had to sit and watch.

I was dancing, too, or better to say making some awkward movement, trying to fit into the rhythm. Around 3 a.m. the slow dances started. I retreated. Most girls were dancing with guys then, and the guys with girls; however, I could observe some exceptions as well. Nobody paid attention anyway... everyone was too busy with dancing. Watching and observing is for the wallflowers like me.

I noticed Laura in the crowd. She was dancing with Renars, Janina's crush. After a dance he kissed her on the cheek. Janina was near to tears. She looked so desperate I was forced for an instant to forget about my own fate. I knew nothing else than to pat her hand compassionately. She stared at me with her eyes large (maybe the only objects that are beautiful in her body) full of unshed tears. I felt so worn out and tired. I went out for a while to get some fresh air. Suddenly I felt somebody's arm round my waist, somebody breathing straight into my face. I could sense alcohol. It was some drunk Swede trying to tell me something in his language.

"I don't understand," I said in English.

He looked puzzled. He asked me, "Where are you from? Germany? Finland?"
"From Latvia. It's right across the Baltic Sea."
He let me loose and walked away.
I saw Ingo walking around all by himself. I didn't have the courage to approach him. I was so scared of being rejected. I felt sick. I wanted to throw up, although I hadn't been drinking anything besides Coke.

71. We are back in Riga, and Sweden, with its cold breezes, fairyland towns (in comparison with our dirty villages with falling apart houses) and blondee freckled teenagers seems like a beautiful dream. Well, yes, there is no doubt now that Ingo has developed a huge crush on Janina. Of course, how could it ever be different? Ingo likes Janina even though she is short and plump, with no waistline, always smiling in that silly, irritating way. Yet apparently she is more special than I am. Maybe I am trying to find faults in other people which are not there at all, yet which are necessary for my own comfort. Maybe for him Janina appears to be beautiful. After all, guys seem to have different eyes than girls. Guys always fuss over things which girls consider nothing special. Maybe Ingo, like the majority of people, is attracted to the unreachable, which always seems to be more appealing and tempting than the reachable, and for the reason that it is unreachable, which means you can dream about it, you can have the craziest fantasies about it, you can live and thrive on the pictures created by your imagination, and usually they are far more beautiful than reality. Ingo, the tennis player, likes Janina because she is unreachable. She has a huge crush on Renars, who does not notice her at all. He is something unreachable for her. While I, so very reachable, am right next to Ingo, and he doesn't care. The kiss on the top of my nose was just a joke from his side, and I took it so seriously! I allowed my heart to take the upper hand and stir up all these bittersweet emotions, exactly the same way as it happened that time with Cook and his hug.

I am not going to think about it because it spoils my mood. I am a big girl now and I have made a resolution that I will not let the stupid emotions like love ever occupy my mind and heart. I am just not going to like anybody, for nobody will like me first. I am more than sure about it, and since it is so, I am going to protect my heart. After all, one can live in this world without love. It is not fun at all, but you can pull through. I know I will survive even without love, like some people are living without one leg or one eye or even without both.

Of course they cannot enjoy life completely, but what can they possibly do about their situation? I wish I had guts to commit a suicide, but I guess I don't. I am very scared that it will hurt. Death will hurt, and

I am scared also of what will happen to me when I die. Will I be rotting in grave not feeling anything? Will I disappear like foam? Will I have a soul which will go to heaven or hell?

Yeah, hell is more likely. I suppose I am just such a bad person. I am so envious of anybody who is prettier than me, of anybody who is more liked than me. Well no! I will not commit a suicide! I will just try to find fulfillment and meaning in something else. I will go to some church and pray to God. Maybe He will help me. Maybe He will fill me with Himself and I will not need any human love. I will be strong and happy, and I will not need anybody. I have heard of such things happening.

72. The family where I am babysitting is on a vacation in Norway, which means I have three weeks all by myself. I am not excited about such prospects, for I do not know what to do with myself for such a long time. Today I was simply wandering up and down the city streets observing people. I find enormous pleasure in staring at people, observing the way they are dressed and they way they carry themselves. Maybe it's impolite, but I don't care. Well, I was observing people when suddenly in the crowds I noticed a very nice lady. She was tall and thin and frail, dressed in a black rain coat and sunglasses. She was a very beautiful lady, and I was staring right at her. Incredibly, she was staring back at me. On the street corner she passed me, then quickly made up her mind and turned around. She walked right up to me and asked, "Do you speak English?"

I told her yes, although my English is very bad.

She took off her sunglasses and smiled. Gosh! She was the most beautiful woman I've ever seen. Her eyes were large and blue and very kind.

She asked me also if I believed in God. I said yes, this time more securely.

"Do you read the Bible too or maybe you go to some church?"

"No, but I was going to."

She was looking at me very carefully, as if waiting for me to say something more.

"Yes, I am having some tough times currently. That's why I thought maybe God could help!" I said it all very fast, as if I had said something stupid.

"I see," she said and paused for a while, as if trying to remember something. "If you would like, we could study the Bible together. I would love to share with you my own life and how I found God and why I found Him. Would you be interested?"

"Yes," I said quickly, thinking, "I would love to talk more with this wonderful woman."

"My name's Lisa," she said, extending her hand. I took it and smiled, nervously saying my own name. We chatted for a while about nothing. She told me about her little daughter Catelyn and about the wonderful husband God had provided for her. I didn't have anything wonderful in my life to discuss with a stranger, so I just kept quiet. Then a dark cloud covered the sun, and it seemed as if it was going to rain, so we parted. We arranged a meeting tomorrow at Laima clock.

I am very eager to talk with this Lisa. Maybe I will learn something about God, and certainly I will improve my English. I think Lisa is American, so maybe I will also learn something about America.

73. Today I met with Lisa again. I cannot understand why she was smiling all the time when there is no reason for it. When I asked her, she looked at me funny and said in a serious voice, "This is not a joy that world gives me; this is the joy that comes from the Holy Spirit."

I just stared back at her with my mouth half open.

"Have you ever heard of the Holy Spirit? Do you know what it is?" she asked me.

"It must be something connected with God or religion?"

"Oh, you're absolutely right!" she exclaimed with so much enthusiasm that I jumped a little bit. I didn't expect such a reaction on my stupid answer. "The Holy Spirit is the spirit of God."

I nodded.

"We could find some little cafe and sit down and talk if you would like." She showed all her teeth again. I have never met anyone who smiled as much as Lisa.

We found a cafe near the Laima clock, and Lisa bought me a Coke and a pastry. It made me feel like in seventh heavens. She was opening up her heart and soul for me. She told me about her life. How she was born and grew up in New York City. How her parents were taking her to some old traditional Dutch church and how boring it seemed to her; how she met her first boyfriend at the age of fifteen and how very scared she was when he offered to have sex in some cellar (they weren't able to find a better place). She told me about all her boyfriends (she has had a lot of them because she is so beautiful) and how she had always been so terrified when it came to sex. I couldn't get the point why she was terrified, being so beautiful and so much wanted. I would be terrified if it ever came to sex in my life, but not about being beautiful and sought after.

Lisa told me about her career too. For many years her job was singing and dancing in city clubs and bars. She told me about her long-term relationship with Rick, her singing partner, and I guess her partner in sex as well. She told me about the tough and depressing times in her life when she was seeking help from somewhere above. How she was studying Bible all by herself. How she became a true Christian and how she met her husband Danny. It was all very crazy. She was still performing in clubs and pubs with Rick, but she was dating someone else at that point of her life. That someone else was her present husband's friend. One night Danny had invited him to some sort of a Christian meeting. When he came back from the meeting he said to his girlfriend Lisa, "We are living in sin! We will stop it right today!" Lisa didn't know how to respond to that.

The very next day she also was dragged to that meeting and then God's miracle happened. Lisa got touched at the very depth of her heart. Suddenly she became painfully conscious of her own sinfulness and immediately made a decision to repent and be baptized, just as the Bible tells us to do in Acts 2: 38-39, to be able to start a new and wonderful life. She dumped her boyfriend, through whom God had brought her to Him, and fell in love and married Danny.

Her story showed what wonderful and incredible things God can do in a human life.

Then she asked me to tell something about myself. What could I tell her? There was nothing exciting or wonderful about my life. I simply told her that I have also had numerous guys willing to sleep with me, but I never slept with any of them because I was terrified, but I wanted to make an impression.

She smiled and said to me, "You are a very smart girl for your age. Not many girls at your age have that much common sense."

I am not at all smart, but it was nice that Lisa thought so and I will leave her in those illusions until she finds out the truth for herself.

She looked at her watch. "I am sorry. I have to go now. We had such a great talk. Thank you very much for finding some time for me!"

What was she thanking me for? After all, she found some time for me, not I for her.

"Yes, and thanks for being honest with me and opening your heart to me."

I blushed. I had invented stories, and she was thanking me for me being honest with her.

"Would you like to get together some other time?"

I told her yes. I liked Lisa very much, and I also like the fact that I can practice my English by talking to her.

"I will leave you my phone number," she said. "You can call me any time day or night. You are my very special friend now."

I spent the rest of the day in raptures. What a surprise that this wonderful lady wanted a white crow for her friend! And what a surprise when mom made no objections to my meeting with Lisa in the future!

74. Today I met Lisa again. This time we met at McDonald's, and Lisa had brought with her a large Bible in English. She made me to read certain Bible scriptures. After I read them, she asked me certain questions. She was in raptures about my wise answers. She was trying to make me see what it means to be a true Christian, which is equal to being a true disciple of Jesus Christ. She drew all sorts of pictures and spiritual formulas on a sheet of paper. I remember only one, but then this is the main one: Christian = Disciple of Jesus = Saved.

That made all the matter serious, for it turns out that if you are not a Disciple of Christ, you are going straight to hell after you die, for the Bible says that only God's children will be saved.

When I asked Lisa how I could become one of the God's children, she got very excited. "That's the simplest thing ever," she said. "All you have to do is to get baptized into our church."

"Why into your church?"

"Because then we can continue to study Bible, and you will see with your own eyes that we are the church that lives according to all the God's standards. You are lucky that God sent me in your way, for through me God is revealing to you the great mystery of the salvation. He has has decided to show compassion and mercy on you. He doesn't want you to perish. See how many people are sitting in this McDonald's, how many people are passing us by? They know nothing about their Creator and their Savior. If that last day comes today, they will all go to hell! Can you imagine this? Doesn't your heart ache from pity and compassion for those people?"

Wow! That was something! I was listening to Lisa as if she were the Heavenly Father Himself talking to me.

"God has prepared you for something great. He's got a wonderful plan for your life, more wonderful than you could ever imagine in your craziest dreams. God has chosen you to save the lost people of this world. This is the only job with an eternal significance. All the other are just temporary ones. Money, fame, beauty, all will fade away on a day you die. All you will have to present to God will be your soul. It's the soul you should care about first, for that determines your eternal destiny. Unfortunately, people are so engaged in making money that they have become blind to see God and deaf to hear His voice calling them to repent. Look at the people around you. Look at the people out there."

Lisa was speaking like a real preacher. But she is a preacher's wife after all. I was in a daze. I felt as if something great and incredible is about to happen with my life. I have been thinking about God a lot lately and asking Him questions. Could I imagine that God will answer my prayers so fast?

After a while Lisa had to go again, but we made another appointment for tomorrow. I came home with a feeling of being in another dimension. I felt so full with my new knowledge about God and about the IMPORTANCE of the salvation that I wanted to talk to somebody who would listen to me.

Dad was not at home, and mom was definitely not the best option, so I chose to go and visit my aunt. Olga is a spinster, a very attractive one, but fussy too. In the recent years she has become my best friend. I trust her. I always tell her things I cannot talk over with my mom, for I am frightened by my mom's weird reactions.

I was preaching to Aunt Olga the way Lisa was preaching to me, and I was wondering where all those wise words and expressions came from. Was God really talking through me so that my aunt could hear the message of salvation and could be saved? Merely imagining that God was using me as His tool for other people's salvation made me tremble from excitement.

Despite my eloquence, Aunt Olga remained unmoved. She was rather worried and warned me to watch out from all sorts of preachers pretending to be innocent lambs but actually being wolves. Yeah, Lisa warned me already that Satan will work hard sowing fears and doubts in people's minds, in that way trying to prevent them from accepting God's truth. Anyway, I am so full of hope and God's wonderful power that my aunt's skepticism just makes my resolution to convert her even stronger.

75. I just came back from my meeting with Lisa. Today we studied Bible again. Basically we looked at the scriptures which talk about who God and Jesus Christ really are. Today I learned that God and Jesus Christ are actually one and the same. Lisa was smiling a lot as usually, and she called me a smart girl again. It turns out that she and her husband Danny are leading the International Church of Christ in Moscow. They came to Moscow in 1991 during the putsch, when the Soviet empire was falling apart and tanks were on the streets. Lisa brags that all the other American preachers and Gospel teachers (a vast number of them had come to bring the good news to the Soviet citizens, so to say to the pagans to save them from the fires of hell) left Russia during that time, trembling about their own mortal skins, while she with her husband and another American couple stayed, committing their lives into the hands of our heavenly Father.

I can only admire Lisa and her faith and endurance. I will have a chance to meet her husband and her little daughter. They have come here as a whole team from Moscow, an international team of Americans, Russians, Finns, Lithuanians, Estonians and one Latvian guy named Salvis. He was converted in Sweden while playing for some badminton club. He used to be a famous badminton player some years ago in Latvia. Now he's quitted playing badminton, and for the past five years has been faithfully serving the church. Lisa said he wasn't able to come back to Latvia because there was no church here five years ago. Saying this, Lisa made a serious face. "Do you understand all these years Latvia has been completely under Satan's rule, and now God has taken mercy upon the people here and has sent a team to Riga to plant His own church here, for He wants nobody to perish and everybody to be saved?"

Lisa wants me to understand the importance and seriousness of the matter. She wants to meet my parents and she wants me to be baptized into the church as fast as possible. "You will be the Rock, the foundation, that the God's church here in Riga will be built upon, just like Peter was 2000 years ago. You are one of the God's chosen." Lisa says this frequently to encourage me to make the decision about the baptism.

76. Despite my great liking Lisa and all her convincing and powerful words, there still is a little seed of doubts in my heart which keeps on nagging me in that painful unpleasant way. What if this church is some sort of cult? All kinds of religious practices are permitted in post-Soviet Latvia, and many wicked people are taking advantage of the situation, creating all sorts of dangerous and destructive sects and involving young and innocent people in their practices. When I shared my doubts with Lisa, she was understanding and supportive. "Of course it is scary to commit your life completely into God's hands. Everybody feels like this at first. For from now on you will not be the king of your life anymore. Instead Jesus will be the manager of your life, and you will have to submit to His will in everything with a humble heart, for He is the one who knows best what you need. Yes, what concerns the cults, there are plenty of them around; however, if you truly believe and trust in God that He is leading you on the right path, you shouldn't have any doubts. Do you think that God, who loves you, would ever allow you to get involved into some sort of cult? Do you believe that you are on the right path?"

The question was too straight for me. With trembling knees I answered "Yes!" I feel scared to commit my life to God, but even more scared not to do it. I do not want to be damned to eternal sufferings and fires of hell. I think I have had enough sufferings and hurts while living in this world.

77. I am so excited I cannot fall asleep! Today I had a chance to meet Lisa's family. Her husband is very handsome and apparently loves his wife very much, and her little daughter Catelyn is a cutie. She wasn't shy at all like most kids are meeting with strangers. I also met the rest if the team. They are such awesome people. We were playing volleyball, telling jokes and laughing all the time. They all were kind and attentive towards me, and all of them wanted to know me better. For the first time of my life I was the center of everyone's attention. I also got to know the other married couple, Shelly and Craig Cooper. They are helping Danny and Lisa with the church in Moscow.

Shelly seemed a little weird. Of course she, like all Americans, was constantly showing her beautiful white teeth. I wonder if this is some sort of an American habit, to smile all the time. Or maybe it is characteristic only of Christians, who cannot help putting all their overflowing happiness into their smiles in such a way trying to impress the so-called pagans.

Yeah, besides Shelly has got HUGE blue eyes. Of course they are beautiful, but a little scary too. I think I wouldn't be able to trust Shelly the way I trust Lisa. Shelly's husband Craig is very handsome too and appears to be a kind and harmless soul.

Among the team members there are also two Estonian girls who were converted to Christianity about a half a year ago. Both of them are plump, good natured and hopeless at speaking Russian, so I had to communicate with them in English.

The two Russian girls, Katja and Anja (also from the Moscow team), seem to be the sharp ones. They were dressed in shorts (a little too short according to the Christian virtuousness) and T-shirts, and spent most of their time chasing guys. Every time they managed to catch one, they giggled and squeaked from joy. I wondered if this was some sort of a Christian game or it was their own invention, coming completely from their own initiative.

I noticed also that Katja was constantly flirting with the Latvian guy who had spent the past five years helping to grow the Moscow church. Maybe they are dating. Katja told me that it had been her biggest dream for the past five years to come to Riga and to help to start the church here. She said she had been praying for Riga and the people here all these years, and now she was seeing the fruit of her tireless prayers.

Katja's friend Anja is nice, too. Stylish, I should say, with her short jet black hair, her funny sunglasses and her short, bright red shorts which revealed a pair of athletic and nicely tanned legs.

The guys? Yeah, what should I say about the guys? The tall and dark-haired Lithuanian guy Rikardas is a cutie, no doubt about that. The other guy is Russian named Dennis. Originally he is from Riga, but he has been studying for past two years in Moscow, and there he was converted. Now as he assured to me it was his honor to start the God's church in his own country.

The Finnish representative named Anti is handsome and little simple-minded, but that doesn't spoil his charms at all. He is also smiling most of the time, however not in an American way. He greeted me so as if we had known each other for the most part of our lives and even hugged me. I blushed and didn't hug him back. He couldn't pronounce my name at first, but he still thinks I have a very beautiful name.

I also made friends with a Latvian girl named Lasma. She had met Shelly on the street. The rain had been pouring, and Shelly had forgotten her umbrella, so Lasma let her stand under her umbrella. While the rain was pouring they were talking. Shelly had told her a lot about the church in Moscow and about how wonderful it is to be a part of God's Kingdom already here on this earth. Lasma had been intrigued and curious; that's why she had decided to come and find out for herself.

78. This afternoon Lisa and I were inviting people to the first service of the Church of Christ in Riga. We got to talk with so many people, starting with the local Latvians and Russians: girls, boys, uncles, aunts, kids, couples in love, tramps and homeless people—in other words the representatives from all societies. Lisa can speak very good Russian, and we also talked with Swedish, French, British and American tourists. Most people were positive, and I suspect it was all because of Lisa. She's so beautiful and she knows how to make people to like her. She has a warm smile and beautiful eyes. One Latvian guy, who couldn't speak English, asked me to translate to Lisa that he would come to the service not because he was interested in God or religion but only to look into those beautiful eyes one more time. Lisa was laughing when I said it to her. The guy was trying to touch her, but she escaped his touch very successfully, and we crossed the street at the red light. The guy wanted to follow us (better to say her), but cars were driving back and forth, and the guy wouldn't risk throwing himself right under the wheels, not even for the American lady with the beautiful eyes.

Lisa thinks that I have a heart for God, and that I would make an awesome servant in His Kingdom here on the earth, and that through me many people will come to the knowledge of God and to the salvation.

Her words make me very happy. Now in the evenings when I go to sleep I always remember those words, and I fall asleep happy, for my life has meaning. Now I know why I was created. Now there's even an explanation to my ugliness. If I was beautiful and admired and adored by everyone, I would have become very conceited. I probably would have a boyfriend by now, and I would have never come to God and to His truth. As Lisa says, "God lifts up and helps those who are despised by the world." God made me ugly to be able to show me His infinite mercy! Besides what are the looks? They will perish anyway. All of us will die, no matter how beautiful or ugly we have been during our lifetime. All of us will have to stand in front of God and give an account about our lives, and would good looks save me then? No! There will be not good or bad looks there. There will be just my soul, and God will see if I had been walking his ways during my life time on the earth or not.

Such thoughts comfort me and instead of hating my appearance they help me to accept myself the way I am, the way God has created me.

79. Today—oh!

Today Lisa told me that I will have a very special Bible study with Katja. Katja will read to me a medical report (some American doctor had made a research) about what Jesus had to suffer on the cross. How horrible and painful it had been for Him from the physical point of view, for since He came on the earth in a human appearance He used to have the same type of body as we are having.

Gosh! The report was horrifying! Katja was reading in Russian, and I was glad that my Russian was not good enough to understand everything. All I understood was that his flesh was soft like a peach from beatings, and there could be seen open nerves and tissues. People had put a crown of thorns on his head, and there was blood dripping from his forehead when He was carrying His own cross to some hill, I do not remember the name of the place. People were spitting at Him and making fun of Him. When He was already hanging at the cross he could hardly breathe from the horrible pain in His lungs. Of course the description was much more detailed; everything was mentioned, every damaged part of His body was described up to precision (almost as if the doctor himself had been there and had examined it all). I couldn't understand all the Russian medical terms. Anyway it was horrible enough.

When Katja had finished reading she put the sheets aside and stared at me in silence. I didn't know what I was supposed to say or to do. After a ten minutes silence Katja asked, "How do you feel now?"

I didn't know what to say.

Katja's gaze was piercing and very unpleasant.

"Don't you feel bad? Don't you?" She questioned me as if she was a judge and I was a criminal. "Jesus had to go through all this because of YOU! Because of your very sins! Don't you feel bad at all about what you had done to Him?"

I really did feel bad, but not because I had done something to Jesus. I felt bad because of Katja's piercing looks and because of the tone of her voice. I felt paralyzed by some mysterious fear. I was scared like a rabbit confronting a wolf.

"Don't you realize what you have done? Didn't the description break you? Don't you feel that you should ask Jesus for forgiveness? On your knees you should ask Him for the forgiveness of your sins with tears streaming down your cheeks."

I really started to cry, not because of my sins, but because I didn't really understand what I was supposed to ask the forgiveness for. I started to cry because I was scared, and because I felt sorry for Jesus that he had to suffer so horribly. Katja seemed to be satisfied with the outcome. She hugged me and said to me in a kinder voice, "I felt the same way too after reading the description. Now you are broken, and now you understand who you really are. You are a sinner who cannot save herself unless you ask Jesus to forgive you and to save you."

Right after the Bible study with Katja I met with Lisa again. She hugged me and asked me how I felt. I said I was crying. I didn't even have to explain why I was crying. Lisa threw her arms around me once again and exclaimed, "Oh, I know, I know, darling! I felt the same way after reading it. It just struck me what a mess I was. Of course I felt pretty bad about myself, but this realization brought me to repentance and, in the end, to salvation. I got baptized into God's church. I got baptized by immersion, which is the only right baptism, the only way of baptism which can save you. Do not ever listen to people who tell you that you can receive the forgiveness of your sins only by accepting Christ in your heart. Instead, you MUST be baptized with a water baptism, which means you must be completely covered by the water. For only in that instant do you receive the free gift called the Holy Spirit."

Lisa noticed my horror. "What is wrong, Sweetheart?"

"You mean that all those people who do believe in God but are not baptized by immersion are not saved?"

Lisa grew quiet. "I hate to say so but that's true, dear." A shadow of sadness passed over her face.

"In other words, all those people, even if they are believers and are leading Christian lives, are going to hell anyway? Their faith doesn't mean anything?"

"That's what the Bible says. The truth is sometimes harsh, but that's the way it is, and there is no point of deceiving yourself with illusions of your own imagination. You may think it's not true, but if the Bible says it is true, then it is, and there's nothing you can do about it."

"I think it is horrible!" I whispered.

"Yes, but you must be a very lucky person, then. Can you imagine what grace God has showed to you by letting you to meet with me that day on the street corner? So many churches and so many people are living in illusions, thinking that they are saved because they have accepted Christ into their lives. So many people think they are saved because Christ has died for their sins almost two thousand years ago, and that's why now they can relax and enjoy life. However, God expects us to live a life of a disciple. He will not accept into heaven anyone who hasn't lived a life of a disciple on this earth. This life means permanent confession of your sins to God and to your spiritual leader, daily sharing your faith with the lost, sacrifice of your own selfish desires by putting God's desires at the first place, constant Bible studies, Christian meeting attendance, and so on, and so on."

The list didn't sound very encouraging. Noticing my indecision, Lisa asked, "After hearing all this are you still willing to give up your life to God to seek and save the lost? Are you still willing to die for yourself to live for God?"

Since I didn't have any other choice but to accept it or burn in hell, I had to say yes to Lisa. Of course, I do truly believe that Bible is God's word, and what it says must be true. I have always believed in the Bible since I was a child.

Lisa was in raptures. "I knew you had a heart for God! God will do incredible works through you. Through you He will make the difference in many people's lives. I just believe it!"

I felt happy again. Even if living the life of a disciple will be difficult and painful, it will be worth it. First I will start with my parents. I know they believe in the Lord, but since they are not baptized, they are not saved. And my dad could die any minute! But I have faith that through me God will come into my parents' lives and will reveal them the truth.

80. In these recent days I am walking around like a person obsessed! Everywhere I walk I see crowds of people who are not saved: on the streets, in the busses, trolleys and trams, in the shops and movie theaters. What if the last day is today? This thought gives me the courage to approach any person on the street, in a shop, on the trolley. I share my new faith with them, trying to make them understand how important the information is. I am giving out the invitations for the first official meeting of our church in Riga. Some people engage in conversations; some just stare at me cynically; some tear the invitations into pieces right in front of my eyes. I do not care what people think of me. I do not care, for Jesus didn't care either.

At home things are kind of tense. Mom seems to be more supportive than Dad. Of course, both are afraid that I may be involved in some sort of a cult. My explanations that those people live very strictly according to the Bible teachings and that they are the true people of God because their role model is nobody else but Jesus Christ himself do not help much. I offered Mom to meet with Lisa, and she promised she will.

81. Today Mom met with Lisa! I was a little anxious about her reaction. Would my mom be able to see that Lisa is a God-sent person to save me and maybe her and Dad?

I waited for Lisa at Laima clock. I first saw her far away, talking with that Lithuanian guy. They were hugging. Yeah, that's another custom of the church: whenever the disciples meet, they hug each other. That is a sort of a greeting form and also a demonstration of God's love among the disciples. God's people must love each other as Jesus Himself loved people, and Lisa claims that so far this is the only church where she has seen the true display of sincerity and love among the church members. That is something!

When Mom arrived, I was watching her from a distance. She was walking up Bulvaris Iela, from the direction of the Opera. She looked so exhausted and so sad, I felt sharp pain in my chest. My mom! There isn't such a day when she is not mad at me about something. I am so happy when she is not at home. Sometimes I think I hate her for annoying me with her constant nagging me and blaming me for some silly unimportant things. Yet apparently I love her, and I love her more than I thought I did.

Mom is always so clumsy and shy when meeting with strangers, it embarrasses me.

"Hello. My name's Lisa!" Lisa was speaking in Russian.

"Gaida." My mom took Lisa's extended hand into her own large palm, damaged by hard work, and smiled awkwardly.

"Your daughter told me that you wanted to meet with me, that you had some questions concerning her joining our church."

"I would like to know what sort of a church it is my daughter is so determined to join."

"We are just Christians. We are a nondenominational church. We are people who sincerely and truly follow God by living out the Bible's principles in nowadays world. We are a living proof that it is possible to live according to Bible even in our twentieth-century world."

"Maybe we could go and sit down on the bench over there," Lisa offered kindly and took my mother under her arm.

We sat on the bench in a shade of an oak tree. Lisa was trying to answer all my mom's questions as well as she could. At the end of the conversation my mom was so overwhelmed that she couldn't help weeping. I felt awkward, but then my mom always wets her eyes with or without a reason, just as Americans always smile with or without a reason.

82. Tomorrow we are going to celebrate Lisa's little daughter's birthday. Alona, some Russian girl who was also invited on the street by Shelly, is trying to make friends with me. She suggested also that we buy a present for Catelyn together. I think Alona is a hypocrite. Of course, what right do I have to think so? The Bible tells us not to judge others; then we won't be judged ourselves.

Anyway, I can't help not liking Alona. I think she is one of those people who are doing things only for their own welfare and convenience. I know that she is coming to these meeting because she wants to practice her English (these meetings are a wonderful opportunity) and not because she is really interested in Christ. Lisa told me once lots of people at first come to their meeting out of curiosity or for some selfish reasons and later become true followers of Christ.

We bought a present for little Catelyn, a soft furry dog. Of course, I had to pay more because at the counter Alona realized that with the money she had she also needed to buy some sort of medicine for her pimples. She has huge, ugly pimples all over her face which make her look hideous. She is not beautiful either, and I am glad about that.

Now I truly see how nasty, selfish, and horrible I am, but I cannot make myself to like Alona.

83. Last night Catelyn's birthday was celebrated at the Hotel Riga conference hall. All of the team were there and of course many new faces, the people that we met and invited on the street.

Little Catelyn, dressed in a pink dress with her long blondee hair unbraided, looked like a princess on a throne. She was almost buried in wrappers and boxes, the remains of the countless presents she had received during the night. She was sitting all by herself and observing the crowds in the hall. Such a little kid! What was she thinking about? She must be a very happy kid, loved, petted and admired by everyone.

Because of her there was candle light and romantic music and an enormous cake. Alona and I couldn't pluck up our courage to give Catelyn our present. It looked ridiculously poor in comparison with all the other expensive gifts she had received. Someone even gave her a real, live kitten! We looked at Catelyn. She gazed back and smiled. Her smile gave us courage. Alona was the one who handed her the present. She made it appear as if the present was only from her, so I had nothing to give. Well, I gave Catelyn a hug. She stared at me for a while with her eyes so large and incredibly blue, just like Lisa's.

"Thank you! It's so beautiful!" she said. She was gently petting the dog. "I have never had anything like that before!"

Alona was green with envy because Catelyn didn't say thanks to her, only to me.

The party was fun. Catelyn sang for us a couple of songs written by her mummy and left everyone with an impression that there are no better and nicer people in this world than the representatives of the International Church of Christ!

84. Today was Lisa's last day in Riga. They are leaving tomorrow afternoon. I met with Lisa in one of those small cozy cafes in the old town. To my unpleasant surprise she had Shelly with her this time. I shuddered a little at the sight of her and immediately asked God for forgiveness for having a bad attitude.

They both greeted me with a hug, and Lisa even bought me some Coke. After asking how I was and obviously not expecting an answer to such a question, they both opened their Bibles and showed me several scriptures talking about sin. They made me read them carefully. Then they one after another started to confess their deepest darkest sins to me. After having confessed, or better to say having brought everything out into the light, they suddenly fell silent. Were they expecting me to open up and confess? What was I supposed to do? I just stared at them dumbly, not knowing how to start.

Shelly was examining me with her scary eyes, as if scrutinizing every detail about me. Her gaze made me feel even more uncomfortable. Lisa noticed that, patted my hand and spoke to me gently.

"Honey, your sins are the wall that is between you and God. God cannot reach you and help you unless you break down this wall by bringing your sins out into the light, which means you simply confess them to your brothers and sisters in Christ."

"Do I have to confess everything? Absolutely everything?"

"If you do not bring into light all your deeds, if you do not confess them to me or to some other sister in Christ, you are nourishing darkness in your heart. And this darkness brings you further away from your heavenly Father, which means your heart slowly gets harder and harder. Satan gets more and more hold of your heart and life, and in the end you simply fall away. I hope you understand why it is so important to confess."

I nodded, but a lump of fear blocked my throat and made me unable to utter anything.

Shelly smiled cheerfully. "Well, it is scary at first, but once you find out that you have such awesome Christian sisters all around you, whom you can trust completely, you become willing to confess your sins to get this darkness out of your heart."

"Well. . . ." I was able to speak again; somehow I had managed to swallow the lump of fear in my throat. "I probably have very many sins, but I really do not know with what to start." Inwardly I was still shivering from Shelly's gaze.

"Let's start with the ones which are mentioned in Galatians 5," Shelly suggested.

"The first one is so-called sexual immorality. Do you know what the Bible means by it?"

"Not exactly."

"Under sexual immorality one can subordinate any sexual relationship outside wedlock. So have you ever had sex with anybody?"

"No," I said very quietly casting down my gaze, so full of shame and embarrassment. "I lied to you that time, because I wanted to impress you. I have never had sex with anybody in my whole entire life."

Lisa patted my hand once again. "It's all right, Sweetheart. In fact I am very proud of you because you had enough courage to confess that you had lied to me."

"I have had impure thoughts. A couple of times I have tried to imagine how it would be to have sex, but I have never even had a boyfriend. I have never even kissed with anybody."

"That is so wonderful darling! That only means God has prepared for you somebody very special, only exclusively for you, and you will belong only to him, which means you will have only one man in your life. And that is exactly how God has intended it to be for any of us. You are such a good and sweet girl!"

"All right, Lisa we have to go on!"

"Yes, sure. The next sin is debauchery, which includes drinking, overeating, and laziness. Have you ever had any of this?"

"Well, I have drunk several glasses of wine and a little bit of beer throughout my life, and probably I have overeaten at times. We do not have a lot of money for food in our house. Of course I have been lazy."

They both smiled. "A couple glasses of wine is okay, but you haven't been drinking too much have you?"

"No. I . . . I don't remember."

"All right. Well the next sin is . . . ."

So we went through the whole list of sins, and I could not help feeling totally rotten by the end of my confession. I have had impure thoughts, and I have been touching myself, I have read and believed in horoscopes, of which God strongly disapproves in Bible. I remember at school we used to have this history teacher who was trying to foretell my future according to the lines on my palms. I have believed in reincarnation, which is also wrong according to Bible, for Bible says there is only one life given to us.

I had been envious of other girls in the class because they were better looking than I am. I had been horribly jealous of Janina because Ingo preferred her to me despite her nonexistent waistline and her fat butt. I have hated my parents at times for not allowing me to do certain things and go to certain places. Especially I have hated my mom for constantly yelling at me for trifles like torn pantyhose and dirty slacks. I have even hated my grandmother, who is now on her deathbed. Nobody believes anymore in her recovery, because she is too old and weak to be able to overcome the disease. When she dies, she will go straight to hell, for she was never baptized into the Church of Christ, the only true church on the whole entire earth. The very thought terrifies me. And now it's too late to try to convince her, for she is already sort of disconnected from the world.

Yeah, these are all my sins. I have always tried to find some excuses for my evil ways. How could I possibly be a good person, always subjected to other people's cruelty? I have been laughed at by girls and mocked at by boys. I have been yelled at by my mother for my numerous shortcomings. How many times I have been told that I am tall and ugly and clumsy and good for nothing? Of course I have become hypersensitive, always ready to attack and bite back, easily irritable, unnecessarily suspicious. Insecure and miserable. I always considered myself a victim, an unhappy girl who was born by mistake. Yet now it turns out that my hatred, envy, jealousy and bad thoughts all are my own sins, which means I cannot blame anyone else for it. To my horror I am becoming aware of the fact that there is actually no excuse for my wrong doings. And if it wasn't for Jesus, I would be burning in hell after my death.

Well, I confessed everything to both of them. They were listening carefully, their piercing gazes on me. When I finished, Lisa suggested to pray. They both were praying for me. They were asking for God's protection and His support. I must admit it touched me deeply—those two Americans were praying for me, not even properly knowing me.

Anyway, I had confessed all the deepest darkest sins of my heart to them—maybe that is why I felt so strangely close to them. Now they know everything about me, and now I do not have to hide anymore, or make up fairy tales to impress them.

Lisa consulted her watch. She had to go. Danny and Lisa and little Catelyn are leaving at six tonight on the train to Moscow. I won't see her anymore. Lisa gave me a big hug and a little beautiful box with something in it (it was a green necklace). She even kissed me on the cheek.

I watched her leaving, and I couldn't help thinking that God has given her everything: a purpose and meaning to her life, strong convictions upon which she has built her life, faith in Him, a stable and honorable position in the society, inward and outward beauty, many talents, a loving husband and an adorable daughter. And above everything, the eternal life.

Well, I adore her too much to let any bitterness enter my heart.

I did not confess one gnawing thought which doesn't want to leave my mind. If God is righteous and infinitely good, why doesn't he give His gifts to everybody equally? I cannot understand that question. But Bible says that grumbling leads to nothing good, so I just smiled at Shelly. She returned my smile, showing her strong, beautiful teeth. Maybe Americans have got such good teeth because they do not have to drink water from the River Daugava, once praised in the Latvian folk songs, now totally polluted.

"So is there anything else you want to tell me? Anything you didn't manage to tell in front of both of us?" Shelly sounded like a prosecutor questioning the accused in the Soviet times.

"No, there is nothing else I could tell you that I haven't told already to both of you."

"Good!" This was uttered in an extremely cheerful voice. "Tomorrow you will have to confess your sins again to a few more people . . . of course, not so detailed. Those will be not disciples either; those will be couple of girls just like you, who are also going to be baptized next Saturday. You probably have met Anna and Alona, have you?"

"Yes," I stammered again. It wasn't that I was afraid to confess my dark past in front of others—now it didn't matter anymore. What puzzled me was the weirdness of it all: the Bible classes, Katja trying to break me for the satisfaction of seeing my tears, Shelly's constant and persistent gazing at me, the whole confession thing, all the requirements concerning the meeting attendance.

Why do I feel so frightened? God is in control, from the moment of my baptism. He will guide me and protect me in all my ways. Shelly thinks my fear is very understandable—everyone is scared to let go control of their life into God's mighty hands; however, later when they learn what the life with God means, they do not want to go back to the ways of the world where everything is so insecure and so corrupted.

I came home and prayed very hard. God knows what's going on in my life now and He will show me if I am doing right by joining this church or not. I want something to change in my life so bad. I am even trying to be nicer to my mother.

85. We are all gathering in the Hotel Riga conference hall, where in Soviet times important Party people used to have their meetings and banquets. I am wearing the green necklace, Lisa's farewell present to me. Today is our most serious meeting before the baptism on Saturday. Today we are going to confess our sins one more time publicly in small groups. I am in one group with Shelly, Alona, Anna and a couple of other girls I do not know so well.

Shelly begins, her eyes shining. "Well girls, now let's go through all the sins one more time. I know you have been confessing your sins already, but in case there is anything still left there. So let us open Galatians 5: 22. Sexual immorality. Who of you have had sex outside marriage?" Two girls raise their hands. "OK, good. The rest of you haven't."

Alona and Anna haven't had sex either. Wow! I am not the only one at the age of seventeen. But then Alona is ugly, and Anna is plump. That explains everything. Besides, like me they're both timid with guys.

Shelly continues until the very last word in the sin list.

"OK girls," she says and smiles broadly. Everyone feels embarrassed except Shelly herself. "Now we have confessed everything, we feel clean and free again. By the way, maybe you have done something which wasn't mentioned in these scriptures but which you know wasn't good?"

"Well, I slammed the door in front of my husband. We are going to divorce soon anyway. I feel sorry!"

That is Lurissa, one of the married women, who is going to divorce her husband and marry her current lover if the church will let her do it.

"Anything else?"

"I live in a communal apartment. I share the kitchen with two other families. Once I stole a couple of pickles from my neighbor's plate. I am glad I remembered that. . . ." That is Tanja.

"OK. Anything else?"

No one says anything more. Shelly declares the confession is over. I look around. The other groups are still confessing.

I feel tired and somehow depressed, just the opposite of what Shelly promised we would feel after having confessed all our dark deeds. Trials, sufferings, self-denials. Sometimes I wish I'd never known the truth, but then I would go to hell without even knowing it. I think I miss Lisa. I know it is very childish, but since she left I do not feel good about all this church thing anymore. I cannot get over my fear of Shelly, even though she hasn't done any harm to me. Yet.

86. Today I was inviting people, together with Alona. Shelly had put us together for this assignment. Alona doesn't like to approach strangers on the streets, so Shelly set me as a good example for her. Alona confessed me something today: "You know what worries me the most?"

"What?"

"The fact that we cannot have sex until marriage. I was planning to get married only when I will be about twenty-seven, but of course I was planning to have plenty of sex until then. Now, however, it turns out that we cannot have sex unless we are married. Can you imagine waiting until you're twenty-seven?"

I shrugged. "Why do you think you will have to wait until twenty-seven; maybe you will get married earlier."

"I don't know, but don't you think it's crazy?"

"I don't know." What could I have said to her? I had thought about that myself. What if I do not get married? I do hope, however, that God will have mercy upon me, for I want to love someone so much and I want that someone to love me too. In God's kingdom all sorts of miracles are possible. I have seen ugly Christian girls married to quite handsome guys. Ugly people also want to be loved and cared for.

Suddenly my doubts about the church came back to me again. "Well, Alona, don't you feel somehow weird about all this thing?"

"About sex?"

"No, I mean the church. Do you thing it is really the only one in this world that is the right one?"

"I guess so. They live according to Bible; everything they do or teach is according to Bible. Don't you see it yourself? Besides, the Bible tells that there is only one God's church, and this must be the one. We must be very lucky, as Lisa said once."

"Yes, of course."

I didn't want to talk about that anymore. I do not like Alona, and I cannot help it. God forgive me that.

87. Tomorrow we will be baptized together. Four girls and four boys. Lilita, a girl with the eyes like the witch's, will be also baptized tomorrow.

She once accompanied me to my trolley stop. She told me all about herself. Lilita is my age but she is not one of those green inexperienced girls, virgin types who cannot find their place in the cruel and wicked world because they are too timid and too frail for the rough touches of the worldly men. She has gone through heaven and hell at her age. She was raped when she was about eleven and she didn't even know about it. She was having fun with some older boys. They all were drinking and apparently they had given her some sort of sleep pills, so she dozed off and they raped her. When she woke up they told her what had happened, but she didn't understand that. Later her mom took her to the doctor, and it turned out to be true. She was raped a second time on the some road at night—she told she likes solitary nightly walks on remote streets and roads.

Besides, she has had countless boy friends and has slept with all of them. She had visited magicians and fortune-tellers, she had practiced some magic herself, she had been drinking and even using drugs. She has had plenty of everything, and now she has come to a realization that she wants to change her way of life. She has very strange eyes. They are dark, and there is some sort of a wicked spell in them.

Well, she will be baptized with all of us tomorrow.

Yesterday I called my best friend Signe from the school and told her all about the great changes in my life. Instead of being skeptical and negative she seemed pretty impressed. She even promised to come and see my baptism.

I secretly wish that she also joined the church—of course because I want her to be saved, but also for some very selfish reasons. If she was there I wouldn't feel so scared in the church, and in case it is the wrong place to be in, at least I will not be alone there. There will be someone with me whom I have known before I came to the church.

88. Today was the great day. I got baptized, which means I am saved. I was the first one from the girls who were baptized today, which as everyone believes is significant enough. The first one! I have the responsibility to lay the foundation for the others who come after me.

I am trying to memorize every singe detail about today. Lisa claims that the baptism day is even more important and more significant than the wedding day, for the baptism means signing an eternal contract with Heavenly Father himself.

Signe, my ex-classmate, came as she had promised. She was holding my hand and comforting me. I was trembling throughout the whole sermon.

I remember crossing the bridge, the whole church marching over the bridge like pilgrims to the baptism place at the little beach of the River Daugava. It was a beautiful day, sunny and the sky was exactly the color I love. I remember two planes each flying in different directions and leaving long white stripes in the skies. The stripes crossed each other like a cross over the skies, which of course made the event even more significant.

Aija, a girl whose boyfriend was going to be baptized along with all of us, was crying hysterically because her boyfriend was deserting her for the sake of God. They are not allowed to date anymore, because Imants now is a holy man reborn through the baptism and redeemed by the very blood of Jesus Christ for the new life; Aija is just a girl from the wicked world, lost in her sins.

Shelly was trying her American best to clam Aija down, yet it wasn't helpful at all. The people sunbathing and swimming at the little beach obviously freaked out seeing the enormous crowd approaching. Many of them took their blankets and disappeared. The most curious stayed. They wanted to witness what was going to happen. Shelly ordered me and the other girls who were to be baptized to hide somewhere and get dressed for the baptism in our pink T-shirts and black shorts. The five male would-be disciples were already ready. There was Imants, the one Aija was crying for, with his long hair and fat girlie ass (I can't figure out what Aija finds so special about him). There was Alex, one of the handsomest guys I have ever seen in my whole life, tall, strong, beautifully tanned with shining blue eyes and a row of strong white teeth. There was also that Georgian guy, Ahmar. He seemed to be the most excited and the happiest of all, jumping from one foot to other. And Norman, the guy with reddish hair and funny smile. God forgive me for such thoughts, but I do not believe that he is sincere and serious about what he does. And another dark haired guy whose name I do not know yet. He looked a little scared too.

The girls—Alona, Lilita, Anna and Zinta, a funny, freckled and a little plump, a year younger than the rest of us, a typical teenager—and I were all standing in row opposite the guys.

"Let us sing a couple of songs for our dear would-be sisters and brothers in Christ," Craig said. He was leading the whole ceremony. Everyone started to sing. I felt dazed from the bright sun and from the whole affair.

"We are all very happy to gather here today knowing that this is a very special day for all of us, not only for our would-be brothers and sisters in Christ, but for all the church members and for this city and of course for our heavenly Father. . . ."

The speech was followed by a long prayer. Everyone was standing in a circle, holding hands with their heads bowed, far away from the world, absorbed in prayer. I was just observing the people on the beach. Fat ladies showing their tits, little boys running around without underwear and all sorts of dogs lying quietly in the afternoon sun.

The first guy baptized was Imants. Salvis, the only Latvian Christian for so many years, baptized him. Salvis was recruited and baptized in Stockholm by Danny. Since at that time there was no church in Riga, Salvis couldn't return to his own country. Instead he had to go to Moscow with the rest of the team and stay there for five years until the leaders in Moscow got an order from their leaders in States to come to Riga and establish the church here. Then at last Salvis also could come back home. Craig baptized him. Wet, clumsy, and happy, Imants was surrounded by the many hug-givers.

The next was Alex, and then Ahmor, and then the rest.

When it was girls' turn, nobody was brave enough to step first. Shelly was already waiting in the water.

Somebody pushed me, so I was the first. Shelly was telling me something. Somebody was taking a picture of me. Then there was a moment of darkness short and scary, and I was already out of the water baptized, born for a new life. So were baptized all the other girls. Afterwards we were asked to step in the middle of the circle. We were given the Big Mac of love. We were squeezed by others in the outer circle with a lot of yelling and noise. The savage-like custom scared me a little, maybe because I was suspicious about all this affair; the others, however, seemed pleasantly surprised.

After the baptism all the new disciples returned to the Hotel Riga for a lunch. I parted with Signe shortly after crossing the bridge; she seemed to be pretty impressed by the affair. I silently prayed to God that she also joined the church one day.

"Bye, Sweety," Shelly said to my friend in her honey sweet voice. "Hope to see you in the church on Tuesday!"

Signe smiled back politely but said nothing. She winked at me in an odd way and off she went.

89.
Today the new disciples met together at Pizza Lulu before going out into the street to evangelize. The whole way up Brivibas Street Shelly was chatting about the Church of Christ, praising it for its righteous and radical ways and telling us how we all together will turn the world upside down one day.

I started to ask her something: "Tell me if your church...."

She interrupted me impatiently. "Honey, not 'your church' anymore! It is 'our church,' mine and yours. You are a part of the powerful God's movement now."

Her words brought a dark cloud in my mind. They made me feel chained to the church with chains of fear and doubt. Somewhere deep within me lay the thought that I will never be able to break away from this movement. I scolded myself: "Do I want to break away? Do I want to break away from God's movement?" Yet I could not get rid of the dark feeling that my freedom is lost forever.

"I am sorry, Shelly. I wanted to say 'our church.' All this is so new to me. I need some time to adjust. It is like when a child who has grown up in the house of his stepparents suddenly has found and has to face his real parents. He cannot immediately address to them as to mom and dad."

"Honey, that is such a vivid comparison. That's so wonderful! So what was your concern about our church?"

"I just wanted to know if our church also has the Lord's Supper . . . the communion . . . how do you call it?"

"Of course, Honey, every Sunday. In fact the Communion is the most essential part of the service on Sundays. That's the moment which makes you remember what Jesus has done for you and why he had to die for you. That's the moment when you concentrate on and confess your weekly sins silently to the Lord only and ask for His forgiveness. Later, of course, you will need to confess them to your leader in case you didn't have a chance to confess them before that."

In front of the glass window of Pizza Lulu Shelly let my arm go. As we walked in and sat ourselves around the small, round tables, she approached Alona and whispered something to her.

Pizza Lulu is cozy and very new. With its bare brick walls and chalkboard decorations, it looks like a true American pizza place. It is becoming a very popular meeting place for university students and foreign visitors. But Pizza Lulu is not God's kingdom. There was some nasty song playing on the radio in English. The words were like "if you suck my—I will lick your—."

Most of the new disciples were not familiar with English (since Shelly and Craig speak such good Russian it is not necessary for them to learn English to be able to communicate with the couple. I am the only one who communicates with them in English) so they probably could not understand the words. I was observing Shelly and Craig. Had they noticed the song? What were they going to do? To leave the pizza place? No! Obviously they were pretending that they did not hear anything.

We ordered our pizza slices; each could choose two. It was a treat from the church for the special occasion.

The pizza was ready in five minutes. Alona grabbed one of her slices and bit a piece. Yet she realized her mistake immediately. She blushed beet red and quickly put her slice back on the plate. She was nervous. Accidentally she knocked over her glass of Sprite. She dared not to raise her eyes on the others anymore.

I had also forgotten that since now on I have to pray before each meal. I was glad, however, that it was Alona and not me who grabbed and bit the pizza slice before praying. What a bummer!

"Let us pray that God blesses the rest of this day and that he blesses our daily bread," Craig began. I liked to listen to Craig's voice; it was low and very masculine. He was praying in Russian so that everybody could understand. He had that funny but pleasant American accent when speaking Russian.

The prayer was over and everyone, without any special ceremonies, attacked the food and gobbled it down fast. Then the meal was over and we left for our work.

We parted by hugging each other . . . just the same as when meeting. I think it's a very nice custom.

When I got home, Mom had prepared a special dinner for me. The neighbor girl, who is five, had come to play with me. I felt the same, yet I felt different at the same time. I felt excited, beginning my new life with the Lord and working in His vinyard, although the mysterious fear hasn't faded yet.

90.

Today I met with Alona and Shelly again. Shelly ordered us to go and evangelize on the streets. "I am sorry, girls. I cannot go with you. I have a Bible study with Karina, the lady who is in charge of the Hotel Riga conference hall. She has heard Danny's preaching and fallen in love with God's word. She wants to be baptized as soon as possible. The only problem is that she's got to get rid of some sins."

I vaguely remembered a lady with brown hair in light blue jeans fussing over little Catelyn, Lisa's daughter. She gave Catelyn a kitten as a farewell present. It had to be left in Latvia because of complications on the border.

"Do you want to come with me girls?"

Alona said she had plenty of things to do. I was hesitant. I did not have any plans for the afternoon yet, since it was my holiday. Finally Shelly persuaded me to go with her.

Karina was at work. She was beaming at our arrival. Shelly opened her large, stylish leather bag and took out her pink Bible. She reminded me of a doctor who had come to visit a sick person. She had that half compassionate, half determined face expression.

"So I have come to you to talk about some serious things. This is our new sister in Christ." She pointed at me. "That's why I think she has all rights to hear all about your situation."

I was embarrassed and proud at the same time. Now since I am a part of the church I am allowed to look into other people's sinful souls. Well, I know it sounds morbid; however, if to be honest we all have this sick interest in ugly things. Karina didn't seem to mind my presence, and I was thankful to her for that.

"Actually," Shelly started a little insecurely, "I wanted to talk about your current relationship with Michael."

Michael, it turned out, is Karina's current lover. He is still married but is ready to divorce his wife because of Karina.

"Yes . . . and?" I could sense a light tone of defense appearing in Karina's voice.

"I just wanted to warn you that if you want to accept our Lord as your Savior and start a completely new walk with Him, you will have to stop your current relationship with Michael." Shelly's voice sounded stern and determined.

"But he is going to get divorced soon. He has already handed in the documents, for his wife has nothing against the divorce."

"Well, yes, but currently he still is his wife's husband and your relationship with him turns out to be adultery, and there are pretty radical words in the Bible about the divorce!"

"Yes, yes, I know that, but he does not love his wife anymore, and she does not love him either. His wife does not mind our relationship at all. She is living with another man anyway."

"The fact that his wife is sinning is not an excuse for you to sin too. Karina, I want you to understand that it does not matter if Michael's wife loves him or not. Currently you and Michael are committing adultery. Do you understand what that means? Do you understand how serious it is?" Shelly was excited and a little impatient already. Her cheeks were turning light pink and her eyes had that odd shine again.

Their whole affair was starting to turn out quite interesting for me. I did not for a moment regret I had come.

"Today we were eating lunch together, me and Michael." Karina was talking in the quiet voice of a scolded and intimidated child.

"We were praying before meal, praying God together for the first time in our lives!"

"Well that's all very nice, but I want you to understand."

Karina interrupted Shelly this time. "Do you believe that God can change Michael?"

"Of course He can. God is almighty. You only have to make the first step. You have to show Him that you have become aware of your sinful and wrong ways of living. You have to admit that to Him from the very bottom of your heart, and then you must regret and repent sincerely. Only then God will start doing miracles in your life. As long as you live in sin and refuse to change your ways, God will do nothing about your life!"

"But we do want to change our ways of living! We have started to pray already and to read Bible."

"God has invented sex for married people only! Isn't that clear and obvious enough?"

"And what is wrong if people have sex but are not married?"

"It is wrong because it is sinful!" Shelly said abruptly. She was running out of patience, which surprised me. She is a Christian, which means she has to bear with people patiently. "As far as I see it does not make any sense for us to continue our Bible study unless you repent. I have to go now."

"Come!" she said to me. "Karina, we will be praying for you!"

We left Karina sitting motionless in her small office.

91. Mom's getting a little suspicious about all that church going, and so is Dad. Shelly says I should not take it close to heart, for Satan is very smart, and of course he wants me out of church. He wants me to skip the meetings and prayers and confession times. Besides he is well informed about all my weak points, and he knows pretty well when it's time to click the right button. He will speak through my parents and my dearest friends if it will help him accomplish his mission, which is to lead me astray.

I could not imagine that Christianity will be so complicated. I know my parents love me, even my mom, who cannot live a day without scolding me for something. It is kind of painful to tell them all the time, "Mom, dad I love you, but I love God more, and I have to follow to where He leads me." My parents think I'm a psycho. Well, I have to be ready to look a psycho and a fool in other people's eyes for His sake.

Mom is losing her job at the trade center. It used to be one of the most prestigious ones during the Soviet times, but now with the times of changes, the center is being bought by some rich private company. It is going to be rebuilt, and all the current staff will be out of there, for they are going to hire young and charming bookkeepers and secretaries with good teeth and nice tits.

My mom is very upset. She feels old and hurt. I can understand that, for she has been working there most of her life, and she has come to love the place and her job. I remember in Soviet times it was a very convenient place to work. The workers often could get foreign goods like candies from Czechoslovakia and preserved fruit from Hungary. Also all sorts of clothing like sweaters and slacks and even panty hose. Mom's colleagues made themselves rich by selling those luxuries to their friends and distant relatives for a much higher price than they paid. My mom, however, was too honest. She never raised the price, so she never profited anything from those little helpings out.

Besides, with the gradual change from Soviet rubli to Latvian rubli and now to Latvian lats, my parents lost all their savings. All the thousands of Soviet rubli they managed to save working hard all their Soviet lives have turned into mere santims.

I often hear my dad asking, "Where did all the money go that I had saved for my funeral? I know I am dying, and you folks won't even have the money to bury me!"

I hate when he talks like that. I hate it when he talks about his death, because we live in constant terror of the possibility. I am especially scared now that I know that all people who are not members of the Church of Christ are headed straight to hell. I do not want my dad to die and be in hell. But he does not want to hear about Christian teachings. He is worried about how we are going to live and meet the ends of this world.

At least my parents do not have to worry about my educational expenses. I got accepted at Foreign Language Department of the University of Latvia. My major will be German. I passed the entrance exams in listening, writing and speaking, and somehow got among the group of those lucky twenty-five students who will get state tuition. Of course I was last on the list, but maybe that proves that I am not such a God's mistake after all. I have got purpose and meaning now, plus I have the university, which means I will be able to study and get a degree and maybe a better paid job later. Then I will be able to help my parents, and I will also be able to evangelize to the people around me. Last Friday at family time we were told that all we do in this world—whether it is work, studying, cleaning our house, washing the dishes after the dinner or walking our dog—is done to the glory of the Lord.

92. Yesterday we had a huge rainstorm, and it turns out that we have a leak in our roof, so the water came through our kitchen ceiling. The kitchen looks pretty ugly, and Dad is upset and feeling sick again. For him the water problem seems like the end of the world itself. I am not worried about that at all. What one could possibly expect from those

large ugly block apartments? First they are ugly. Second, they are so very alike each other! Third, they were built in Soviet times, so they are shit. Probably they will all fall apart in twenty years, and where will we live then? The people inhabiting them are like the houses themselves. Most of them are Russians, and not very rich ones. Their permanent outfit is blue sports slacks with one either red or white stripe and some sort of a dirty T shirt with some incorrect English words, probably made in Turkey and sold by Polish peddlers. They usually wear a black jacket (imitation of a leather and therefore very cheap) and worn-out sports shoes. Their faces are gray, and their stares are dull. All they think about is food and beer or a stronger drink. They are faceless and perfectly fitting into the buildings. It so depressing!

93. Well, I am worried about my dad. He has not looked well in the recent time. He is worried about that damn kitchen ceiling and of course about me and that church thing. I feel horribly guilty for making him sick with worry, yet what can I do? I have to give God the first place in my life, and that is not at all easy. You have to sacrifice so much... your old friends, your girlfriends and boyfriends (now I am glad I did not have one before I joined the church), your free time, your job, your personal wishes. You have to watch your parents and relatives worrying about you. You do not even have your privacy, for all you have in mind you are supposed to talk over with your spiritual leader, whether it is a trip or a new job opportunity or friendship. You have to confess all your sins, your wrong doings, even your thoughts. You cannot even sin in private anymore and then confess it to God only, as my parents do. If it all wasn't for God sake, I would say this deal stinks.

There is one more interesting thing about the church, the Saturday night dates. Saturday nights are the night when guys are allowed to ask the girls (only and exclusively from the church) out. All this, of course, happens under close supervision of the church leaders. Dates can never be one and one. They must be at least double dates. The larger the number of people, the better. People are allowed (in a large crowd) to go to the movies or to have a nice walk in the park. Later they can go and have some pizza or some SOFT drinks. The date must be over at 9 p.m. Then the guys accompany their dates home. They must not step further into the apartment than the threshold of the building. Accompanying the girl up to her apartment door is out of question.

When I asked Shelly why is it necessary to go in a large group of people, she looked at me with a look of a person who knows everything and said, "This way it is much safer, dear! You are young and do not know things. However, it is very easy to fall into a temptation! You know what I mean. Since this church is the very establishment of the Lord, we are strongly submitted to the law of chastity. NO impure or immoral person can be a member of this church. Of course we all are weak, and we fall, and there are people who have sinned in this area. Nevertheless, we have been there for them, and they have repented. That is why we are trying our best to avoid falling into a temptation by dating in large crowds, which is also a lot of fun."

I do not know where I had the guts to ask Shelly if she had ever sinned in this particular area, but I asked her.

"I hadn't slept with anyone before my marriage to Craig. I hadn't even been dating anyone else, for I have been in love with Craig since I was thirteen. We used to be neighbors before his family moved away to a different state. Nevertheless I kept on thinking about him . . . and sometimes my thoughts about him were not as pure as they were supposed to be. So sometimes I tried to imagine how it would be to kiss. I could not imagine it very well, since I had never kissed with anyone. Then I had this temptation. Oh, it's very embarrassing to tell that! I had this temptation to touch myself, to masturbate, and I did it couple of times in the bathroom while taking the bath. I felt so horrible after that; however, I continued to do it. It was all very embarrassing to tell that to Craig.

"Why did you have to tell him that?"

"You are supposed to tell everything to your husband the night before you get married—all your sins in detail, so that he knows whom he is marrying. It all happens under the supervision of two leaders, yours and his. They just make sure that you do not omit anything. Your husband just must know everything about you, so that there is nothing between you two. You probably know the scripture in Corinthians 13 where it says that love covers everything. If he loves you, he will accept everything that you tell about yourself."

"I had always thought that my past is nobody's business."

"In the world, yes. But not in God's Kingdom. In world darkness governs everything. People lie and cheat on each other; they have affairs being married; they have sex before marriage; they have abortions; they do all sorts of filthy things which are considered deeds of darkness in the Bible.

"In God's Kingdom, people walk in light. They do not hide their dark deeds; instead they reveal them by bringing them into the light by confessing them and repenting. I am glad that the world has not managed to do too much damage to your young mind. Here among us, your brothers and sisters, you will come to know the truth. Your mind will be transformed completely, and you will learn to separate the truth from lies that world is constantly telling us all."

Maybe Shelly is right. She is twenty-three, after all, older and more experienced in life. What judgments can I make? Certainly I am less experienced than girls normally are at my age, and if this dating thing seems a little crooked to me, I have never had any dates in my life, so how can I possibly judge?

94. Signe also got baptized last Saturday, and her mom is coming to the church frequently enough. Shelly is praising me up to heavens, because Signe is my friend. She even wrote a letter to Lisa that through me one more soul got saved. A few days later I got a sweet card with a puppy next to the flower pot with the text: "God is doing amazing work through you in other people's lives! I am so proud of you! I am sure you are incredible investment in God's kingdom! I have been praying for you and will keep on doing so! Your sister in Christ, Lisa."

For couple of days I was walking around like a gobbler, all my feathers in the air. Then other people started to be praised too for bringing their friends, relatives and even strangers to the church and baptizing them, and I became small and insignificant again, as I always have been.

95. Signe likes Salvis, the badminton player. He seems to like her too, even though he is much older than she is. He is about twenty-seven and she's only eighteen. Salvis asked Signe for a date this Saturday, and of course I am jealous again. I am jealous also of Signe being elected as my spiritual leader. She came to the church after me, and she hasn't brought anyone to God yet. However, she is so enthusiastic and excited about everything that they (particularly Shelly) think she would make a better leader than I would because I still have all those doubts and reservations and questions. It does not help, either, that I try to be as honest as I can. If I chose not to tell, I would probably be a leader by now. But then I would have that dark spot in my heart, and then God would probably decide to cut me off. We are always being threatened with God cutting us off if we do not try hard enough. I do try hard to please God. I evangelize every single day. I meet with Signe and study Bible with her, since she is my leader now. I even confess all my sins. I even told her about me being jealous of her, for the Bible teaches that there must not be anything between the brothers and sisters in Christ. Yet I do not seem to find the promised fulfillment and peace in God. Or maybe I am too selfish, thinking just about the reward. Or maybe there is something wrong with me.

The brothers in the church do not seem to like me, either. Nobody ever asks me out for a date. I thought that in God's Kingdom I would have a chance.

96. Today is a Saturday, and we all gathered for the purpose of evangelization in the city. The whole church goes out on streets on Saturdays to speak to the blind and deaf about God and about His marvelous offer.

Saturdays are also the days when the brothers ask the sisters for dates. First we all come together at the top of Bastejakalns, make a circle, sing and praise the Lord, pray, and get the invitation cards from our leaders. Then we split up into small groups of three or two people and, filled with the Holy Spirit and with a well-rehearsed smile on our faces, go out on the streets and start talking to the by-passers.

Between the distribution of invitation cards and splitting up into small groups, guys usually manage to arrange the dates. Sarmite is smiling shyly and happily as Andrejs is approaching her, asking is she's got any plans for Saturday night. I feel crappy because nobody is asking me, but I am not going to cry. A fat girl approaches me—I think I remember her from Sunday—and asks if I would like to evangelize with her. I do not feel like talking to people at all today. When I tell that to Shelly, she just shrugs. "Not all days were pleasant for Jesus either, but he took his cross and carried it till the end. He should be your role model!"

Why is it so difficult for me to deny myself? I am probably a very selfish person.

I can see Gatis, the freaky one with tanned glasses, who just got baptized last week. He is evangelizing alone too. I guess nobody would want to go with him either. So God's Kingdom is not much different from the world. Here people are also judged by their appearances.

Gatis has noticed us. He is coming to say hello.

"I would like to talk to you. . . ." He is talking to me a little hesitantly, completely neglecting Olga, the fat girl. "I . . . . just wanted to ask you what your plans are for tonight. Do you have a date already?"

"No." I blush.

"I don't either." He keeps on staring. I know nothing else except to stare back. He pulls himself together and says, "I would like to ask you out tonight for a movie or something. Shelly and Craig will be with us." Two guardian angels. Or maybe two body guards, since they are supposed to guard us from falling into bodily lusts. Although lust would be quite difficult with the freaky Gatis.

"Sure," I hear myself saying. So this Gatis is my luck and my honor! Well, the Bible teaches us to be humble and thank God for everything. Besides, white crows cannot afford to be picky.

97. Since the date with Gatis was my first real date, I was very nervous. I washed my hair and borrowed a fairly decent sweatshirt from my mom. What a misery! All my slacks are too large and baggy for me so that none of them look really good on me. Anyway, I chose the least bad looking ones from all and put them on. I threw one last look in the mirror. What a mistake! A tall and clumsy girl was looking at me. She tried to smile; however, realizing that her slightly crooked smile did not improve her looks at all, she became sad, and the corners of her mouth dropped.

"Maybe I should use a little make-up," I thought frantically. "And lipstick and eyeliner."

I sneaked into my parents' room. Dad was watching TV and Mom was making dinner in the kitchen. Wonderful! Dad never pays attention to what I do or take from the room; it's my mom who always demands the explanations.

Mom has a few cosmetic things. They are ugly, carrot color lipstick, a stinky tonal cream for face (it stinks because it's old and has never been really used), and a bottle of cheap perfume. The carrot color lipstick looked like a disaster, but I thought I could put it on just a little bit, to make my lips look a little more fresh.

I do not have eye liner, and my mom does not have one either. Maybe I could use a black pencil. I quickly returned to my room. What an advantage it is to have a room of my own. I smeared the lipstick carefully over my lips and rubbed the one against the other. The orange paint made my lips look worse rather than better, so I wiped it off. I found a black pencil and tried my best to draw a small dark line below my eyes. My eyes immediately looked larger and more expressive. I need to buy an eye liner. That will definitely contribute to my beauty.

We were all meeting at Laima clock. I did not want to arrive the first one, for I have heard that a girl should always be a little late, not to expose her eagerness to see the guy. Was I eager to see Gatis? No, but I was eager to go out for a movie or cafe.

So I was five minutes late. As I approached the Laima clock I saw Shelly, Craig, Alona, Aleksej, Signe, Salvis and Gatis all standing in a circle.

"You are late!" Shelly snapped.

"I am sorry," I said blushing from my ears to toes. Apparently in God's Kingdom all things are different, even coming to a date. Well, we learn from our mistakes. If I ever have another date at all, I will be punctual.

We all split in two and obediently followed Shelly and Craig, like kids from the kindergarten. Craig and Shelly were holding hands. Since they are a wife and a husband, it is legal for them. For other daters, however, it is strictly forbidden, because holding hands is considered as the first step to falling into a temptation. I would not want to hold hands with Gatis anyway.

The movie was a boring action movie. I could not wait until it was over. Afterwards Craig suggested to go to some cafe and hang out a little bit. That sounded like an appealing perspective.

We found one right opposite the movie theater. For the whole evening I hadn't said a word to Gatis, or he had to me. We both felt awkward. Alona felt awkward too, so we started to chat with each other. Shelly rebuked us, reminding us that we were on the date not with each other but with the brothers. So we turned away and kept on walking in silence besides our dates. For Signe the situation was even worse. Salvis was apparently engaged in conversation with Craig, and she was left all alone.

In the cafe Gatis finally spoke to me. He asked me if I wanted a piece of pie with my tea. To be honest I did not want anything at all; however, to avoid surprised stares and questioning, I nodded that I wanted both.

We moved the tables together and made one big table for us. We drank tea and ate our pieces of pie, listening to the little silly jokes Craig was telling in Russian with his funny American accent. Salvis was trying to be original by making us guess his riddles, which were as stupid as Craig's jokes. Maybe that is why we did not guess any of them.

When the evening was over, the guys were supposed to accompany us home. On the bus home the situation between me and Gatis loosened a little bit. We chatted all kinds of nonsense. He accompanied me to the very door of my apartment, yet when I asked him if he remembered the way back to the bus stop (it is kind of confusing among those numerous monster-like block houses) he looked confused. I explained to him one more time. He smiled nervously, yet he did not convince me that he knew the way back to the stop, so I asked him, "Do you want me to walk you there?"

"Oh, no! Of course not! I can find it!"

"Okay." When we parted, he hugged me as it was proper among the brothers and sisters who love each other and give their own lives for each other.

In the elevator I thought to myself, "Is this the way the dates are supposed to be? Is that how it normally happens, or is that how it happens in the God's Kingdom? Of course in God's Kingdom everything is upside down."

98. Last night we got a call from my grandma's neighbors that she is very sick and had been taken to the hospital. Mom was in despair and Dad too, but then he's been in despair for as long as I can remember. Today we wanted to leave for the country, which meant I would have to

skip the Sunday service to see grandma before leaving Riga. I hope God forgives me for that. When we arrived at the hospital my grandmother was already dead. It was a shocking experience for me, for I had never seen a dead person before. She looked so strange and remote. This could not be my grandma, the one who was always grumpy with something, yet for whom I was the dearest of all the grandchildren.

My grandma used to be weird at times. She liked to invent stories which never happened in real life. That used to drive nuts to everybody. She was very concerned about her food. She had to make sure that she got the best piece of cake or the biggest meatball, or the ripest strawberry. She would fight with my mom a lot. They both have that silly stubbornness which makes no sense. I think I have inherited a bit of that. However, on the whole my granny was a good person. She loved me and used to take care of me when I was just a baby, when my dad's heart disease was discovered in 1978, and my mom had to work hard so she did not have time to look after me.

I think I loved grandma too, and still do. She is dead, but I still love her. How could I stop loving her just because she is not here with us anymore?

Death takes people away from us, but where does the love go? Where did her love for me go? Does love die along with the person? How can it possibly die? I am trying to think about love so that I do not have to think about something else, something too horrible to be true. My grandma was not baptized into the Church of Christ, which means she is not saved. Which means. . . .

This cannot be true. My grandma will not be in hell. I cannot help the tear. How little one human being can help another. One cannot suffer another's pain, or die for him. One cannot even make this person be baptized if the person does not want to.

I did pray for my grandma, but maybe God decided that she is one who does not have to be saved. Bible talks about people who are lost and will never be saved. Why is it that some will be and some won't? What if my grandma did not have a chance?

99. The funeral is over and everybody is relieved. It is always like that after a funeral. Most people shed their tears before the funeral, some more, some less. When the ceremony is over and people are seated at the tables with food and drinks, everyone seems to revive. Although people are a little reluctant to show that, they are all hungry and can't wait for the official permission to attack the bowls of soup and pans overloaded with potatoes and meatballs. When they eat, they try to pretend that food does not interest them at all because they are still very much wrapped up in the sorrow. However, when the glasses with all sorts of drinks are raised, all the reservations fall away immediately. The more bottles are emptied, the louder the voices get. Some even start joking and making the others laugh. Mom seems to have calmed down a little bit. She was a little frantic about all the arrangements: the coffin, the gravediggers, the flowers, the religious ceremony, the food and drinks afterwards.

Since none of the other grandchildren or cousins could come, I was the only one there. Of course I was bored to death sitting at the table, stuffing myself full and gazing at all the guests, mostly elderly people.

When everyone was stuffed, they all suddenly became interested in me. I pretended I needed to go to the restroom and sneaked out of the room, leaving my mom and dad to answer all the questions. I know it was rude and silly of me, but when I sense the danger of becoming the center of everybody's attention, my basic instinct is to run and hide.

All I could hear through the door was, "Oh, she's grown up so much!" "Oh sure, I remember her as a little girl eating apples from my orchard when you were visiting!" "Yes, she is very tall!"

"Of course," I thought sulkily. "That is all that can be said about me. Tall, clumsy, shy—that's me."

At church, the people prayed for me and my family. That was touching. I was even exempted from the Wednesday night Bible study, which was a great relief for me. I am ashamed to admit that fact, even to a diary, but I prefer honesty to hypocrisy.

100. Since Signe was baptized into the Church of Christ my relationship with her has become worse. We used to be the best friends in high school, but now she is my leader, and I cannot help thinking that all this leader-disciple relationship is pretty stupid. One month ago we used to talk about topic most teenagers talk about—like how it feels to kiss or have sex for the first time, or how to behave near your crush. Now she is supposed to ask a daily account from me

"How many people did you invite today? How many responded positively? How many phone numbers did you get? [I always feel uneasy asking strangers for their phone numbers; I cannot help thinking it is impolite and obtrusive.] How many did you call today? What are your sins for today?"

I think that all those questions will gradually ruin our friendship.

When I told Shelly that I have no desire to tell Signe about my sins, she said, "You are proud! Your heart has become hard! That is a warning sign to you! You are slowly starting to fall away from God!"

I was terrified, of course. With tears streaming down my cheeks, I ran to Signe to confess all my recent wrong doings and wrong thinkings.

101. Last night I got home very late. Friday devotions always end at about 10.30 p.m., but last night was even later. Mom was waiting me in the hall. It was half dark and I couldn't see her face very clearly. She was sitting there motionless.

"Hi, Mom!"

She jumped up like an enraged tigress. "Ha! What do you think you are doing to me and to your father?"

I was totally taken aback, for I did not expect the attack. "What's wrong?"

"What is wrong? You are asking what is wrong? Do you have any sense of shame left in you?"

"I don't understand."

"You do not understand! We are sick with worry about you being somewhere out in the city in the middle of the night, and then you come and pretend to be a holy innocent! Well, when you get your father in the grave you will understand! Then you will understand!" She was hollering at me.

"But what did I do? You both new I was at the Friday night devotions!"

"The hell with all your devotions. Your father has been taking pills every five minutes. Every five minutes he's been running out into the staircase listening to the sound of the elevator. And every time it stops at the different staircase he comes in, pale, terror in his eyes, and he has to take medicine again to keep his heart beating! Do you understand what you are doing to your family? You know how your dad exaggerates things and how he worries and becomes sick when he worries!"

I started to answer, then stopped my defense abruptly, seeing my dad coming out of the room, his face twisted with pain.

"Let's just drop it here. She is at home now. Everything is all right now!"

I looked at Dad, tears burning my eyelids and tickling my nose. Seeing how much my parents love me made me feel small and guilty. "I am sorry, dad. The devotional ended late. You know I had to be there. For God's sake I had to be there."

At the mention of God's name my mother exploded again: "That isn't God that keeps you there. They are all crazy there. This cannot be God's establishment. Who knows what filthy things you all do there!"

"Mother!"

"I won't leave it like this. I will go there myself. I will tell them!" My mom was furious.

"Mother, you do not have to go there! We do not do anything that could be dishonorable or filthy. Instead we praise God with songs and chants and pray together and talk about spiritual things. If I miss the meetings, my heart will become hard and I will fall away from God!"

"You are either bewitched or brainwashed," Dad said wearily.

"I am not!" I exclaimed, running into my room slamming the door behind me. I fell into my bed, squeezed my face into the pillow and wept. That's exactly what Shelly told me . . . she said, "Sometimes you will be persecuted by your dearest and the most loved people."

I know I am hurting my parents by spending most of my free time in the church and by coming home late and exposing myself to all sorts of dangers. What if my dad dies worrying about me being out late? Then I will have to walk around with that huge pile of guilt for the rest of my life. What if he dies and goes to hell?

"Oh God, please help!" I prayed. "Please do not let my dad die! I am staying at devotions because I want to please you, but I want to please my parents too. Please help me to reconcile that somehow!" I was praying with tears running down my cheeks, wetting my pillow. Tomorrow I will look especially ugly. I always look ugly after crying. Oh, how can I be so selfish and think about me being ugly when my parents are suffering because of me? They think I have made the wrong choice. They think I am crazy. God, please help me to convince them that it is the right choice. Please help me to love them more and help them more with the household and talk to them about. You and about what a wonderful life I am having together with You!"

Finally I prayed, "God help me to talk to my parents about what a difficult but meaningful life I have together with You." That sounded better. "Yes, God, I forgot to say I am thankful for what you have done for me, and I am very sorry for not really feeling thankful."

102. I have started my studies at the university. They are nothing pleasant, however. We have many classes, old and grumpy professors with horrible German pronunciation and heaps of boring home works. Classes start at 8.30 a.m. and are over sometimes at 4.00 p.m., sometimes at 6.00 p.m. I am worried for not getting all my home works done on time. And I still attend all the church meetings.

I am especially terrified of Frau Misinja, the German conversation teacher. Conversation classes are one big nightmare for me. When I close my eyes I still can see Frau Misinja's stern face and her fat body moving like a ship through the classroom, back and forth, back and forth.

Every class she starts with her favorite maxim, "Liebe Studentinen, man muss viel mehr arbeiten . . . sonst kommt man nie auf den gruenen

Zweig!" We always make fun of her behind her back by imitating her voice and her body language.

The other professors are not so scary, but they are dry and boring, and since I wake up at 6 a.m. every morning to have enough time to read the Bible and pray, I am always having a trouble with keeping my eyes open during the class. Once I really fell asleep, dropped my pen, which I was holding ready to put down the teacher's words, and woke up. A couple of my classmates were staring at me in amusement. I was very embarrassed. What if the professor noticed that I am falling asleep during her classes?

103. **S**helly and Craig have left for Moscow. They are not coming back. Now Salvis is our official church leader. A couple of more people have been baptized, including that chick Sabine. I would never think she will ever get baptized into this church. She is stylish and beautiful, and she loves discos. Such people do not wind up in churches. But she got baptized after last Sunday's service. She came to the church because of her friend, who is also a stylish and beautiful girl with lots of boyfriends. The friend got baptized and to the great horror of everybody left the church within two weeks. To all the warnings and threats her response was, "I don't like it in here. It's too damn boring!"

Sometimes I wonder what girls like Sabine and her fiance are looking for in a church like this. Of course every one needs Christ and everyone needs to be saved; however, these girls are good looking and picky concerning guys. They have parties and fun. They certainly do not need a shelter or protection from the harsh world. Neither they are looking for the meaning of their existence. They just exist and have fun, and when the time comes, they drop dead.

Well, I am almost sure that Sabine will leave the church soon too. I would like to make friends with her. She is cool, but I am not sure, if she wants me to be her friend. I keep my distance.

104. **M**om has found a new job. Now she works as a secretary for the boss of an old Soviet-time half-fallen-apart perfume factory, which will probably go bankrupt in the near future. Anyway Mom's happy for now. She likes the boss, who is an old, good-natured guy. Besides, the factory is close to where we live. Maybe next month we will be able to change our oatmeal diet to something better, like rice or pasta with ketchup. Oatmeal porridge with butter (sometimes with jam, since mom likes to pick berries in the woods in summer) has been our special diet for more than three months now, and we are getting a little fed up with it. Dad's already become very skinny. He used to have quite a belly (let's call it a cheese belly, since he does not drink beer), but now it is gone completely. He's also lost a lot of his hair. He is very upset and disappointed with the new government. I am tired of hearing his daily complaints about the new leaders, who are doing nothing to improve the lives of the population, but everything to provide themselves with fancy cars, nice summer cottages and trips abroad.

Dad grumbles. "In Soviet times we used to eat ice cream every Sunday afternoon; now I soon will not be able to buy a loaf of bread with my pension. What the hell of a life is this? Was I born to die of starvation in the new independent Latvia?"

"Don't be so bitter about everything!" I tell him. "It does not help much anyway. You know what the Bible says about grumbling and complaining?"

"I don't want to hear anything about your Bible!" he shouts back at me; "look how far you have gotten with your Bible. You are about to be expelled from the university!"

"I am not!" I say defensively. Boy, do I hate it when the conversation takes this direction! I do not like to talk about my study achievements. The winter session is approaching fast, and, to my own horror, I am starting to realize that I won't be able to pass all the exams. I have too little time to prepare for my classes properly. I come home from the church meetings very late, and I am very exhausted. I try to do my home works or read some boring and dry stuff about theoretical grammar; then I fall asleep on my desk and wake up at 2 or 3 o'clock at night. Then I quickly brush my teeth and crawl under the blankets. In the mornings I wake up from the sounds of our Soviet-times alarm clock ringing with a sound that one could raise the dead. My eyes are swollen and my head aching.

"You do not study enough. You do not have time, because all your free time you are spending at your sect!" Dad says reproachfully

"It is not a sect. It's God's own establishment! You don't understand anything!"

I always defend the church, although I have started to doubt that this church is God's establishment. But I better keep quiet, for what if my heart really has grown hard and Satan has taken hold of it?

My basic instinct is telling me not to trust my leaders either. It is saying to me, "Do not be open about everything with your leaders. They may harm you if they know everything about you. Watch out!"

Is this Satan's wisdom or merely instinctive self-protection? How can I figure it out? I pray to the Lord, but so far no revelation has come upon me. I must be patient and wait. Obviously I have been drifting into my own thoughts for a while, for I hear Dad's voice somewhere from the distance saying, "Well, if you want me in the grave, that is what you will get with your church! Will you be happy then?"

"No," say quietly holding back the tears.

"Then get the hell out of there!"

"I can't."

"Why can't you? Have they hypnotized you or what? What have they done to you?"

"I'm afraid I will be in hell if I leave!"

"Well, we all will be in hell," Dad says. His voice calm again. "We are not good enough for heaven. None of us!"

"What do you know of heaven, Dad?"

"I don't know anything. I just know I won't be there."

Is that a chance, given by God Himself, to evangelize to my own father?

"Heaven is for everyone," I start carefully; "all you have to do is to accept Christ, repent from your sins, get baptized and. . . ."

"And," my dad interrupts me, "sit in the church all day long, and skip your classes, and not get home works done, and argue with parents and make them sick with worry. Is that all what's necessary to get into paradise?"

"Dad! I was being serious."

"I am serious too, daughter! Do you think that Mom and I want to harm you or to forbid you something that's natural for your age? No! Of course we want you to go out and have fun, meet new people and make friends. But all this church going. . . ."

"Dad! It is my life! My fate! I was chosen by God!"

(Or was I simply recruited by Lisa, a woman with an impressive life story and teeth like from the toothpaste ads?)

"That's all nonsense! Do not make me sick!" Dad turns away and walks towards the kitchen.

Nobody seems to understand what I am going through. I am torn between doubts about the church, fear of being cut off and sent to hell, and the desire to please the church leaders and my parents as well . . . and in the midst of all that I still have to somehow manage those damned German studies, or Frau Misinja will fry me alive. A pretty tough situation eh?

105. Signe has left the church.

She got too stressed out with the church duties and the school and her volleyball trainings. Her mom used to come too, but she did not like Shelly. After every conversation with Shelly she used to say, "What a nasty woman!" Signe had something like a nervous breakdown, and her parents came to the church and cursed all the leaders and everybody else as well, and took Signe away. Of course her mom blames me too for involving her daughter into all this mess. Nobody in the church is allowed to talk to Signe now, because she is a doomed one.

Alona left too recently. She just freaked out, because some American Latvian guy had told her that the Church of Christ is a dangerous and a destructive cult. So Alona stopped coming to the meetings, and when her spiritual leaders tried to call her at home, she was never there, or pretended not to be. When the whole bunch of people went to visit her, she refused to let them in.

The crazy Lilita left too, or better to say she was cut off and thrown out, because she was being immoral and did not want to repent. She had sex (and several times) with one of the newly baptized basketball players. They both left.

Oh, I forgot another girl named Marita was, thrown out too because of sexual immorality. Before she joined the church, she had lived together with a guy, who was much older than her. They have a little baby girl, but they are not married. When Marita joined the church she was ordered to break off her relationship with the man. When she told that to the guy, his response was, "You are a psycho, and I am not leaving our little girl with you." So the father took the kid with him. Marita was allowed to visit her daughter once in a month, but of course she was not allowed to stay at the place overnight. She did, however, and apparently she had sex with the father of her child. Salvis decided that it was immorality, and she was cut off too.

There is something cruel and inhuman about Salvis. I have a vivid picture of him walking back and forth the stage of the Hotel Riga conference hall and shouting at his full voice, "Since there has been sexual immorality in the church that concerns the three doomed ones, Lilita, Juris and Marita, we are forced to take some measures and enforce a new rule in the church in regard to Saturday night dates. Now brothers, attention please, for that concerns you more than the sisters! If any of the sisters becomes a special sister to you, which means you like the particular sister or even want to offer your friendship to her, until you officially become a boyfriend and a girlfriend, you are allowed to ask the sister out to a date only ONCE a month. Is that clear to everybody?"

The offering of friendship usually happens in a big hall with the whole church sitting around; the guy who is offering the friendship comes in with a heap of flowers and approaches the sister, to whom he wants to offer his friendship. At that moment they are officially declared as a boyfriend and a girlfriend and can date only each other. The process is rather complicated. If the guy decides that he likes the sister, first of all, he has to have long talks with his spiritual leader. Then his spiritual leader has to consult the girl's spiritual leader, and they both decide if the couple is ready for the relationship. In that way wanna-be couple's fate is completely in the hands of their leaders.

Salvis was getting hot from shouting. I could see the beads of sweat on his temple and face. His speech was often interrupted by exclamations like "Amen, brother! Go, brother! Preach, brother!" These are the same exclamations we hear all the time during the sermon. The people who exclaim the loudest and in such a way inspire the speaker the most, are considered to be the most spiritual ones. Those, who do not exclaim even once, are considered to be spiritually weak and selfish, because they are not willing to yell and inspire the speaker. I wonder if party members shouted the similar words in a similar manner in this same hall during the Soviet times. Maybe this church is just another People's Party.

I did not hear the end of the sermon, because I had to rush home. I didn't want Dad to get sick again because of worrying about me.

106. Apparently Salvis noticed my sudden departure last Friday. On Sunday, before the service, he approached me and asked, "Why did you leave earlier on Friday?"

I am always terrified when he talks to me. He makes me think about a God who revenges and punishes.

"Well," I stammered, my heart beating fast, "I promised my parents to be at home earlier."

"Why did you promise such a thing to them?"

"Because they worry when I am out late, and I want to please them."

"Whom do you have to please first?" I could see he was annoyed, for his eyes had become narrow and the gaze piercing.

"God, of course."

"There you go! God! Did you please God leaving the church in the middle of the sermon?"

"I thought it was the end!"

"You definitely lack one thing that God greatly approves of. Do you know what it is?"

I looked at him puzzled.

"That is humility. You are proud and stubborn. God does not like people like that. Besides that, you are not putting God at the first place in your life. The Bible's greatest commandment is 'Love the Lord with all your heart and soul and strength and mind.' "

"But the Bible also says to honor your parents and take care of them, for the one who does not honor his parents is worse than a non-believer!"

"God is at the first place! But He definitely isn't at the first place in your life!"

"I am trying."

"You are not trying hard enough. And now you will promise me one thing. You will promise me that you will never again promise to your parents to be at home earlier!"

"I cannot promise you such a thing to you," I said. "I cannot promise you that because I have to be at home. My dad gets sick when he worries about me. He has a serious heart disease, and what if he dies worrying about me? Then I will have to walk around with that feeling of guilt for the rest of my life."

"You forget that everything, including everyone's life and death, is in God's hands. He will take care of your father. If God does not want him to die, he will not, and if He does want your father to die, he will die, regardless of your presence or absence. You just have to trust God. If you make the right decision, which is to be at the sermon, and if you do God's will, He will take care of the rest. The same thing with you. God is watching over you, when you go home. Nothing will happen to you if He does not want anything to happen to you."

Those words made sense. Only how can I convince my parents about God's almighty power?

107. Kristine, a girl with shiny eyes and clean complexion, a law student at the University of Latvia (Oh, she's got so much energy and potential!) seems to be liked by Salvis. She and I got an invitation from Lisa to come over to Moscow and visit her, Danny and little Catelyn. Lisa even called me and said that she would be very glad to spend some time with me. I was in seventh heavens. Everyone in the church envied me, because I have such a wonderful friend, a role model to every woman in God's Kingdom, Lisa. I was never in Moscow, and I was very excited to see Lisa and little Catelyn again. The Church was even paying for my train ticket. Finally, my mother said, something good was coming out of the Church of Christ for me. But when we got to Moscow, after a long and uncomfortable ride on the train, Lisa barely noticed that I was there. She talked to Kristine for hours and hours about the things in the church (Kristine has moved pretty high up since her baptism; she is already leading the women Bible study on Thursdays). Lisa even took Kristine into her room; they closed the door behind them and talked and talked. I was left to play with Catelyn and the dog. On our way back to Riga, Kristine confessed to me that Lisa had asked her to marry Salvis.

So that was the deal! Kristine was sent to Moscow to be matched up with Salvis, because Danny and Lisa have decided that Kristine with her energy and charms could make a perfect church leader. Besides, Salvis needs a wife really. I have heard that he has some serious struggles concerning a certain forbidden area. Kristine is smart and beautiful and a leader type; she will be perfect for Salvis.

My mission on this trip was to provide a sense of safety for Kristine, for those Riga-Moscow trains are full of Gypsies and all sorts of dangerous elements. They can be pretty scary if you have to travel alone. How could I be so conceited to think that Lisa wanted to see me?

108. My winter session has started and I am pretty much in trouble. I have passed couple of tests, but I am not sure I will be able to pass the theoretical grammar exam, or the Latin (I do not even have all the notes, for I have skipped some classes because of the church) or — oh, my God! — conversational German with Frau Misinja.

The conversational grammar exam is tomorrow, and I am supposed to know more than a hundred specific expressions and idioms. I am so scared of talking in German. All the girls in my course have been to Germany at least twice, and some of them have even lived there for one or two years babysitting.

109. I woke up at 4.30 a.m. unable to sleep. Whenever I closed my eyes and tried to sleep, out of somewhere floated Frau Misinja's stern face, her lips twisted in an evil grin. I know she hates me. I think she hates all the insecure and weak ones, because she has never been one herself.

I took a shower and found it difficult to swallow Mom's fried eggs for breakfast. Then I remembered my weekly prayer appointment with my disciple Maija at 7 a.m. at Laima clock.

I arrived (to my own shame) at the clock five minutes late. It was an ice cold winter morning. I was relieved to see that Maija was not there yet. I was frozen and worried and sick, my eyes hurt really bad for not getting enough sleep, and I looked pretty horrible at that point. I was trying my best to gain some more self-control and to pull myself together. I certainly could not appear like this before Maija; I am supposed to be her role model at everything.

Well, at 7:25 there was no sign of Maija. My hands were frozen stiff even through my granny's hand-knit mittens, my face was burning in the sharp wind. I started to pray, asking God for courage and comfort. When it was 7:40 I realized that Maija was not coming. Either she slept over or forgot all about the appointment. Well, that would be forgivable for a young disciple of Jesus Christ. I felt a little disappointed, though. I could have spent the time studying, and it would have been nice to pray with somebody before that horrible exam.

I knew nothing else but to slowly start my way to the Foreign Language Department. Before that, however, I decided to have a cup of coffee at McDonald's. It is right across the street from Laima clock, and it is usually crowded with all sorts of folks. People in Latvia seem to love McDonald's food, even though it is considered to be not very healthy. In the early mornings, however, McDonald's is empty and has become one of the favorite hang out places for the Disciples of Jesus Christ. They meet at McDonald's for their morning prayers and so-called quiet times. But Maija was not at McDonald's either.

After I left McDonald's, I felt a little calmer. I decided to go in first to the examination hall. I wanted to be finished, the sooner the better, for I could not stand the tension anymore. I had to go first also because there was supposed to be women's conference today at the church, and of course my presence was mandatory.

The university was empty. I was too early. I sat down near the examination hall and took my notes out. I tried to remember the meanings of the expressions and the idioms, but there was a big empty hall in my head. I could not remember anything.

I saw Egita, coming from the other end of the hall. She is one of the smart ones.

"Hi!" she said, smiling at me. "You look pale like a ghost.

"Do I?" I rushed to the mirror. I looked hideous. Pale, large dark circles under my eyes. "Oh, my God!" I whispered.

"Hey, we all look like that. That's because of that monster woman Misinja."

I smiled. I felt very tired and very worried. I had stomachache. I could sense the disaster approaching, yet it wasn't in my power to prevent it.

Soon came the other girls. They all held their notes out, testing each other's knowledge.

I saw Misinja slowly crawling up the stairs, and my heart sank.

"Guten Morgen, Frau Misinja," all the girls said at once.

"Guten Morgen," she murmured back and glanced with the white part of the right eye on us. I could not help imagining her as a large hovercraft drifting in tempestuous waters. She slammed the door in front of our noses. Suddenly all the girls stopped chatting. There was a silent terror in the air.

After a while Frau Misinja opened the door of the examination hall and shouted out, "The first five, please!"

The first five ones were usually the five best ones from the course: Kristine, Egita, Kristine, Sanita and Irita. Sanita said she needed some more time, so I plucked up my courage and asked the girls if could answer the first one, because I was in a hurry. "Sure," they said, a little surprised at my desire.

We all went in. I was the first to draw a ticket. My hands were trembling. I thought maybe Frau Misinja would appreciate my courage and be kind to me.

I drew the number 13. Of course I am not superstitious, I believe that all is in God's hands, yet I couldn't help the tiny shivers running down my spine.

I got my text, which I was supposed to read and retell, plus the expressions and idioms to explain and use in my own sentences. The text was about some car crash or about some tragic even, yet there were so many unfamiliar words that I could not figure out what was actually being told, and if the person involved in the crash survived or died.

"Please, calm down," I whispered to myself, staring at the ceiling, maybe hoping to see God's face up there. The text wasn't so difficult after all, neither were the idioms I had to explain, yet I was so stressed out and scared (because I know Misinja does not like me) that I could not figure out the heads and tails of it.

"Are you ready to answer?" I heard Misinja's voice and felt her glance on my face.

"Not yet," I whispered.

"Well your time is out. I am not going to waste my time because some people who do nothing during the semester cannot prepare their tickets on time."

I rose from my desk slowly and walked towards the chair next to the professor's desk meant for students. "What a nice beginning," I thought ironically.

I sat down slowly, trying to control the shaking of my hands and my knees.

"So what type of text it is?" The question came like a bullet from the gun.

"I think . . . it's . . . a . . . story."

"Wrong. It's a novel! What are the main characteristics of a novel?"

"It is long. A lot of text." For heaven's sake, what nonsense I was talking! I used to know the characteristics of a novel.

"The story could be a lot of text too."

"I don't know," I whispered.

"Tell me what the piece of text you read was about."

"It was about a car accident." There was along silence. I did not know what to say. Misinja did not ask anything, just stared at me. I wanted to run out of the hall and slam the door. I knew it would be childish. I am a grown person now. I am a disciple of Jesus Christ. "Christ! God! Anyone, please help me. I am in a mess," I thought to myself.

I stayed there sitting. It was so humiliating. I saw the other four girls exchanging glances and whispering something to each other.

"Hush up everybody!" Frau Misinja yelled at the four. "Show me your sentences with the idioms, please!" Her voice sounded even colder than before.

I handed to her my page with the sentences.

"Could you please the next time write so that it is readable?"

"Yes," I whispered. No, I would not cry. Not in front of Frau Misinja and the others.

"This is hopeless! Now you tell me please, because I know you are not stupid, what is it that does not let you to prepare for the classes properly? Do you work besides your studies?"

"No."

"Do you have some sort of a romance in your life at the current moment?"

"No."

"Then why is that that you appear in my classes always unprepared? Did you come to the university to sit, stare and rub your butt against the chairs? If that is so, then I do not see the point of you being in here."

"I did not come to the university to sit and stare. I came to study."

"Then what is it that prevents you from dedicating your time to studies?"

"I am attending a church. It takes a lot of time. That gives my life a whole different meaning!"

"Holy heavens! The church! Now, people, listen to this! The church gives her life a whole different purpose!"

"Do you understand at all what you are doing with your life, child? Do you understand that you are ruining your life? Your very life that you cannot live twice?"

I couldn't help the tears. Suddenly they were streaming down my cheeks. I knew the girls were watching and later probably will make fun of me, but I could not help it.

"I will call your parents, and I will tell the whole department! I will not leave it like this! That is too horrible to see how young and smart people are messing up their lives by involving themselves with all sorts of wacko organizations! Do your parents know at all that you are involved with that church?"

"Yes," I whispered, rubbing my teary eyes. Some girl handed me a tissue.

"What do they say about it?"

"Nothing." God forgive me for lying. I did not mean to.

"Then they do not know! I can't believe that any decent parents, who care about their children—and yours do care about you, don't they?—that any decent parents, knowing that their child is in a sect, would leave it alone!"

"It is not a sect! It is the church of God!"

"Nonsense! Of course it is a sect. I can bet on my head it is a sect. Where does the organization come from?"

"From America originally!"

"That is what I suspected. In the Soviet times the religious activities were strongly prohibited. In the free independent Latvia, however, where everyone can do what he pleases and all sorts of religions are officially allowed now, we have gone into another extreme. Religion is supposed to be what saves the world, and that is why we have so many world-savers from all over the world invading our little land and bombarding it with all sort of idiotic teachings. And young people absorb it. Now listen, girls, and remember, most of all the evil in the world comes from America, including all the crazy religions like Mormons, Jehovah's Witnesses, all sorts of Christians, life-savers and life-givers and moral teachers. If it was my authority I would wipe them all out with a shitty broom. Do they really think that here in Latvia we like the cave men? That we know nothing of God or moral or ethics? Well, we can do very well without all that crap they claim to be true, and without their McDonald's too. We do not want them polluting our land with all those destructive teachings and brainwashing methods, which make young and naive people lose their heads. I have heard of many people who go into those sects and are lost to their families. Many of them leave their parents, their spouses, their children, their good jobs and houses to follow some crazy ideas, which leads them to their own destruction.

"Do you also want to ruin all your good chances and your whole life?"

"Can I ruin my life by believing in God?" I asked her back.

"Apparently one can. Look at yourself. You are far back of the other students with your studies. You look stressed and worn out and have no self-confidence. You are not even able to defend your religious convictions in front of me and your classmates. How can you possibly be a testimony to others?"

I felt a failure again, a complete failure. I am far back with my studies. I am no testimony to others. I have no self-confidence. I hadn't been able to defend my convictions in front of those people.

I had failed the exam.

Who told me that in God's Kingdom nobody is a loser or a failure? Who was it?

"I will tell you what, girls," Frau Misinja said as she got up from her chair and started to walk back and forth the room. She always does that when she wants to make an impact on us. "Religion was invented by people who were too weak-willed and too narrow minded to fight themselves for their place under the sun. So they invented God and religion to lean on in hard times so that they would not have to work their own brains to find a way out of the mess, and that they could blame all their misfortunes on some higher powers which seem to determine their lives.

"I'll tell you what. I have never believed in all this nonsense. I have fought my way through life myself, and I have fallen and hurt myself, and I have gotten up survived. Nobody can shake me or brainwash me. I do not take it on. I think with my own head and do not let anybody mess with my life."

Somebody in the church told me that Christians are strong people. Frau Misinja was saying that Christians are the failures. Everything was all upside down. Of course Frau Misinja is an atheist and from Satan. I should not get influenced by her speeches. Yet something deep down within me was telling me that she is right. Was that what we call common sense? Didn't I got to the church because I felt out of place in the big world around me? Didn't I seek a shelter and protection in the church because I could not cope with my problems and insecurities myself? Maybe I am doing too little myself. I am just waiting for God to do everything for me.

"Well, I will see that you get out of there, for I am not going to leave it like this!" I heard Frau Misinja's voice from somewhere. I thought it was a dream, a nightmare. I was seeing everything from a distance.

"I will call the whole school together. I will call your parents. Do you want me to do this?"

I shook my head.

"I just want them to be informed what is going on with you!"

"NO!" I shook my head violently. "Frau Misinja, please don't do this! I will tell them myself!"

"For heaven's sake, what binds you to this organization so much? What obligations to you have with it?"

141

For heaven's sake! That was the answer. I was there for heaven's sake, for I do not want to go to hell after my death, but I could not tell that to her. I could not make myself a laughing stock to all these smart and sophisticated girls. I said, "I am there to help people find God."

"That is ridiculous. Do you think that your classmates after they have seen this will ever consider going there?"

She was right. I have been such a horrible example.

"OK, you can go now. I have already wasted enough time by giving you all this sermon. At least I hope it was of some use to you. You just saw what happens with people who let themselves to be drawn into organizations like this."

"Have I failed the exam?" I asked quietly.

"You have, but I will give you the lowest satisfactory mark because I feel sorry for you, and you must promise me that you will get out of there and will start to study. Now you may leave the room."

The lowest satisfactory mark. What would my parents say? Mom would kill me! "Can I take the exam one more time please?" I pleaded desperately.

"No, you cannot!" Misinja snorted. "You are free to leave. Next please!"

The exam was over. I could do nothing to make the situation right again. I had received the lowest satisfactory mark, and I had to accept that fact. How was I going to present this to my parents?

I walked out of the university, my cheeks burning from the salt of my tears. The wind was warmer and the snow had started to melt. It was gray and dirty around. The air smelled like hopelessness and misery. I stood at the bus stop and shivered. Across the street was an old abandoned building from the Soviet times which workers were starting to tear down. The wood was rotten, and plaster was falling off the walls; piles of garbage could be seen in the old rooms where workers had stripped off an outside wall. Once this had been a beautiful apartment full of happy people; now it was a garbage dump and smelled like pee. I felt just like that building.

110. I tried to pray, but I was mad with God and had lost all the hope that He is willing to help me at all. Just when I was about to turn into a stone of ice, the bus came. I crawled on it. It was wet cold and nasty in the bus. I put my head against the ice flower ornamented window and closed my eyes. I was too worn out to worry of what awaited me at home.

I was glad that when I came in only Dad was at home.

"How was your exam?" he asked immediately, his face serious and concerned. "You look horrible! What happened?"

"I got the lowest mark on the exam," I said quietly.

Dad did not get angry. "I warned you not to spend all your time in the church," he said. "Now you see the results."

"What if they deny a state tuition to me?"

"Then you will quit the university and go and clean the streets. We cannot afford to pay for your studies. You are not a child anymore. You should think more about how you live and what you do. If you want to ruin your life, go ahead, but it hurts me and Mom. We have always wanted the best for you."

"I will study. And I will pass the other exams!" I said, full of determination again. And I will. For my dad.

"Good," he said, trying to be cheerful, but I could sense he was very sad and disappointed with me. I will do better. For Dad and for myself.

I went into the bathroom to wash my face and to change for the women's conference. I was glad Mom was not at home and I did not have to see her. In the evening I would be calmer and will have more confidence.

I grabbed my backpack and was about to leave when dad appeared in the kitchen door.

"You look exhausted," he said carefully; "why don't you come and eat something and take a good rest afterwards?"

"I have to go now."

"Again? Today? Again?"

"We are having women's conference tonight."

Dad did not say anything. He just went back into the kitchen. Was he mad? I did not have time to care about that. I had to be there soon.

The conference distracted me a little bit, yet on my way home all my horrors came back to me. How was I going to face my mother? What could I say to her, and what would she say to me? Those questions tortured me on the bus home. I knew she would be furious and she would yell and burst into tears, blaming me for being a good-for-nothing daughter. And maybe she is right about that. Then my dad would beg her to stop. The evening would be a disaster.

I wasn't wrong, even a little bit. Everything happened exactly the way I had imagined it. Mom attacked me already in the hallway (Dad had told her about my failure), ordering me to pack my bags and leave, for she did not need the daughter like me. I have heard those threats before, so I was neither surprised nor intimidated.

I tried to sneak into my room, yet Mom came after me yelling, "No, wait; I want to talk to you! I want to hear your excuse why you failed at the exam today."

"Gaida, please stop!" I heard my dad's begging voice.

"Stop! She needs a good spanking! This lazy brainwashed brat! She is eating our food, we are giving her money, buying her all sorts of things, and she chooses to be a parasite. I won't tolerate parasites in my house! She and her God...."

"Oh, please, do not talk like that about your own child! You may regret that later!"

"I won't regret anything, and please stop playing that savior's role! She needs a little lesson, since she does not understand when we talk to her in a human way!"

Mom barged into my room, slamming the door behind her.

I was sitting on the couch, knees to chin, and staring at the little moth on the ceiling.

"Now you! Listen to me carefully! If you fail one more exam you are out of here! You go to your church and stay with them. Let them feed you and buy you things. Am I clear enough?"

I nodded.

"You have to promise me that instead of going to Sunday meeting you will stay home and prepare for your ... what's the exam on Monday?"

"Latin."

" ... for your Latin exam!"

"I cannot promise that. I have to talk with my leaders first, but I promise I will be well prepared for the exam."

"Who is a bigger authority for you: your leaders or your parents?"

"Well, God actually, and our church leaders are His servants."

"They are parasites and brainwashers! They are too lazy to work or do anything reasonable. That is why they have chosen brainwashing as their major occupation. Look at your Salvis—a big fat buffalo. All he does is brainwash fools like you!"

"Salvis is working for the church, and that is an honorable occupation," I said quietly.

"What work does he do? What? Recruits fools on the streets? Then he arranges meetings, or, better to say, brainwashing sessions with them, and the fools fall for it. That is all he does, but he gets paid for it, and I suspect he is much better paid than I am working hard from dawn to dark. Otherwise he would not be able to live in a large, beautiful, downtown apartment all by himself.

"He is a parasite, like all of them there, like our old leaders. Like our new leaders! I cannot watch without my heart breaking that my child has become one of them! I don't want to hear those parasite theories anymore. I cannot sit and watch how you are ruining your life by dedication all your time and energy to them.

"I want you to take our conversation close to heart." Mom had calmed down a little bit. She was still yelling, but not as loud as before.

"I promise I will do better on other exams." Mom gave me a stern look and left the room, slamming the door behind her.

I will pull myself together. I will prove to my parents and my teachers and my church leaders that I can manage it. I will need a lot of strength. God will you help me?

111. I was studying Latin all the Saturday from dawn to dark. I thought I was doing pretty well, yet I need one more day to repeat everything. I thought maybe I could skip the service just once. I had to consult my leader on this, so I called Astrida. Astrida never went to college. When I told her I had an exam to study for, she just said, "That is not an excuse and you know that! You have to learn to plan your time better. You cannot blame the church for your laziness, carelessness, and lack of organization abilities. Skipping the meeting is out of question. She hung up on that note.

I wanted not to go just because she was making me to, but then I remembered about God cutting off the proud and the arrogant ones, and I was frightened. So I went anyway.

When I got there, I met Sabine, my friend, a tall, blondee, skinny and beautiful girl who seemed to be conceited at first. I dared not to approach her. Yet to my surprise she approached me. She just came to me and said, "I want to be friends with you. I have wanted to get to know you already for a long time."

When I started to talk, Sabine was very frank about her life. She is as scared and as insecure as I am. She is also shy, and she has never had a boyfriend either. When I told her that she is very beautiful and that is why she should not be so insecure about herself, she just rolled her eyes and said in return, "I thought the same about you!"

"Then we both are very beautiful . . . at least in each other's eyes," I said and laughed. That is how our friendship started, and now I can say that Sabine is probably the only person in the church whom I trust completely. We have become life savers to one another. Whenever one of us comes into the huge conference hall, full with fifty or sixty disciples of Jesus Christ, whom you have to greet with a hug, which is quite tiresome and unnecessary in my opinion, first we look for each other and when we see each other, we wave to each other and quickly disappear into some corner to escape the whole damn hugging ceremony.

Coming to the Sunday meeting after my conversation with Astrida, I saw Sabine at the wine table. She was appointed to be responsible for wine distribution at the communion. I was relieved, for that meant I will have to hug maybe only some ten people on my way to her, because the wine table was placed quite near the door.

"What's the matter?" Sabine exclaimed when she saw my face. "Your eyes look as if you have been crying."

"I was."

"What happened?"

"I almost failed one exam. I got the lowest mark, and my parents consider it equal to failure. I didn't have time to prepare. I promised my parents that I will do better on my other exams, and tomorrow I have Latin, and I need to learn a lot for it. I was studying all day long yesterday, but I still need more time. When I called Astrida and asked if I could stay at home today and study, she said it was out of question. When I told her I do not have enough time to prepare for my exams, she blamed my laziness. When I begged her to listen to my arguments, she hung up."

Sabine nodded sympathetically. All she could say was, "I'm sorry."

"I was mad at her. I think she is a heartless monster."

"I totally agree with you," said Sabine.

I offered to help Sabine with wine, and my mood brightened up a little bit. However, neither Sabine nor I had noticed that there was a third listener to our conversation, obviously who obviously reported our conversation to Astrida, for after the sermon she approached me and Sabine and asked us to come with her. She led us to her small private office (where Karina used to sit when I visited her in the early days of my disciplehood. Karina never got baptized; neither did her lover Michael. One day they just stopped coming to the church, and Karina changed her office to avoid the disciples).

Astrida was straight to point: "Girls, there is an unpleasant event we have to talk over. You both at the wine table were slandering me."

"We were not," I broke in.

"Can you please wait until I finish, and then I will give you a word," Astrida snapped at me. I could tell she was annoyed, even though she was trying to conceal it.

"So you two were slandering me behind my back. One was complaining and calling me names, the other was listening and accepting it as an absolute truth. Now let me ask you is that how this happens between the disciples of Jesus Christ? Is that the way people solve their conflicts and misunderstandings in God's Kingdom?"

We both kept silent. I was too pissed off and too proud to say anything. Sabine just said, "No."

"Now you tell me please how we act if somebody has something against somebody. How does the Bible teach us to do?"

"We go and talk it over with the person," I started quietly.

"Correct. Did you act as the Bible tells you to?"

"No," I said with a slight defensiveness in my voice. "But I did not mean to slander you."

"Apparently you did! Doesn't the Bible tell us to tame our tongues?"

"We are all just human beings, and we all sin and make mistakes," I said with so much conviction in my voice that Astrida stared at me for a while surprised. She did not expect me to be able to say anything to justify myself, for I have always been the quiet mouse. However, the numerous quarrels and fights with my parents and Frau Misinja have made me tougher.

"I see your point about us being human and sinful," Astrida said slowly, as if considering what to say next. Then she turned to Sabine and became stern again. "And you? Instead of refusing to listen to it, you not even listened to her but even supported her. Did you act right?"

Sabine licked her lips and spoke carefully. "I think Iveta was right. She needed to stay home and study, but you did not let her, and that was wrong from you."

Astrida's cheeks turned a little pink, but she tried her best to keep her voice under control. "Let me ask you, who is leading the church at the current moment—you or I?"

"You."

"What does the Bible say about the church leaders? What are the members of the church are supposed to do when confronted with their leaders?"

"To obey their leaders in all things."

"Is that obedience from your side if you are questioning my decisions?"

"Everyone is allowed to question. That is why we are given a brain," Sabine replied.

"A truly submissive person, who is a person after God's own heart, obeys without questioning, because she knows that leaders are appointed by God and that every word from a leader's mouth is like grain of gold. Leaders are appointed to help you, and if you disobey them you are disobeying God!"

"I do not see any help in a leader not permitting me to prepare for the exam, which is also important. I believe it was God's plan for me to study languages," I said, encouraged by Sabine's daring.

"I see that you fail to understand the priorities. Your education is important, I do not deny that, yet which is more important for you to hear God's message through Salvis or to prepare for your exam?"

"In this case, prepare for my exam, because I hear Aivar's message— I mean God's message—every single day, and every single day I hear the same words about us being lukewarm and about not inviting and baptizing enough people. Is that all God wants us to hear every single day of our lives?"

Now Astrida was really angry. "You are proud and arrogant. God is disgusted with people like you! If you do not repent, God will cut you off from the tree of life!"

With those words, she released us.

112. I passed Latin with an 8, and I got good marks on my other exams. Now I study mostly at late nights, since all the evenings are occupied with church activities. I feel sick now and tortured by headaches. I am constantly tired and somehow depressed. Sabine and I are not supposed to communicate with each other anymore, because we influence each other in a negative way. Regardless to the prohibition, we still remain friends. When we go out of the hall together, Astrida always comes after us and drags us back. My parents have been talking to Salvis several times, trying to make him understand how exhausted I am, yet they get little results. Salvis, jlike Astrida, assures to my parents that all my problems are manageable and that I should work more on planning my activities ahead. My parents are trying to persuade me to leave the church before it is too late. I have considered this idea myself, yet Astrida's and Aivar's threats about being cut off and thrown into hell are very real to me. They can always find a passage in the Bible about that and show it to me, and I do respect Bible and believe that Bible is the word of God. Part of me, my logical part, is doubting that the Church of Christ is the only true church in this world; however, my emotional part is afraid to leave the church.

I keep on evangelizing daily. I keep on telling people about Jesus because I am afraid not to. I pray hard in the mornings and read my Bible trying to penetrate through the surface of the text and discover some hidden meaning some revelations. Yet nothing happens and nothing gets clearer. My life seems as senseless as it used to seem a couple of years ago. Has anything changed? No. I am still that same ugly ducking, even though nobody ever mentions me that, because I have grown up. Grown up people do not make fun of other grown up people who are ugly.

Every Saturday people go to those silly dates, but nobody ever asks me or Sabine out.

She has a crush on the handsomest guy in the church, Kaspars, who is also a big leader. That is why she does not have any chances on him. He is considered to be spiritual, but Sabine is not. She is considered to be a struggler in the church, one of the weak ones, and it is just because she often chooses to think with her own brain instead of the ones of her leader.

Yeah, and people in the church cannot date whomever they want to or chose to. They are matched up with each other, and if they disagree, they are considered rebellious and arrogant. If a guy likes the girl, he asks his leader first, and the leader is supposed to turn to Astrida, who now decides whether to let the guy to date the girl or not. In most cases the answer is no, and that is very understandable, since Astrida herself is thirty-five and a spinster and all the guys in the church are younger than her. She has no chances of ever getting married while being in God's Kingdom. In fact most girls don't have any chances because there are more sisters than brothers, and sisters are not allowed to date the guys they like.

113. Sabine often confesses me her desire to go back to the old life and have fun. She remembers the discos she used to go to before she came to the church, and slow dances, and kissing, Martini with Coke, and cigarettes. Well, that all belongs to the past. Sabine has had more fun that I, and now we are cut off from any kind of fun forever. This raises some sort of a wild rebellion within me. I want to have some fun before I die. The Heavenly Kingdom is no fun at all, I have learned already a long time ago. The discos we sometimes have at the church are ridiculous, with lights on and only fast dances. Mostly girls dance with girls and boys support the walls. We are young and craving for some sort of adventures to make our monotonous lives in God's Kingdom a little bit more colorful.

Last Saturday we decided to go out to a bar near Sabine's house, just for a little while to have couple of beers. Salvis says that moderate drinking is OK in God's Kingdom, so we were not sinning actually.

I had never been to a bar before, so that was another step towards the big life. Arabika is a small, dark and cozy place where the smell of women's perfume mixes with the smell of alcohol and cigarettes. It is a nice smell, I must admit.

Since I had never been to a bar, I did not know how to behave or what to order; Sabine, who was more experienced, settled everything. She ordered a 50g. vodka with black current juice for both of us. We found a quite table at some corner and sat down.

We did not have to wait a long time before a bunch of guys surrounded our table, eager to make friends with us. A tall and quite good-looking man in his late twenties maybe was staring at me all the time, and that made my heart beat faster. Somebody was noticing me after all, and somebody who was quite good looking. The problem was that we had decided to be reserved and cold towards the everyone who tried to communicate with us, for despite our desire to be appreciated by men, we felt uneasy about all that bar thing, because all of those men there were worldly and carnal people who probably know nothing about God's Kingdom and Jesus Christ. Church teaches us that we belong to light, and all the other people in the world belong to darkness and light has nothing to do with darkness. We have been warned of the outcome of dating the worldly guys. We have to save ourselves for the men of the light who will marry us and be our only sex partners in our whole entire life. The thought of having something to do with a non-Christian guy, although tempting because non-Christians seem to be more fun, is unacceptable to both if us. That is why we have to be so careful about those bar visits. We do not want to go away from God or the church; we just want to have a little fun. Play a little bit in darkness, and with darkness, and then come back and continue to live in the light, which means boring sermons every single day, Bible studies, prayers, meetings with leaders, evangelization sessions, etc. No wonder darkness is more appealing, even though it may be tricky.

So we were pretty careful. We finished our drinks feeling much better afterwards, more relaxed and more self-confident, chatted with the guys for few more minutes, then excused ourselves. They guys wanted to accompany us, but we said we live not far from the bar and that we would be fine. The guys let us go, even though I could sense they were sorry we had to leave. That made me feel very happy. We came home in quite a good mood, and the future did not seem so colorless and dull anymore. We decided to try our best to be faithful servants of Jesus Christ ... and just sometimes (VERY SELDOM!) we will allow ourselves to have a little fun going out to some bar or maybe even to some disco. So far disco has been the taboo. Well, what if we take with us a bunch of other liberal girls from the church who want to have some fun too? It should not be as dangerous then.

114. I have become more responsible what concerns my studies, especially what concerns my classes with Frau Misinja. I do not want her to call my parents. They already are furious enough. I study all my little free time that is left after attending church activities. I am very tired, and my falling asleep problem during the classes has become worse. My classmates have noticed my tiredness and my constant exhaustion.

Some have asked me a couple of times, "Why are you always so tired and so short of time? Do you still attend that church?" I do not like to answer that type of questions. I just nod and walk away.

Dad has become a real pain in the neck with his constant grumbling and complaining about the new government. He keeps on cursing a long list of people, whose names I never remember. I do not worry about our government at all. I do not care who is governing the country, or if the economic situation is getting better or worse. It matters so little to me. I have always been poor, and I am pretty used to wearing out-of-fashion clothes, eating oatmeal or pasta with tomato sauce, or the mystery meat and boiled potatoes and cabbage that those fat old ladies with the purple hair serve at our miserable university cafeteria. I am used to having no money at all, and now I have money to buy tapes. If I do not have money and I am not able to buy a bus ticket, I just walk eight kilometers home.

In fact I think that the situation is better than in Soviet times. Young people have more freedom and more possibilities. They can travel abroad; they can even study there if they get a scholarship. We are allowed to say what we think and to write about what we feel. Besides, all sort of foreign music and books are available. The stores are full with imported clothes (from Poland mostly, but also from Germany, Sweden, Denmark, Holland), which used to be the great treasures in Soviet times. I do a little translation for the project called ECAT (Environmental Center of Administration and Technology). It gives me a little money, and now I am even able to buy a pair of real jeans for myself, which was my Soviet times dream.

The main thing and the big thing is that we are allowed to believe in God and not be persecuted for that by getting fired from the job or getting excluded from the Communist Party and losing all the privileges or, worse, being put into jail for expressing our thoughts and opinions openly and poisoning the air of sacred Soviet ideologies.

However, Dad is grumpy about everything and unhappy with everything. He hates the large luxurious stores which are opening one by one in the center of the city. He hates the beautiful houses on the sides of the road to Jurmala and the black Mercedes and Toyotas parked at the every corner of the street. He hates the car alarms that are going off at all hours of the day and night. He thinks those belong to corrupt and dishonest people. Maybe he is right, but you cannot get far in this world if you are honest, can you? Unless you believe and put your trust in God. The Bible promises us that God will provide for the righteous. My dad thinks is it a lot of bullshits. He is full of bitterness and resentment about his own unsuccessful life. I try to convince him that it is not his fault that he became sick and that's why could not do more about his life, yet those words aren't much help to him. He thinks we are all failures in life and victims of poverty and injustice.

"This is ridiculous," my dad grumbles every single morning. "In Soviet times we had enough money to buy food, but there was no food on the shelves in the stores, and when there was, people were ready to cut each other's throat for a pair of sausages or a piece of red meat. Now when the stores are overloaded with all kinds of food from all parts of the world, we have no money to buy it because all our pension goes for rent, heating, electricity and phone, since Lattelekom has monopolized the phone business. They know they are the only ones in the phone business; that's why they can put prices for communication services as high as they want and nobody can stop them. The government does not care that elderly people are dying in the country unable to pay all the taxes, unable to buy the necessary medicine and pay off the medical bills."

Well, what concerns medicine and education my dad is right. In Soviet times medicine and education were free, which meant they were for everyone. If people got sick, they could stay at the hospitals and sanatoriums as long as they pleased. Now they have to save money for months and months to be able to afford a dentist visit.

The same is with education. In Soviet times everybody could go to college. After graduating they all were provided with jobs, and those who did not attended colleges were also provided with jobs. Now only few lucky ones in each department get state tuition. The others pay large sums of money to be able to study. Besides, there is a large competition, so that only the richest with no brains and the brightest few get to study. Thousands of people willing to study never get the chance, and if you do not get some sort of a college degree you won't be accepted to work for any good company, which means you won't make money. That is why most kids study law and economy, because they see opportunities in these areas.

Unemployment has increased enormously in the recent year, since all the large Soviet-time factories are liquidated, bought by some shrewd money bag and remade into large private companies with their own staff, which usually consists of relatives of the owner. All the simple people get fired, and if they are over thirty they have a very slight chance of finding another job. Due to this there are more burglaries, thefts and shoplifting in one day than we ever heard of in Soviet times for years. The car stealing is very common nowadays.

If in Soviet times everyone made about the same about of money per year (of course there were exceptions, and people who had relatives abroad were better off than the usual mortals). Most people lived in communal apartments, either enjoying or suffering through the communist dream. They all dressed the same because they could buy only the clothes that the Soviet shops were offering them. They had the same cars: Lada, Moskwitch, Neva or Zaporozhjetz. Now Latvia has split into two large groups: the extremely rich and the extremely poor. The middle class is gone.

My family, of course, belongs to the extremely poor, and dad feels betrayed by the government he trusted at first. Everybody believed that the brave freedom fighters would be effective government men; that is why everybody voted for them. Yet like all sinful people, they could not resist the temptation of sliding some of the money from the governmental funds into their own pockets. Yeah, my dad feels betrayed and robbed and abandoned by the people he put his trust in, plus he has his incurable illness, and those are reasons enough for being resentful and negative towards the whole world.

If I could only make him believe in God and cast all his troubles and worries upon the mighty shoulders of our heavenly Father! Yet it is not within my ability; all depends of God Himself. Besides, I have been such a bad example. Instead of becoming stronger and calmer and slowly turning into a person after God's heart, I have become a frightened, neurotic, depressed creature failing at everything I start to do. I do not believe that God really cares how I feel and that it really matters to Him. Maybe He has already cut me off a long time ago and all my constant failures and misfortunes are merely a result of it. Do I trust God enough to teach others to trust in Him? Do I cast all my worries upon His shoulders?

115.

Zinta is having Bible studies with a girl named Dina. She is a student at the Academy of Culture and seems to be a nice girl in all the possible ways. We have talked couple of times, and I think she likes me too. She has been to America for a whole year, and that of course makes me admire her even more.

There is also some boy coming with her; they are classmates. He is staring at me when he thinks I am not noticing it. He is good looking and strong . . . that's why I plucked up all my courage and last night at Pizza Lulu I asked Dina, "Is the guy, your classmate, your boyfriend?"

"Roberts? Oh no. We are just very good friends . . . we go to the library together and have lunches together, but nothing else. I used to like him a lot some time ago, and he kind of liked me too, but then nothing happened between us, and now he is in love with my friend Everita."

"Shit!" I thought. "I was born never to be happy!"

Dina noticed my face changing and asked, "Is anything wrong?"

"I was just thinking . . . that I must have left my grammar notebook at the library." God forgive me those lies, but I could not tell her the truth, could I?

"How horrible! What are you going to do now?" She expressed so much concern that I had to laugh.

"Nothing, I guess. I will get a new notebook and copy the notes from my classmates and. . . ." I could not finish the sentence, for Roberts was approaching.

Dina did the introduction while two very green eyes were staring at me curiously. "Hey, Roberts, this is my new friend, Iveta. Iveta, this is Roberts, my very best friend."

"Hi," Roberts said smiling at me, revealing a funny dimple in his left cheek.

He looked so cute.

"Sit down have a slice of pizza with us," Dina offered.

"Yes, please," I begged him in my thoughts.

"Thank you, but no. I have my practice in ten minutes."

"What do you do?" I asked him.

"I am a swimmer," he said and blushed a little bit too.

"Oh," was all I could utter. I could not take my eyes off his broad chest and strong muscular arms. I felt something weird at the pit of my stomach.

"I have got to go not," Roberts said very quietly. He was not looking at me any more, he was staring at his sneakers.

"It was nice to meet you," I said even more quietly. When he left I told Dina that I had to go aswell. I felt so full of new sensations and emotions. I thought my heart wouldburst into millions of pieces from that fullness of emotion. I could not stand staying and talking to Dina. I think I am falling in love3. I thought I was in love with Cook, and with that blonde guy in high school whose name I never found out. I never got to express my love. But this is different; this is real. I am eighteen now. I am all grown up, and I am falling in love.

116. Dina got baptized yesterday and told me that Roberts will be also baptized soon. I am very happy. I am happy about Dina, and of course I am happy about Roberts. I figured out that three good things could come out of his baptism: he will be here in the church and I will be able to see him all the time, he will not be able to date that girl he is in love with, and of course he will be saved.

Besides, something else very pleasant has happened recently. Since every day I go out on the streets and talk to people about God and the church and invite them to come to our Tuesday and Sunday services, I meet a lot of people, and lots of them want to be my friends, and guys whom I have invited all tell me that I am very beautiful and that they would come to the service only because of me. They often ask my telephone number, but of course if I gave them my number and Astrida found out, she might call me to her office again. So I offer to give them one of the brother's numbers. When I do that, their faces grew long, and they say, "No, thank you! I do not need a brother's number!" Then we usually part.

I have started to evangelize even in the public transportation. That's a challenge, but I like it, for that way I can meet lots of interesting people.

One day on my trolley home I noticed a blondee beautiful girl sitting opposite me. "I need to invite her," I thought to myself. I stared at her, and she returned my stare. I stared once again, and she did the same. I felt a little uncomfortable. Well, I decided to give her an invitation card if she got off at my stop, secretly hopping that she would get off earlier and I wouldn't have to bother. What a wicked, selfish heart I have!

The girl did not get off anywhere else. We both got off together, and we both stopped at the red light.

"Excuse me," I said.

"Yes?" The girl looked at me. She did not seem angry. That gave me courage.

"I just wanted to ask you to come our Sunday service. We are just Christians—we are not a sect or cult or anything. We are simply people who try to live according to laws of Bible.

The girl looked at me and started to laugh. "Now tell me, are you happy in this church? Are you really?"

None of the people I have ever talked to on the streets have asked me such a question. I did not know what to reply. Am I happy? I guess not. But can I say so? Of course not.

"Yes, I am very happy to be a part of God's Kingdom," I said with a broad smile, the one I have learned being in the church. God forgive me those lies, but I was lying for His own good. If I tell people all the truth about how I feel in the church, I will never get them into God's Kingdom.

"Well, I am not sure if I will come, but leave me the card," the girl said as we started to walk into the same direction.

"What is your name?" the girl asked again.

"Iveta—and yours?"

"Katrina."

"That is a very nice name," I said.

"Are you at college?" I asked her, just to talk about something. She was nice, and I did not want to scare her away by starting to talk about God and hell and all that stuff.

"I am an English major at the Foreign Language Department of the University of Latvia."

"Really?" I was surprised. "I study German."

"Then we both study languages. Where do you live?"

"On Ozolciema 10—you?"

"On the other side of the street! That's incredible! We are neighbors here and we study in the same building at the university!"

155

"Yes, yes." I was feeling hopeful: maybe this meeting shows that God was working through me.

"You could come and visit me some day."

"I would be very pleased," I said a little shyly. I left her my number and did not asked for hers. I did not want her to think that I am from some weird cult or sect, and I did not want to scare her away by asking for her number. I liked her and wanted to make friends with her.

The next day Katrina called me and asked me to come over for ice cream. Before I went, I prayed God sincerely to open Katrina's heart and to work miracles through me so that she could also be baptized.

We had a very nice talk. I told her everything about me, and she told me everything about herself. It turns out she believes in God too and leads a very righteous life. When I told her that, she just laughed and said, "You mean righteous because I am not sleeping with anybody at the moment?"

"Yes!"

"I seem righteous to you only because at the current moment I do not have a boyfriend, for if I did, trust me, you would not think that I am righteous."

But she has had a boyfriend for three years. Had she slept with him? If she had, then how did it feel? I am eighteen, and I know nothing about sex. Neither does Sabine. Those were the questions I wanted to ask her, but I felt somehow uneasy to ask such things.

I did tell her about Frau Misinja and the exam, about all the horrible persecutions I have at home and at school because of my beliefs. Katrina's response was strange, yet it made me look at things from a different perspective: "What if all your persecutions and the ugly scene with Frau What-Was-Her-Name are signs from God that this church is leading you astray? Instead of becoming more peaceful and harmonious, your life has become stressful and exhausting. Do you think that is really what God has planned for you? A life full of stress, worries and exhaustion?

"Besides, I think it is not right to spend all your spare time at the church, leaving your family and your studies behind. I think that your family and your studies are also God's gift to you, and you should learn to appreciate them while you can."

I did not say anything to this. Katrina was sowing doubts about the church, which is considered to be one of the deadly sins, and which means that I should stop meeting with her, yet her friendship ihas already become precious to me, and I do even think of quitting this relationship.

Now we hang out as much as possible. I tell Katrina everything about the church, the events there, about Roberts (who is going to be baptized tomorrow by the way, and whom I seem to like a lot), about the handsome Kaspars and poor Sabine, who has a hopeless crush on him, about the intimidating Salvis and his fiance Kristine (they are engaged now and are strictly forbidden to go anywhere just two of them, since engagement is one step closer to the falling into horrible temptation), about our Bible studies, Sunday Services with Lord's Supper and even about our dates. In Katrina's opinion the dating system in the church sucks. That is exactly what she says. "It sucks. It stinks! It is rotten!"

In my heart I agree with her. I would much better prefer dates one to one. But of course in front of Katrina I defend our dating system as much as I can. I cannot let her see that I myself have doubts about many things in the church.

117.
Roberts got baptized last Sunday. Dina even wrote a card for him. She said it was very difficult and painful for him to say to Everita that they will not be able to go out together, and that from now on he will be able to date the church girls only. Dina told me also that Everita wasn't serious about this relationship anyway—she had just played with him, because she has some other serious boyfriend somewhere, while poor Roberts had taken it all very seriously. But they used to hang out with each other a lot and they even had kissed once, but there had been nothing more than that, because Everita is in love with somebody else. Well, that was a great comfort for me to hear all that.

Roberts is even in my Bible study group! Today I already had one Bible study with my new group, and during the study I noticed that our eyes met more times than is recommended during a Bible study.

Once during one of the women's meetings Astrida said, "We are women of God, chosen by Him to serve Him faithfully and to follow Him, wherever He leads us; that is why our main task is to always keep our focus on God. God must be at the first place in our lives. If there is something or somebody else that we pay more attention to or care more about, it could be our jobs, families, our carriers, goals, desires, money, a boyfriend, a brother in the church, it means our focus has shifted away from the main target, and that is a very dangerous sign!"

I was aware that my focus was slipping away from God and His word to Roberts. I could not concentrate on the Bible anymore. All I saw was him. I knew it was dangerous, but after all God is asking too much of a poor, sinful and weak human being.

How I can stay focused on something abstract and distanced, on something that intimidates me and denies me any pleasure of life? It was much more pleasant to focus on Roberts. To tell the truth, I did not care much if it was dangerous or not. I guess that's because I've grown tired of always trying to perform all the right duties, always trying to stay spiritual by constantly controlling my thoughts and desires, denying myself all things that I like. I know Jesus denied Himself daily and carried His cross, but I am not Jesus, I am not God. I need comfort and understanding.

Probably Roberts's focus also slipped a little bit, but it is forgivable, for he was just a green disciple.

Then a terrible realization struck me. I was an older disciple in Christ, but I was not helping Roberts at all; instead I was leading him astray, being a stumbling block to him. I remembered the words in Bible, which said something like "if somebody causes his brother to sin, a millstone should be tied around his neck and he should be thrown into the water." I had just caused my brother to sin by shifting his focus away from God to me.

My heart was beating fast from fear. I did not hear the question I was asked about some Bible passage. I blushed. The question was asked to somebody else. I felt stupid, because Roberts had just seen my shame. Now he also knows that I am not spiritual and focused on God. God was obviously punishing me at the very instant. When the Bible study was over, Anita asked me if there was anything I would like to confess to her.

I told her all about how I feel recently. She listened carefully then said, "I think your problem is that you are not spiritual enough. Do you pray steadily?"

"Every morning, at the meetings, during the day—the problem is that I do not see any improvements. I don't get any response."

"Well, that only means that you are harboring some dark sins in your heart and are not being open about them. Is that right?"

My heart leaped.

"Are you being open with me about everything? You know what happens to people who carry darkness into their hearts. Satan takes over their hearts and God cuts them off. Do you want that happen to you? Do you know where those people wind up after death?"

I nodded, terrified.

"So what are those things you are hiding in your heart? Any impure thoughts?"

"Sometimes."

"What exactly? What exactly do you think about?"

"About kissing."

"What else impure things do you think about? Are they connected with somebody in the church?"

I blushed. "I like one brother, and when I look at him I have a strange feeling at the pit of my stomach."

"Well, that is lust," Anita diagnosed and kept silent for a while.

Then to my great surprise she opened up and stared to talk about herself. "I have had that, too. Several times. I have had lustful thoughts about certain brothers in the church. Before I became a Christian I used to lead a very loose and filthy life style. I had one-night stands, affairs with married people, all sorts of perversities in my sexual life. That is why it is difficult for me to lock it all out from my life. I still struggle with it.

"Lust can lead us to destruction. So we have to battle against it. When you see that brother and that feeling appears at the pit of your stomach, you just turn away and start to pray God to take it away. OK?"

I nodded.

Anita took her Bible and opened it. She read couple of scriptures about struggling with temptations. I listened absentmindedly; I had drifted away into my own thoughts, when a sharp and direct question brought me back to reality.

"Anything else you are struggling with?"

"I sometimes still have doubts."

"What about?"

"I sometimes think that this is not the right church."

"What makes you think so?"

That was the most unpleasant question. I remained silent, because I never knew how to answer that one. If I say it seems weird to me that we have to meet every day, they find a place in Bible which says that disciples of Christ met every day, prayed together and shared meals. If I say I do not like the blind submission to the leaders, they find a scripture which orders us to submit to our leaders completely. They will also find scriptures about humility and obedience, and in the end they will add that I am an arrogant and rebellious person because I choose to think with my own brain instead of the one of the leader. If I say that this Saturday date thing seems a little queer to me, they will ask, "Are we doing anything against the Bible?" If I say that on Friday nights I would rather stay at home and help my parents or prepare for my classes instead of doing nothing but watching a silly action movie and stuffing myself with popcorn (we do not even pray anymore on Friday nights), their reply will be, "The movie is secondary thing. You are not coming here for the movie; you are coming here to be united to your brothers and sisters in Christ." I have been through this before. They have all the answers ready for you even before you ask the question. In the end they'll rebuke you for not being spiritual enough and make you look like a fool.

There it came already, the question I had been expecting: "Is there anything we are doing against to what the Bible teaches us to?"

I knew I could not prove her anything so I said, "I don't know . . . it is just a feeling . . . an intuition."

"Well that is nonsense! In God's Kingdom we do not trust in our feelings or our intuition; instead we put our trust in God's word." Anita spoke in tone of a caring mother talking to an unreasonable child. "If you trusted God that He has put you in the right place, you would also trust your leaders as people sent in your way by Him to help you and to guide you in your Christian walk."

I did not say anything to that. I just smiled pleasantly. She smiled pleasantly. I left.

As I was leaving the room, a new idea struck me. What if all my misfortunes is a sign from God? What if by making everything fall apart in my life He is trying to show me that I am not in the right place and that this church is not entirely His establishment? Frau Misinja, Katrina, my parents? They all have been talking common sense. What if they are not from Satan after all? If this church turns out not to be from God, then it also turns out that all the people outside the church are not from Satan either.

I was standing and contemplating my new revelation, when I suddenly felt somebody lightly touching my shoulder. I jumped up.

"Hi!" That was Roberts.

"Hi! I'm sorry. You scared me!"

"Did I? Then I am the one now who should be sorry!"

I smiled at him. "I was deep in my thoughts and. . . ."

"What were you thinking about?" he asked curiously.

"Nothing. I mean lots of stuff!" I cursed my lack of wit.

"Problems?"

"Yeah—some really unpleasant ones."

"Do you want me to pray for you?"

"That's very nice of you, really."

"What should I pray for?"

"For. . . ." I could not tell to a young disciple that I am struggling with doubts, so I said, "that I could trust God more."

"OK."

"Do you want me to pray for you?" I asked, happy that this question came to my mind. In fact, prayer requests among two Christians of opposite sex are like life savers. Since you are always told to keep away from temptation, you start to avoid the opposite sex out of fear of the possible temptation, and when you are confronted with the opposite sex it feels like landing on an unexplored planet. You do not know where to step to avoid the possible danger. Yet some topics are pretty safe to talk about: prayer requests, spiritual walks with the Lord, sometimes even the faith trials or some recent spiritual revelations.

Roberts thought for a while and said, "You can pray about the same for me."

"How do you feel being a disciple of Jesus Christ?"

"Wonderful. I am very happy. I like my brothers and sisters."

I sniffed a little bit at the word "sisters."

"Do you like the meetings and the Bible studies?" I inquired.

"Yes, they are great encouragement to me."

"I am glad," I said, but I was not glad at all. Could that really be that Satan has blinded my eyes and hardened my heart? Others, Roberts for example, seem to enjoy the church. However, Roberts is a young disciple. I used to like the church too at first. Besides, Roberts looks very innocent; there is something pure about him. He is probably a year younger than me. You cannot tell that by his physical appearance, for he is big and strong—rather by the way he behaves. He is a fertile soil for the church teachings.

"I have to run now . . . see you on Friday," he said and hugged me. I think held me close longer than it is appropriate for the disciples of Christ. There was that feeling in my stomach again.

"Take care," I said.

He smiled at me in return. "You too!"

118.

On Friday afternoon, I attended a graduation ceremony. One of my sisters in Christ has graduated from some professional school. Since my family in the new independent Republic of Latvia belongs to the beggars' class, of course I could not afford to buy a decent dress for that special occasion, so I had no choice as to wear my old, really ugly, little-beneath-the-knee-length, navy blue skirt, mom's old indigo jacket, panty hose (ugly brown color) and my old high heeled shoes, which are out of fashion by now for sure, besides the heels are a little crooked too.

I was miserable just thinking about wearing such clothes in public. However, when I looked into the mirror, I was surprised to see that my face did not look that bad anymore. Was that really me? I smiled at my reflection, thinking of Roberts. My face lit up and looked almost cute. I felt that strange quiver in my stomach again, like a happy trembling throughout my whole body. Was that lust? No! Lust must be a dirty obsessive desire; this was something very beautiful. I wanted the feeling to continue.

"I will see him tonight!" I thought. I felt excited and happy.

The graduation ceremony was boring: lots of speeches, lots of congratulations, long lists of names. We did not stay for food and drinks.

When I walked past Laima clock, there was Roberts, apparently waiting for somebody. "Gosh," I thought; "I can't appear in front of him like this. I felt like scarecrow in my navy blue skirt and mom's large indigo jacket . . . and the ridiculous shoes with crooked heels." Lately I think a lot about how I look. I think the reason is Roberts. Everything has changed because of him. There is an old song by Kim Wilde: "You came and changed the way I feel." That is true! I feel different now, much different.

Then Roberts noticed me.

He came to me and hugged me.

"Hi!" I said. "Whom are you waiting for?"

"Gatis!"

The freaky Gatis I had once been on a date with! I did not know they were friends.

"I was at a graduation. I thought I will be able to go home and change before the meeting."

"Why do you have to change?" he asked, a little surprised.

"I look horrible in this outfit! Like a scarecrow!"

"I think you look beautiful," he said a little shyly.

I did not expect him to say anything like that. Of course I blushed, and that made my embarrassment obvious. I wanted to run away and hide because I had given myself away. "Now he knows that I have a crush on him," I thought frantically.

"Wait." He stopped me, putting his palm on my shoulder; "You did not give me a good-bye hug." He pulled me close and held me for a while in his arms. He was strong. I put my arms round his neck. I felt that surge of warmth flowing through my body again. This emotion was so strong and new to me that it scared me and made happy at the same time. Yet I jerked away from him immediately. Gosh! What were we doing actually? What if some other disciples had noticed! There is always somebody from the Church of Christ hanging around the Laima clock and McDonald's. What if Anita saw us like this?

"I am sorry!" Roberts said letting me go. "Did I upset you? Was that improper?" He blushed too.

"No. I liked it. I really did. Just what if other disciples noticed?" I was stumbling over my words.

"But you all hug in the church, don't you?"

"Yeah, but that's different. That's just with one arm around the other person's shoulders."

"I see. I'm sorry," he said looking really devastated.

I did not want him to feel hurt. I wanted to encourage him by saying something nice to him.

"It was really great. The whole church should hug like that," I said. A smile lit up his face, but I could sense he was still embarrassed.

"See you tonight," I said. I had nothing else reasonable to say, so I had to leave. Besides, I saw Gatis coming from the other end of the park. Thanks you, God, for making him late!

119. Apparently I have become absent-minded and careless at Frau Misinja's classes, for she is grumpy with me again.

"What is wrong with you? You were doing so well at the beginning of the semester. Is that still that church thing or is that something else?"

"No, Frau Misinja, this is not the church. I am just a little tired."

"Tired of what? Are you out of there or still in there?"

"I am still in there, but I am doing better the second semester. I have proved that after all."

"Yes, at the very beginning. So what is this? A romance?"

Since I am not allowed to lie, I kept silent. In the old days when I wasn't a disciple of Christ, I would have told her a heart-breaking story about me taking care of my ill relative or something like that. Now I could only keep my mouth shut and stare in the ground.

"Well, girls"—she turned to everybody—"this is too much. You are grown-up people and you have to realize that you are coming here not for my sake but for your own sake. These are not the Soviet times anymore, where every fool and lazy bone could find some sort of an occupation to keep himself floating down the stream and not drowning. Now the times have changed. No fool or lazy bone will survive through this period of wild capitalism in our country. The survivors will be people with brains and serious attitude towards work. You, girls, will have to work hard and fight for your place under the sun, and if you are too weak or too dumb to do so, nobody—listen! Nobody—will pity you or pamper you! Life is hard and often unfair, yet the smart and the industrious ones will pull through. If you waste your time and your opportunities you have no one else to blame but yourselves.

"And you, young lady...." She was speaking to me personally. "Quit day-dreaming and floating in some unreal world. Come back to the earth and get your butt in gear, or you will lose your opportunities and ruin your life."

For the first time in my life I was not mad at Frau Misinja. She was a harsh woman, but she was talking common sense. It is time for me to grow up.

120. **Y**esterday we had public confession night. Everybody had to confess his or her deepest and darkest sins publicly, especially the sins of a sexual nature. Attendance was mandatory.

Sisters stayed in the hall, and the brothers went to another room. We had to sit in a circle. Astrida, as the church leader, opened the confession with her story of life. I am saying "story of life" because, before Astrida became a Christian, there was not a day in her life she doesn't need to confess now. She took at least forty-five minutes and gave the other sisters time to calm down and prepare.

Then I heard things I had never imagined before in my life. Girls confessed they have had sex for money. One said that by the age of twenty-one, she had forty-seven sex partners. Some said they were involved with women. Lots of now Godly woman have had affairs with married people and abortions. There were plenty of kinky stories about the ways girls masturbate and stimulate themselves.

I could not imagine that my sisters in Christ could ever have done things like that.

However, some of the most beautiful sisters, including Sabine, turned out to be virgins. Maybe they were lying, but we have been threatened that if we lie, we will be cut off from God's family and go to hell. Those girls are too honest and to sincere to lie.

In my opinion such confession nights could do more harm than good, for now meeting with sisters I will always have in mind: this one has had an abortion, that one has had thirty partners, this one masturbates with a sausage, that one used to be a lesbian. I wish I'd better not known such things about my sisters in Christ. What is past is past. The Lord has forgiven them, and now they are living for Him.

I was glad I did not have to confess much, at least not in the area of sex. However, if I hadn't been ugly and undesirable, maybe I would have had quite a lot of adventures by now and would also be able tell some kinky stuff last night. All I had to confess was stealing pickles and marinated mushrooms from Anastasia's table.

After the confession the whole church came together, and we had coffee and pastries. I had a chance to see Roberts again. He was talking to other girls and seemed not to notice me at all. He did not even say hello to me. That confused me. I thought, "Is he still embarrassed about that hug? Is he mad at me?"

He was whispering something to Zinta. In response she smiled happily at him. He was probably asking her for a date. I felt a sharp pang of jealousy going through my chest. Oh, God, I don't want to be jealous. I don't want to confess to Anita that I am jealous of Zinta, because

Roberts was talking to her. I do not want my leader to know that I like Roberts. I do not want anybody to know that, not even Sabine.

I was observing Roberts with a corner of my eye. He wasn't talking to Zinta any more, he was talking to Daina and Kristina. Maybe he is asking one of them for a date, I thought.

I was absent-minded and careless towards others; I only wanted to see him and talk to him. He is the reason that I have started to love meetings and Bible studies again. I know that's a wrong reason, but I do not care, and I am not going to tell it to Anita.

Anna, a newly baptized sister, approached me. "I would like to meet with you. Maybe we could pray together. Can we do that?"

"Yes, of course," I said without thinking.

"Oh, really? I am so excited. I am so happy I will be able to get to know you better!" Anna was beaming.

Holy innocent!

I wonder why the young disciples like me so much. There have been many times when young sisters have wanted to meet with me and pray together and talk about their problems and anxieties. They seem to trust me more than their own leaders. Usually it makes me happy when people trust me and want to talk to me. However, Anna's innocent smile and shiny eyes irritated me.

"How long have you been a disciple?" she asked.

"A long time," I said absentmindedly. "I was the first sister in the Riga's Church of Christ."

At this Anna's eyes went round like saucers.

"You are really a chosen one," she said with an admiration of a child.

"So are you," I said and smiled reluctantly.

Anna is a year older than I am, yet she is a baby.

Then I saw Roberts coming right at me. My heart started to beat wildly. Anna was chatting about something.

"Hi!" Roberts said. He seemed to be a little tense.

"Hi!" I said, trying to gather a little more self control. This time his one arm went round my shoulders. He pulled me close again. Our cheeks touched, by accident, and we both jerked away. I smiled to conceal my embarrassment.

"I was going to ask you, what are you doing on Saturday night?"

I knew what all this introduction was about. I have heard it so many times when brothers ask sisters for a date. "Nothing.... nothing special I guess," I said trying to make my voice sound indifferent.

"Would you like to go to a movie with me on Saturday night?" Roberts asked.

165

"Yes," I said eagerly, and of course regretted it immediately. I should have said "probably" or "let me think" or something like that.
"We are meeting at five at Laima clock on Saturday."
"OK."
We hugged and our cheeks touched again, but this time we did not jerk away from each other. We just stood like that for a while, holding each other close, dizzy with happiness.

Then Kaspars, Roberts's leader, was coming, so we had to let each other go.

I sneaked into the bathroom nearby. I did not want Kaspars to notice my red cheeks. Kaspars was saying something to Roberts. I waited until they had finished to leave the bathroom.

This will be only my second date since joining the church. Other sisters have dates every Saturday night. God loves me seldom, yet when He does, He really does. Thank you, God.

121. Yesterday was the happiest day in my whole life, my date with Roberts. First we went to see a movie. I don't even remember the title anymore. It wasn't important. All that mattered was his closeness. I could feel our shoulders touching during the movie several times. There it was again, that weird feeling. I feel hot and cold and dizzy and incredible happy, and very scared at the same time. Is that how it feels when you are in love? I don't know. I have had crushes, starting with Pavars, the guy from the middle school, and Ingo, the guy in the high school, but it wasn't anything like that. I thought I was in love because all my classmates were in love with somebody, and of course I could not be the one who wasn't. Yet apparently it wasn't love. Is this love now? Am I in love with Roberts? Those were the questions I was trying to answer during the movie.

Later when the other "couples" (there were a whole bunch of people there, of course) asked how I liked the movie, I could only smile and say, "Oh, it was OK."

We decided to hang out a little bit afterwards, so we went to Pizza Lulu.

Roberts bought me a large slice of pizza and Coke. He was sitting right next to me. I liked the way he smelled. Kaspars, who was also on the date, was sharing his spiritual experiences. Everyone was listening in awe. Kaspars is the legend of the Riga Church of Christ, the star, the girl's favorite, the sisters' beloved brother, and guess what? I am not interested in him at all. Usually I do not even notice him around.

I could not wait until we left Pizza Lulu, and Roberts and I could spend some time together, just two of us. After all, he was supposed to accompany me home. Sitting in the trolley on my way home we were silent again. I guess we both were shy. That made me only conclude that Roberts has not had much experience with women either.

"I have to say something," I thought frantically. What could I ask him? About his training. I would ask about his training.

"Do you still go swimming?"

That was the right question. Roberts started to tell about the classes, competitions, and coaches. Then we had plenty of things to talk about. We talked also about the church and our struggles of faith. I even dared to tell him about my doubts. Roberts promised to pray for me really hard. He has never had doubts; he is sure this is the right place for him. I can understand that. I used to be just like him when I first came, ready to go anywhere and to do anything to save the lost. My idealism has faded away somewhere. I have become skeptic and ironic and faithless. Maybe I'm just tired and disappointed. I could not reveal that to Roberts. What if I sow doubts in his mind, and then I will be accused of causing divisions within God's own establishment?

We touched also the Saturday night date issue. When I asked him whether brothers do not like me because I am ugly, he seemed to be very surprised. "Many brothers think you are beautiful," he said.

"Beautiful? If they really thought I was beautiful, they would asked me for dates on Saturday nights. I am still that same ugly duckling that I always was."

"You are crazy talking like this!" Roberts exclaimed, "You are beautiful! That is why brothers do not ask you out!"

"I do not quite get this."

"They think . . . that is really embarrassing to say."

"What?"

"That you could be a temptation. That they could have those bad thoughts."

"This cannot be true."

"Yes it is."

"There are other beautiful sisters who have dates every Saturday night. How can you explain that?"

"Well, they're not that sexy."

"Sexy?"

"Yes, the brothers think you are sexy . . . you and Sabine."

"Sabine maybe, but what is there sexy about me? I do not have even decent clothes to wear for a date."

"I don't know. It is not clothes or anything. It is just the way you look, move, speak—the whole thing together."

His words embarrassed me, for I had never heard anything like that before.

"I also think you are very beautiful," Roberts said in the end.

I did not know how to respond. I always think that people telling me compliments are just being nice and trying to encourage me. They are lying to me, the same way I used to lie to my fat girl friends, telling them that they are not that fat after all. I do not believe that fairy tales come true, or that ugly ducklings like me turn into beautiful swans later.

But Roberts was a disciple of Jesus Christ. He cannot lie, and he does seem to like me, doesn't he? Miracles happen after all.

Suddenly we were at my station, and we got off. I did not want the night to end. I tried to walk slowly. Roberts was telling a funny story about his coach. I laughed. He was talking all the time. Was he afraid of silence? Was he uneasy about his confession to me?

At the door we hugged again. I like when our cheeks touch. I like to feel his hair brushing against my cheek, to feel his skin against mine, his warmth and strength.

122. I have been in ecstasy for months, which is why I have written so little in my diary. The spring is in the air and I am happy. For the first time I am in love with somebody, and this somebody is in love with me. This sensational feeling has turned my life upside down. Before Roberts came into my life I used to get pissed off about every damn thing; however, my mood is never sour anymore. Frau Misinja's warnings impress me as much as the sound of wind outside. My parents' scolds do not hurt any more. Sometimes when I remember Dad's disease a slight feeling of guilt sweeps over me; however, my happiness is so great and overwhelming that the feelings of guilt simply drown in it.

My doubts about the church have disappeared, or better to say they are pushed into some remote and dark corner of my consciousness. I want to remain in the church forever, because Roberts is there, and he will also remain there forever. Salvis and Astrida do not seem so threatening anymore, or maybe I simply have stopped noticing them around.

The only cloud in my sky is the new rule that allows Roberts to ask me out only once a month. But I accept even it. At least one Saturday night within a month I live out my happiness to the full. In fact my life has become a constant longing for our next date. The very thought that after four weeks we will be able to go out again makes me dizzy. I think about Roberts constantly, and when I pray in the mornings, I pray for him too and feel my stomach quiver again. I love that feeling, and I realize I have started to love my morning prayers and Bible studies. I am overflowing with thankfulness to God and deeply regret my doubts concerning His love to me. I have come to love talking to people on the streets. Many of them even come to the meetings (a miracle that had never happened before!). They say they came because they have been fascinated by my shiny eyes and beaming smile. I have had numerous Bible studies with the recruited girls, and some of them even agreed to get baptized. However, right before baptism they disappeared. However, I did not mourn over them. Absolutely nothing can upset me, for nothing can compare to Roberts' eyes looking at me adoringly and to the warmth of his body when we hug. I could live for months cherishing the memories of his smile or touch. How little it takes to make a white crow happy.

123. Roberts is not being so affectionate anymore. During the Bibles studies he does not return my stares. He does not come and talk to me before meetings, just gives me a quick hug and disappears. When I smile at him or say something nice and encouraging to him, he does not smile back. Sometimes he even forgets to hug me (which was contrary to the rules of the church), and, when saying hello, he sometimes is afraid to look me in the eye. He never asks me to dates anymore, and since other brothers have started to ask me out quite a lot, I often happen to be on the same group date with Roberts. It is painful for me to watch him chat with other sisters and then accompany them home. Even though lately I have dates every Saturday night, I have stopped enjoying them. What joy can there be to go out with somebody you do not care for? I cannot figure out what the matter is. I question myself a thousand times a day, "What did I do wrong? Did I hurt him somehow? Did I offend him? What is wrong with me? Why doesn't he like me anymore?" Just where did I go wrong? I have grown sullen and frustrated with the whole world again.

124. Yesterday I saw Roberts alone in the hall preparing for the Bible study. I plucked up my courage and approached him.
"Roberts?"
"Yes?" He looked up at me with those green eyes I had come to love so much.
"I want to talk to you," I stammered and forced a smile. "Are you available now."
"Sure," he said. "Sit down."
I sat down and licked my dry lips. He was waiting for me to start. I didn't know how to start.

"In the recent times I have noticed that you.... I have got the feeling that you are upset with me about something, and I don't know what it is. Have I hurt you somehow?"

He smiled and looked at me. Even though he was smiling, his eyes were serious and sad.

"No, you have not hurt me," he said softly, brushing his finger against my cheek. It felt like before, when he used to hug me.

"Then why don't you ever talk to me anymore? We used to be friends."

He looked aside for a while. When he looked back at me, I saw pain in his eyes.

"Yes, we did."

"What happened?"

"Nothing." He was staring into his lap.

"It does not make sense to me. You have to tell me what happened. Don't they preach to us that there must be nothing between the brothers and sisters in Christ? Something seems to be wrong between us. I can feel that, and I want to know what I did wrong."

"I told you already. It is not your fault."

"Then what is it?"

He kept silent for a while then said, "I don't know how to explain this. I do not want you to think that I have something against you. The leaders think that it is better for us not to date."

"Why?"

"Because they think we are on different spiritual levels."

Well, this makes a little sense to me. Roberts has grown enormously since he came. He is already one of the Bible family group leaders, and I am still discipling just two people so far.

"So the bottom line is that I am not spiritual enough for you."

"I do not think so. I think you are very spiritual, but they think you are not. They think you are rebellious, and that's why . . . I want you to know that this is very painful to me, a very painful decision, but I had to make it to help the God's Kingdom grow."

His words were painful. I knew he had made the right decision, yet I felt hurt and betrayed.

"It makes sense now," I said coolly. I got up to leave. Roberts grabbed my hand.

"I do not want you to think that I do not care. I do care. And I am praying for you. You can make it."

I freed my hand and left. My heart was aching. The pain was too strong to be washed away with tears.

Now I do not talk to Roberts. I pretend that he is an empty place for me. I do not want him to think that I still care. He rejected me just because leaders told him so. He does not care for me very much. If I was told not to date him for some reason, I would never obey it, not even if they threw me out of the church. I love him so much, that I would be ready—to do what? Even to give up my salvation.

125. One Friday night, right in the middle of the sermon, Salvis ordered everybody to get up and approach everybody else and say, "I love you." So the whole church just walked around hugging each other. I did it very mechanically. I do not love everybody in the church, and it is hypocritical to pretend that I do, and God does not love hypocrites. I cannot say to Astrida that I love her wholeheartedly. I had spent enough time in prayers, asking God to help me not to hate her. I try not hate her, for she is one of God's creatures like every one of us is, but I cannot say I that love her either. After all, love comes from God, and if God has not planted in my heart love for Astrida, there is nothing I can do about it. Salvis is another difficult case. How can I love someone whom I fear? I gave him a just a quick hug.

Roberts? I could not make myself approach him. I was too proud and too sacred, even though I was dying to say those words to him more than to anyone else in the church. But I wanted him to approach me first.

Finally, after I had already hugged with everyone, Roberts approached me. "I have to tell you something," he said and pulled me close. "I love you."

"I love you too," I said, holding back tears.

I put my arms round his neck. We stood like that, squeezing each other for awhile. Then we let go.

Salvis ordered everybody to take their seats and the sermon continued.

126. The spring session has almost ended, and I have done much better at my exams this time. Frau Misinja is proud of me (I got 8!!!). After the exam she said to me, "You are a smart kid; you just need to be pushed and nagged into doing something."

I guess she is right, so I did not comment upon her judgment. I just stood there like a ninny and smiled.

I got 8, 9 and 7 at the other exams. My parents have cheered up. Dad feels better. Maybe it is because of the fresh spring weather, and, since now it stays light until midnight, he does not have to worry about me being out late so much.

Everything would be pretty good, if not for Roberts.

After saying to each other "I love you," things seemed to be better, but now we have started to grow apart again. I go mad when he is cold and distant towards me. Why does he do that? Even if we cannot date, why does he pretend that he hates me? Why can't we at least be friends?

I have made a resolution to cast him out of my heart and my mind at least thousand times. I have tried to dedicate my life to God only, but it does not work. All this situation frustrates me so much! I burst into tears for trifles. I do not want Roberts to think that I care for him. I do not want to be a beggar and a fool.

I sense he does not like my apparent indifference and coldness. Maybe he is suffering too, but why doesn't he do anything about it? Why doesn't he make the first step? Is he waiting for me to do it, or maybe he really does not like me anymore? The thought of him not liking me anymore is unbearably painful. I keep on blaming myself for everything. What can I do to be more spiritual? Would Roberts communicate with me if I was more spiritual?

Besides I am horribly jealous of Melita, a sister who got baptized couple of months ago. She is already leading a women's Bible study group. She's been set as an example of obedience and humility for everyone in the church. Well, she is humble because she lacks brains. She likes to be told what to do. She will never object of anything, just smile and accept. Holy innocence! She seems to like Roberts, and, I am afraid that he has started to like her too.

I feel almost physically sick when I see Melita dedicating Roberts one of her silly virgin's smiles. My heart is so heavy that I could not bear it any longer, so I went and poured it out to Kristine, Salvis' fiance. They are getting married in summer, and then Kristine will take Astrida's spot in the church. The first thing Kristine said was, "You just have to make a decision that you won't be jealous, that you will love Melita no matter what. From now on you are going to consciously work on being friends with Melita. Ask her to have devotions with you, invite her to come and see you," and blah, blah, blah. But she also told me to call Lisa and discuss it with her. That is what I did. I called Lisa, and she said that it was absolutely wrong for them to force to me make friends with Melita, for it will do nothing but make the matters worse. Kristine and Astrida both apologized to me later about their wrongdoing.

127. It is summer and for the first time in my life I am enjoying it. In fact, I have some changes in my life. I have a new leader again, and my leader is Dina, Roberts' friend from the Academy of Culture, and the girl I like very much. I think she is the first of my leaders whom I can trust completely. She seems to be sincere, honest and compassionate. Dina even offered me to work with her at Riga Occupation Museum. They there need girls, guides with good language skills.

So now we spend most of our time together working at the same place. When there are few visitors there we have plenty of time to talk. Besides, we meet lots of interesting people there, and we have chance to polish our foreign language skills. I like the job also because it leaves me less time to concentrate on my unrequited love.

My parents are happy, too, because now at least I am doing something reasonable and making a salary.

128. I am back at the school, watching Frau Misinja walking back and forth the classroom. Yet my thoughts are far away from German. I still cannot completely get over what is happening: Dina is in trouble at the church. It is like a thunder from clear skies. Sabine is surprised most of all, for she thought that Dina's religious convictions are as hard as stone. The irony is, though, that Sabine with all her beauty is still in the church, and the righteous Dina, with all her strong convictions, is in danger of perishing in hell after she dies.

I never knew that Dina had any doubts or struggles; she was a good spiritual leader, always happy and content with the life. I was envying her. Then suddenly there comes this American girl, Bonny, sent from Satan himself to plant doubts in Dina's mind.

One day about a month ago a bunch of American students came to the museum. We divided them into two groups. I was to lead one group, and Dina was left with the other. They were nice kids, very curious, friendly and talkative. No wonder Dina started to chat with that nice girl Bonny. Bonny seemed to be very interested in the life of young people in Latvia. She wanted to talk and to find out more about it. Dina said she did not have time at the moment, but they decided to meet for coffee another day.

Some days later Bonny came in and picked Dina up. I saw them both leaving. When Dina came back later that day, she looked concerned, maybe a little upset.

"What's the matter?" I asked.

"Oh, nothing," she replied, trying to smile, but I could sense she was on the verge of tears. I shrugged and went back to work. My assignment for that day was to greet the visitors at the door. I do not like to inquire people if they are not willing to speak themselves, so I did not say anything more to Dina.

The next day Dina was no better, nor did she get better the following days. From a happy and peaceful girl with lots of self-control, Dina had turned into a nervous and jumpy creature. She did not chat with me or

173

the others anymore. If she wasn't guiding the groups, she crawled into some dark corner of the museum and read the Bible. I noticed also that she was having long conversations with Salvis and Astrida after the meetings. That all seemed very strange to me, but Dina never shares her concerns with me as she used to be just couple weeks ago, and I dared not to ask. I suspected, though, that it had to do something with that girl Bonny and the Church of Christ, and that it was something dangerous or Dina would have shared it with me. It is one of the strictest rules in the church: if the leader has some serious spiritual problems or doubts he/she is not at liberty to share them with his/her disciple.

Eventually I got to know from one of the sisters what was going on with Dina. She was struggling with doubts if the Church of Christ is really the only true *Christian* church. "This American chick has brainwashed Dina!" I thought with much exasperation. Frau Misinja once said all the evil comes from the United States, and the Church of Christ is originally from United States.

129. I feel sorry for Dina. She has been so miserable for these last weeks. She had been always comforting me; now it is my turn to comfort her. Yesterday I approached her and put my arm around her shoulders. "I know what your trouble is," I said. "One of the sisters told me. I have been through this several times. You just have to pray really hard, and God will show you the truth."

"I am praying," Dina said. "I am praying all the time." Her voice cracked; she started to sob.

"It is so unbearable," she sobbed. "I cannot stand that anymore. They are tearing me apart!"

"Who are they? Who are tearing you apart?" I asked softly.

"The church. Salvis. Astrida. All the leaders and Bonny with her friends. Bonny herself was in this church for two years. She left because they were abusing her there; I mean verbally abusing. Something did not seem right to her there. Now she has joined some organization; they are helping people to distinguish the true churches from the cults and sects. Bonny says that our church is a destructive cult."

I had already heard those words somewhere. Oh yes, Alona told me that.

"Salvis and Astrida think that I have come into contact with Satan through Bonny. They prohibited me from seeing her. I am not allowed to answer her and her friends' phone calls. Astrida said that she herself will come to museum today and pick me up."

"Why does Bonny think that this church is a cult or sect?"

"Because this church first of all is very legalistic. They make up their own rules and make people follow them. They limit people's free choice and rob them off their privacy. But. . . ." Dina looked at me with eyes desperate and full of fear. "I was not supposed to tell you all this. I still am your leader." I too felt scared after hearing Dina's confession. What if Bonny is right? What is she is not? What if she is Satan's agent? Dina started to cry again.

"Dina," I handed her my handkerchief. "I have been there before. I know how you feel. Do not worry about anything, but cast all your troubles upon God. He knows how you feel, and he will reveal the truth to you if you will ask him earnestly." Boy, is it easy to preach to others!

Dina was still crying. "Do you want to pray about it right now?" I offered.

Dina looked at me gratefully. "Yes! Let's pray right now!"

We both prayed earnestly, and Dina seemed to feel better afterwards. She even chatted with me a little bit about her new roller blades. We went back to work, but my heart was heavy. I was meditating on what Dina had said to me. What if the church really is a destructive cult?

At five Astrida and Zinta came to pick Dina up.

That night I wasn't listening to the sermon. My mind was drifting around again. I was observing my brothers and sisters in Christ. There was Anna with the eyes like the ones of a child; Melita, the holy innocent; Roberts eagerly taking notes; handsome Kaspars staring out of the window; Zigis whose face is covered with ugly scars and pimples; my leader Dina; my two disciples Astra and Irita; and Salvis on the stage ferociously preaching something. Could all those people have been deceived by false teachings and theories? Most of them—like Anna, Melita, Dina, Roberts and me—were sincerely seeking God. What about Salvis and Astrida? Do they know what this all really is about, or have they also been deceived and brainwashed? What about Kristine, a law student and Salvis' future wife? Has she figured things out, or is she also brainwashed? I could not think about the sermon.

The next day Dina was not at work. She had gone to some town to translate for couple of Americans. I was greeting visitors at the door again. It was a quiet day, and I was bored. I saw a bunch of girls outside, standing in a circle, praying. Suddenly (to my great horror!) I noticed Bonny among them.

She separated from the others. She was coming. My heart leaped.

"What am I going to do now?" I thought. I had never seen Bonny very closely.

"Hi!" the girl in jeans shorts and maroon T-shirt said to me. The girl with large beautiful eyes and a childlike mouth. Could she really be Satan's agent?

"Hi!"

Bonny was wearing a necklace with a large cross.

"Is Dina here?" she asked in a quavering voice. Was she also scared?

"No. She's away translating for somebody."

"When will she be back?"

"I don't know. She is away for the whole week." I was wondering if Bonny new that I was in the Church of Christ too.

"Could you deliver her this?" Bonny asked, handing me parcel wrapped in a brown paper.

"Sure," I said. My hands were trembling when I took the parcel from her.

"Thank you," she answered, giving me an angelic smile. At the door she turned back again and said, "Please tell Dina to call Bonny."

"OK," I said. I was shaking. Had I just experienced the encounter with the Satan or the truth? I knew I was not supposed to talk to her, but after all I had to be kind and sociable with the visitors.

At Sunday meeting I gave Dina the parcel from Bonny. Astrida noticed that. She asked Dina to come aside. They talked for a while. Dina handed the parcel over to Astrida and dashed out of the hall crying. Astrida called Salvis and they went after her.

I thought my heart would stop beating from anxiety and horror. There was something wrong about all this, something dark and terrifying! Kristine asked me later if I knew the person who handed me the parcel I was supposed to give to Dina.

I said I did not know the person. I could lie, because the leaders did not know Dina had told me about Bonny. I wasn't supposed to know anything. I lied because I could not betray Dina. She was my friend, yet if she has handed herself over to Satan, can we still be friends then? I guess not, for what has light to do with darkness? However, what if Bonny is God's messenger to get people out of a destructive cult?

Next day at work Dina told me that she had gotten the final warning. If she ever gets in touch with Bonny again, she will be expelled from God's Kingdom. I could see the spots of tears on Dina's face. She looked pale and exhausted. She told me they had taken her out of leadership.

Later Roberts came to the museum. We never talk anymore, let alone hugging. We rather try to avoid each other. I am doing my best convincing myself that he is not worth my tears, that it was not love at all, just a passing emotion; however, I am still hurting badly. I miss his smiles and hugs and our long talks. But I am mad at him, for I would not have turned my back on him, not for all the threats of our church leaders. I am not the one who should make the first step to reconciliation. It isn't pride, as everyone thinks; it is fear that keeps me back . . . fear of being rejected once again.

When I saw Roberts, I had mixed emotions: anxiety mixed with a wild joy.

He came straight to me. A step away from me he stopped, and we stared at each other couple of seconds. He took me into his arms. I rested my head on his shoulder.

"I am concerned about Dina," he whispered. "I came to you. I thought we could pray."

I looked at him surprised. "Why to me?"

He looked a little uneasy. "I thought you were Dina's friend."

"I am. I am concerned too."

We went outsides the building, hid behind the fence, and prayed. I was praying first. Roberts was praying longer than me. When he had finished, I saw a large tear running down his cheek.

"What's wrong?" I asked softly.

"I do not want her to go. I do not want her to perish. I am worried about Everita, his ex. She will never get baptized, and I hoped that me and Dina . . . that we . . . will convince her, but now when Dina. . . ."

Everita. Of course—he was still thinking about Everita. Probably he still loves her. He never really liked me. I was just a substitute, a nice and supportive sister in Christ to him, nothing more. Everita is the girl who will always hold his heart.

I looked at Roberts. He was crying. I had never seen a boy crying. I did not know how to react.

"Don't," I said, slightly touching his shoulder.

"I am fine," he said and took the paper handkerchief I handed to him.

Suddenly he turned towards me and threw his arms around me. "Thanks!" he said, squeezing me tight.

I was taken aback by such his reaction. "It's okay. I have to get back to work," I said, removing his arms from my waist. I dashed back into the museum. Dina was coming at two. It was five to two. I saw Bonny near the Red Rifle Men Monument. "God help us all!" I thought and rushed upstairs where I was supposed to be.

The phone rang downstairs. I heard the secretary answering in English, "No, she is not here yet."

I had a dark premonition. I rushed downstairs. "Who was that?" I asked the secretary.

"Some man calling from States. He was asking for Dina."

My heart leaped again.

It was a quarter past two when Dina came in. Her eyes had that haunted look.

"Hi!" I said.

"Hi. Bonny is coming here. Tell her I am not here, okay?" Dina whispered to me and fled to the restroom.

I sighed.

I saw Bonny coming across the square. This time she was wearing a long maroon summer dress. She looked beautiful! She opened the door. With a flashing smile she turned to me.

"Where is Dina? I need to talk to her!"

"I don't know—she is not here yet." I blushed because of my clumsy way of lying.

"Please"—I saw despair in Bonnie's eyes—"do not lie to me. I know she is here. I saw her. I need to talk to her."

"She is not...." I tried to explain, but Bonny interrupted me. "Oh, please! You call yourselves the disciples of Christ, yet you turn out to be liars."

My heart was pounding wildly. I was licking my lips. "I can't tell you where she is."

"Okay," Bonny said coolly. She turned around and left.

Her friends were waiting for her outside.

The phone rang again, a call for Dina. I ran to get her.

When Dina hung up, she was pale like the ghost. "That was the guy for whom I was translating last week. His father is a preacher. His father had found some materials about the Church of Christ. It is just a crazy cult! They want to bring the materials to me."

"Are you going to accept them?"

"I don't know." Dina started to cry. "They forbade me to go and visit my parents this weekend," she whispered through tears.

"Who forbade?"

"Astrida and Salvis. They think I am not spiritual enough. They said I should stay with the church."

A group of visitors came and we had to get back to work. I squeezed Dina's hand. "Everything's going to be all right," I said, trying to swallow the lump in my throat.

At six, Astrida and Zinta came to pick Dina up. Then Dina seemed to have calmed down a little bit. Bonny apparently had left for the States.

130. Now it has really happened. Dina has left the church! For a short time she seemed to have calmed down. Bonny left for the States, but Salvis, Kristine and Astrida were working hard to persuade her that the Church of Christ is the place where she is supposed to be. They appeared to have succeeded. Dina did not talk about leaving anymore, and when the whole church went to a conference in Tallinn, Dina was encouraged and full of hope again. She even got accepted back into leadership.

Yesterday morning, however, my life turned upside down again. I had just come in from jogging, had taken a nice shower and was munching down a piece of Mom's apple pie, when I got a surprise call from Astrida. She was exasperated and spoke quickly. "Dina has left the church," she told me. "You are not allowed to communicate with her anymore. You are not allowed to accept her phone calls or letters or anything. Do you understand?"

"What were the reasons for her leaving?" I asked, coughing on a piece of apple pie.

"She was proud, rebellious and disobedient, and she was taken over by Satan. We prohibited her to communicate with Bonny, yet she never listened to us. She accepted her phone calls. Besides, all this time she had been secretly communicating with Agris." Agris was the guy who was attracted to Dina, but who left couple months ago. She even let him come over to her place and brainwash her. Apparently her heart had grown hard, and she had stopped to be open with her spiritual leaders.

"Yesterday she called Salvis around midnight and told him that she was leaving. Salvis wanted to talk to her, but she hung up. Salvis, Kristine and I went to her place, but she refused to let us in. Now you see what happens to proud and disobedient people."

"I have to work with her."

"We know, but we will be looking after you. But you have to promise us that you will be completely open with your new leader, who from now on will be Zinta. In case you have any doubts or any concerns, you talk it over with Zinta, not with anybody else. Is that clear?"

I felt as if I had been fallen down from the seventh floor and was looking down at my own crushed bones with dull eyes. I had to go to work and face Dina that very day.

"Does that make sense what I just told you?" Astrida was still waiting for my reply, and she sounded angry.

"Yes," I said mechanically.

"Have a good day!" With those words Astrida hung up.

Good day? I could not even finish the breakfast. My stomach hurt, and my good mood was gone. "How can face Dina?" I wondered.

I arrived at work my heart beating wildly. I guess I was expecting to see Dina turned into some sort of a monster or something, yet she was the same quiet and peaceful girl, smiling, dressed in her long blue skirt and pink blouse.

"Hi," she said and tried to hug me as we had before.

I pushed her arm away.

"Hi!" I said coldly.

I did not know how to act. I could not avoid talking to her. After all, we were colleagues, and there were lots of things we needed to discuss and to do together.

"Are you mad at me?"

"No!" I said, not looking at her.

"Are you scared of me?"

"Yes."

"I know how you feel. I had to go through the same thing with Bonny. I was scared of her and of the leaders. I did not know whom to listen to. I did not know who was from Satan and who was from God. Now I know the truth, I. . . ."

"Dina," I interrupted her; "I am sorry . . . you know, you are . . . you were my friend. I want you to know that I do not hate you because you left the church, but I cannot talk to you anymore. For God's sake. I cannot. I want to be obedient, and I do not want to get cut off. I do not judge your choice, but please leave me alone."

"I know, I know." Dina came close and hugged me. I couldn't push her away. Tears were streaming down my cheeks. I could not believe she was from Satan.

At six, Astrida and Kristine came to pick me up. They saw Dina in the hall. They both turned away immediately as if they had seen something horrible or disgusting.

That night when Salvis was preaching, his voice sounded like thunder. "Dear brothers and sisters in Christ, I just want you to understand that what has happened in the church today is very serious. Dina has left God and His teaching, and she has betrayed her brothers and sisters in Christ. What a horrible and ugly betrayal! She has been disobedient, rebellious, arrogant and offending. A person with a heart like a stone.

"It was not enough for her to hand herself over to Satan, she also tried to deceive some people in the church with weaker faith and unstable convictions. She caused divisions in the holy body of Jesus Christ Himself.

"This person, brothers and sisters, has committed a crime against God and against all of us and has lost her salvation. Now if any of you attempt to communicate with her in any possible way, you will be expelled from God's Kingdom without mercy.

"Now I want you to read and mark in your notebooks the scriptures from Bible concerning this outrageous case. . . ."

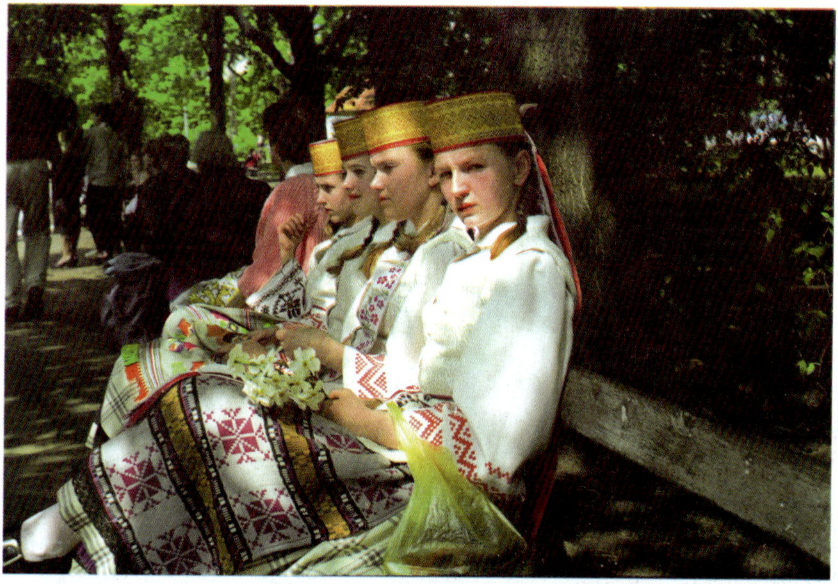

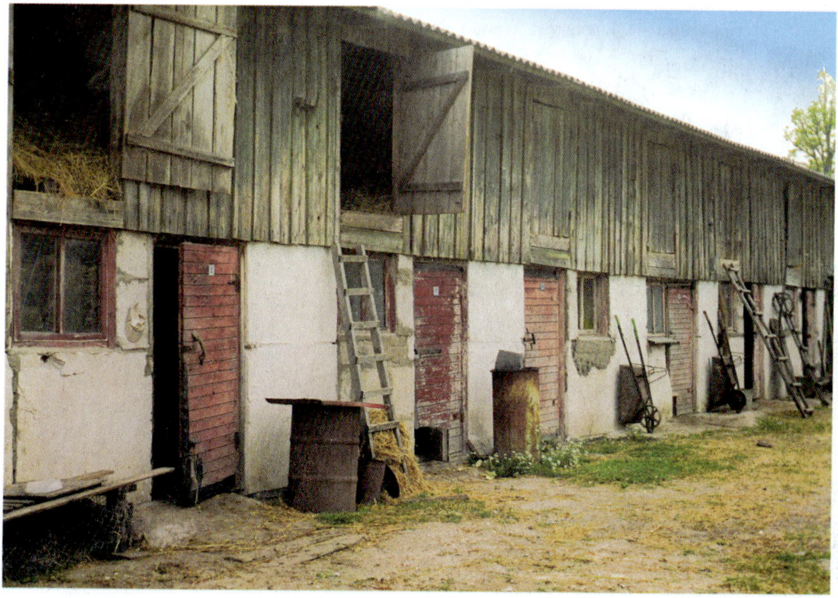

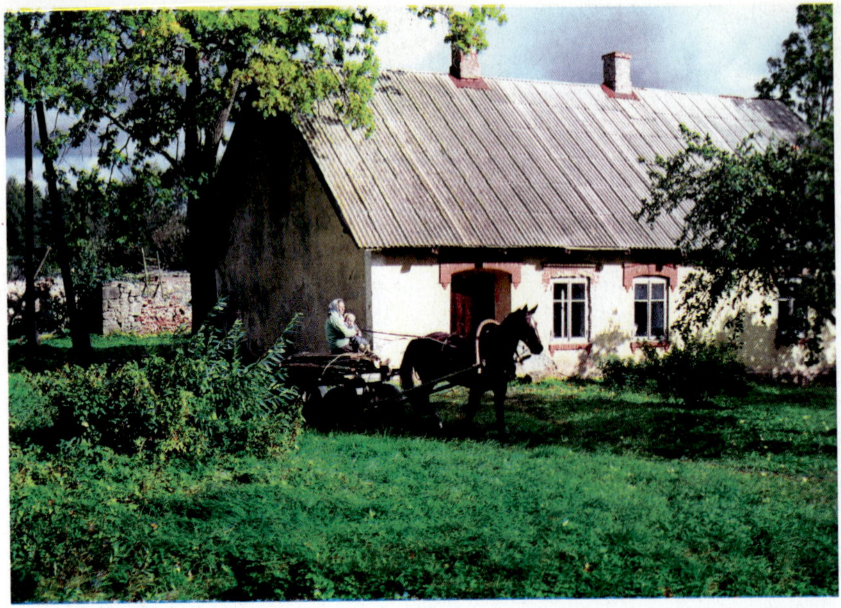

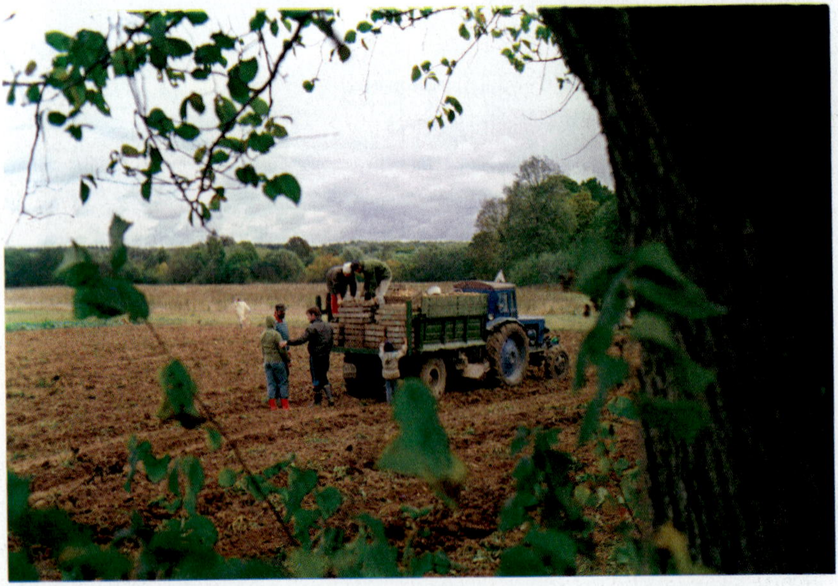

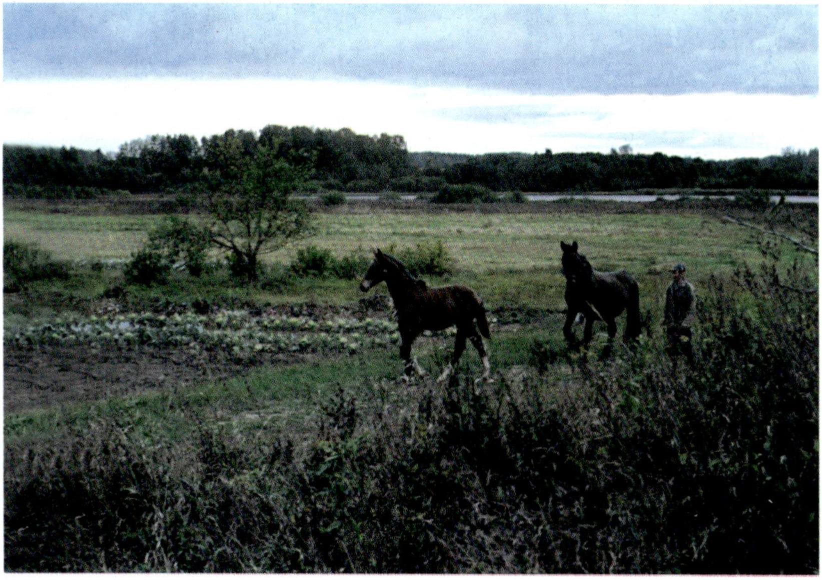

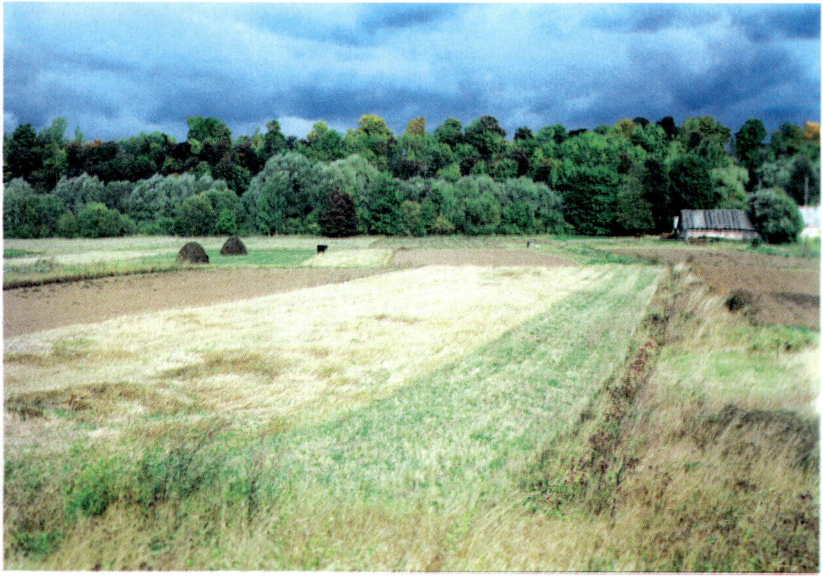

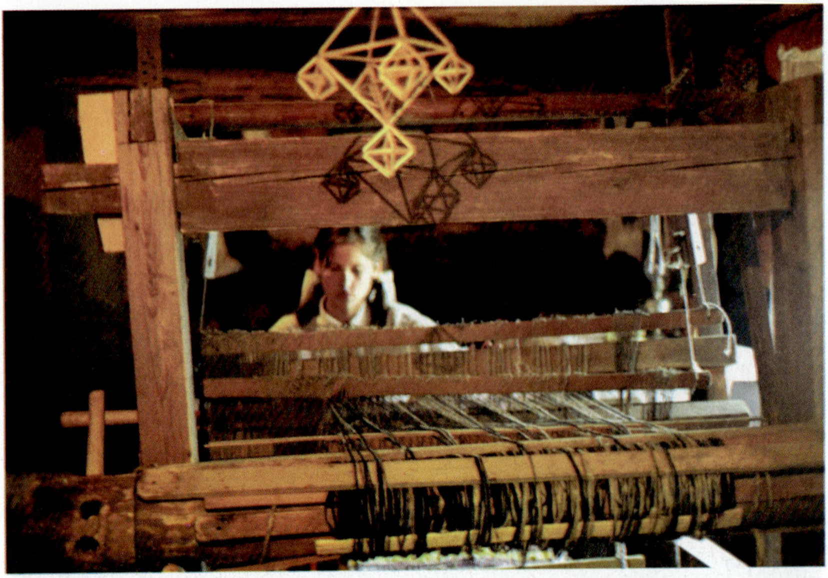

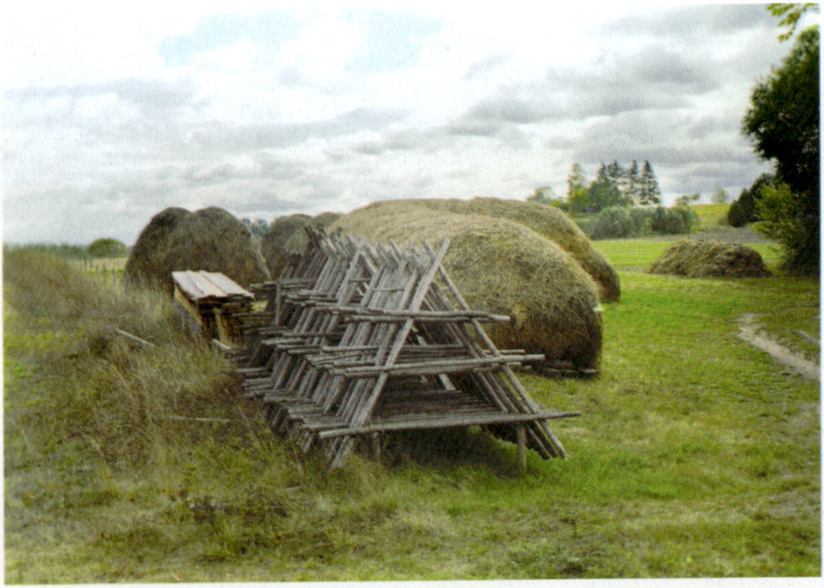

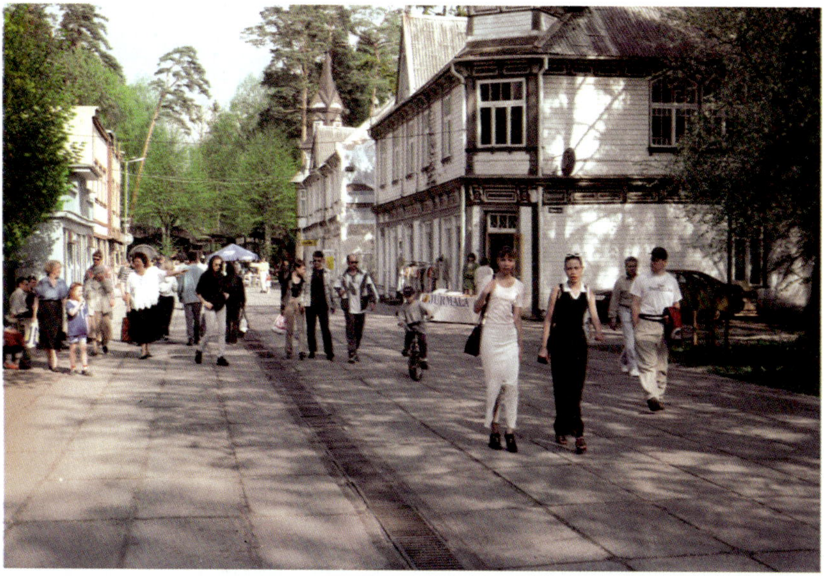

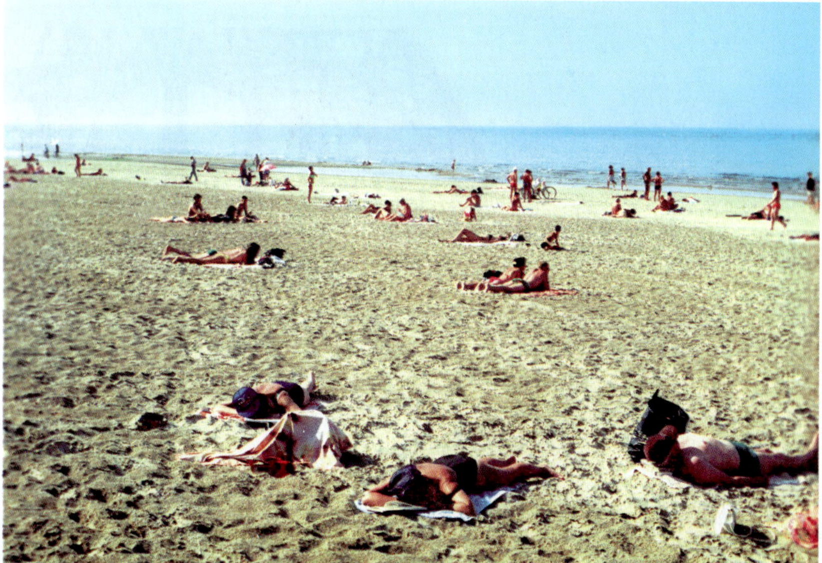

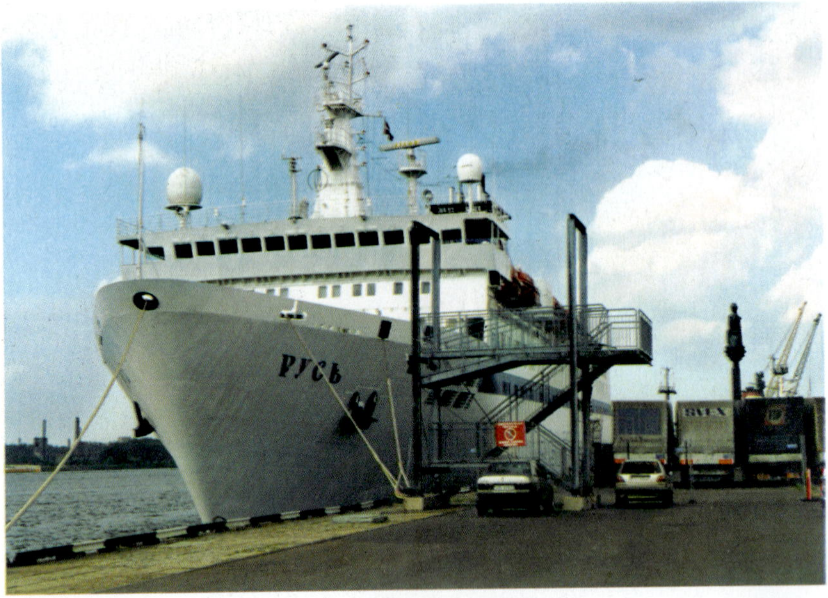
РУСЬ

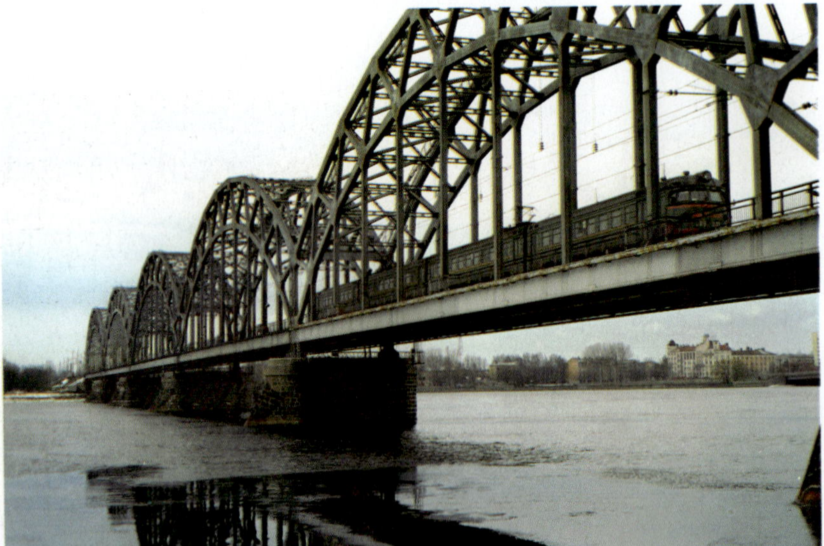

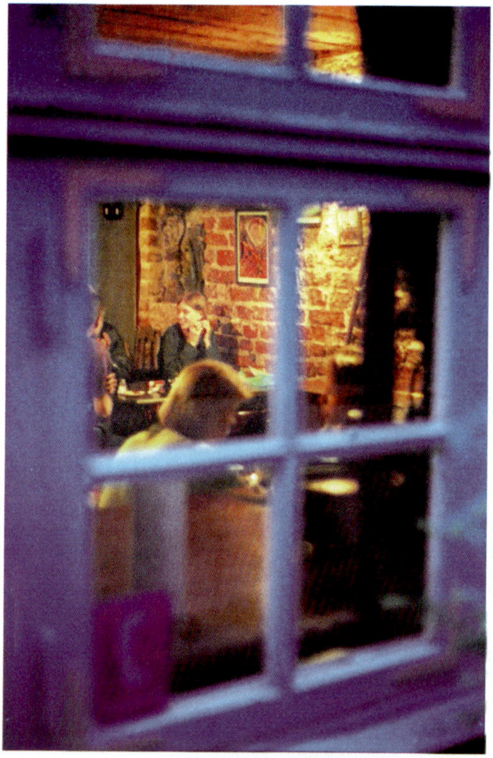

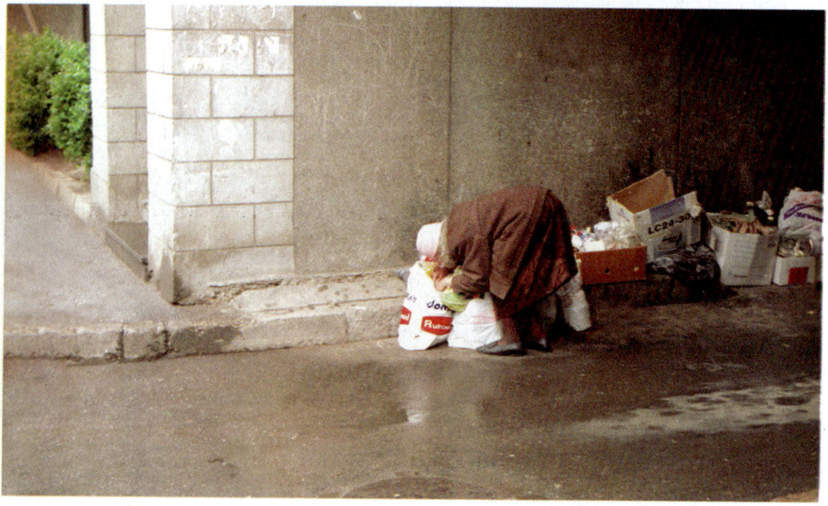
LC24-30

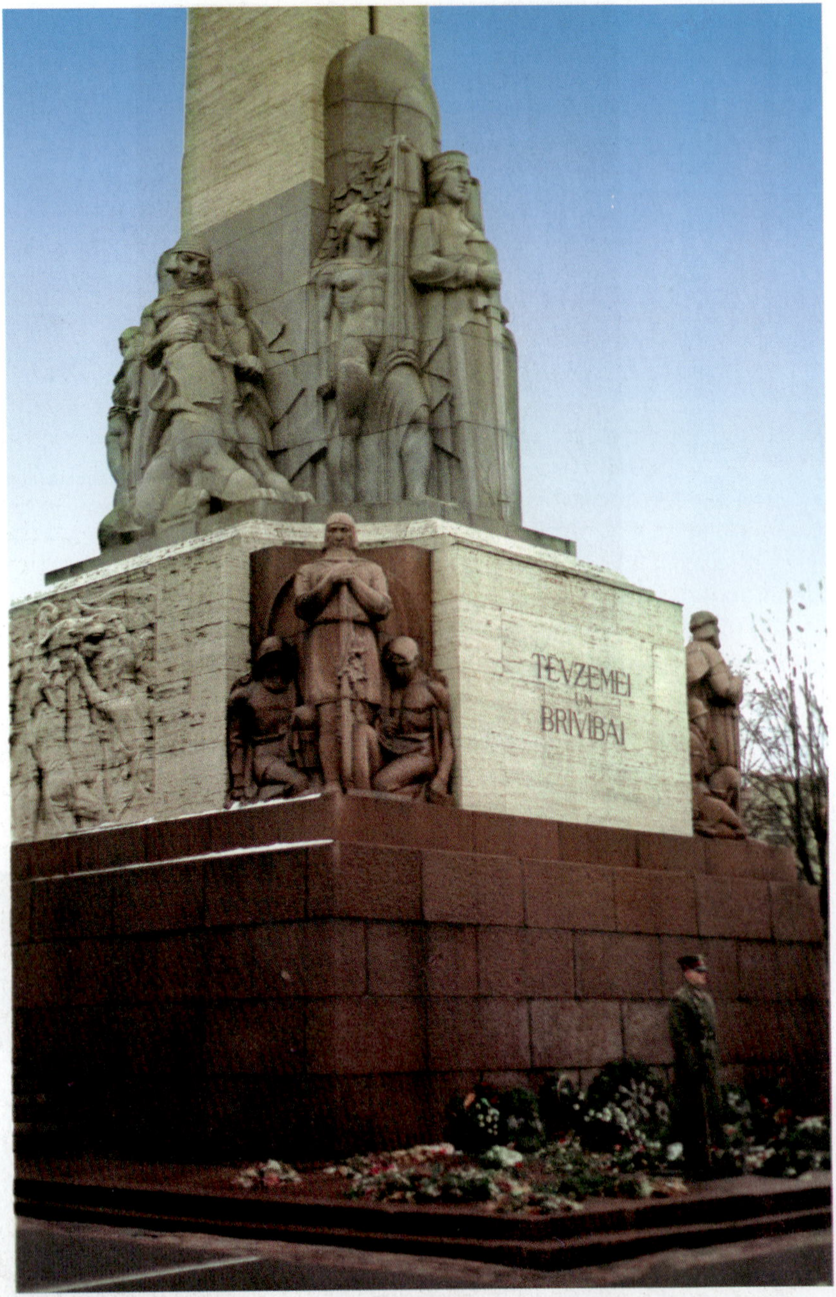
TĒVZEMEI
UN
BRĪVĪBAI

Salvis was reading about fifty scriptures, each at least two times, and every one of them was accompanied by some sort of a threat. His favorite scripture, though, was 1 Corinthians 6:10: "neither the immoral, nor idolaters, nor adulterers, nor homosexuals, nor thieves, nor the greedy, nor drunkards, nor revilers, nor robbers will inherit the Kingdom of God." He read the particular scripture to us at least four times, which confused me, for Dina was neither immoral, nor an idolater, nor an adulteress, or homosexual, nor a thief, nor greedy nor any of those. I noticed also that many times Salvis mentioned sexual immorality in regard with Dina. I just could not figure out what did that have to do with Dina's leaving.

I should talk to my leader Zinta and confess to her that I had talked to Dina, but I am so afraid. What if they expel me form the church?

131. I do not sleep much at nights anymore. I have that heavy burden of sins on my heart. I am struggling with heavy, dark doubts again. I have confessed it only to Sabine. Sabine said she had also questioned the teachings and practices of our church, yet like everybody else she is terrified by the possibility of being cut off from God. "To tell the truth — but this is just between us — I find our meetings and Bibles studies as pleasant as toothache, and if not for the fear of hell I would have left the church already a long time ago. Sometimes I wonder if this is really how God intended it to be. While we are physically alive we are being kept in the prison called the Church of Christ; when we die, however, we are set free and obtain eternal live. I guess it is not much fun to be alive then."

Those were Sabine's words, and I must admit, I have also had such considerations many times. Sabine understands me and my doubts; however, she is not my leader, and would my leader understand? What if I get run over by a car and die and go to hell, just because I have not confessed my horrible sin, my possible encounter with Satan?

When I try to pray, I remember that God listens only to the prayers of the righteous, and I am not righteous, not with that horrible sin hidden at the bottom of my heart. I have stopped praying. God is displeased with me. He won't listen until I repent. I have no one in the whole entire world to turn to.

I have started to lose weight. People in the church are making fun of me, telling me that I look like a model. Not even a compliment like that cheers me up anymore.

Even my parents have noticed the drastic change in my appearance and my behavior. They are attacking me with all sort of questions. Their concern hurts. Everything hurts. I keep on remembering Jesus words, "My sorrow is so great that it almost crushes me." I could say the same.

I hurt for Dina and my parents and those thousands of people daily passing me by, not knowing God.

One day I was working with Dina again, and I talked to her. She told me again and again that she left the church because she felt oppressed and intimidated there (that's exactly how I have been feeling). She also said that a true establishment of God should be governed by love and not by fear. I knew that taking with Dina is forbidden by the church, but I talked to her anyway. It was a sin, a horrible sin. I had encountered Satan; he was talking to me through Dina. Now I am all messed up. God has turned away from me and people in the church will also turn away from me when they find out that I have talked to Dina.

I did tell Roberts. We are back to being friends again, but things are not the way they used to be. The magic is gone. I thought if he loved me he would understand. He did understand. At least he did not condemn me. However, he made me promise that I will go and confess it to my leader.

Roberts is hurting too. Really bad. He has to see Dina every day at school. He said he saw her on the street one day. She tried to talk to him; he had to walk away not even looking at her, his heart breaking from almost physical pain. She keeps on sending him letters. He tears them up and throws them out of the window. The torn pieces keep flying around for quite a time.

132. My contract with the museum is over, and I am very relieved. I do not have to see Dina anymore. She kept on sending me letters with heaps of materials against the Church of Christ. I threw them all in the waste bin without opening. I am trying to do the right thing, just as Roberts had done.

For the first time in my life I am glad to be attending classes. In fact the university has become a shelter to me. I can talk about other things than Dina's betrayal and my doubts.

Now when I happen to see Dina on the street I either cross the street or turn the opposite way. Probably Dina thinks I am a freak, probably everybody does, but I am doing it for the sake of God and righteousness. I hope He does appreciate this.

My other comfort during those terrible times is my friendship with Katrina. Boy, is it great to have at least one true friend outside the church! The irony is, though, that Katrina not being a disciple of Christ is able to give me more help and comfort than my spiritual leaders or anybody in the church. I can tell Katrina all about my struggles, my doubts and my unrequited love towards Roberts without getting rebuked for being selfish and not spiritual enough.

Katrina came to Sunday meetings couple of times. However, she did not like it at all. She thinks that everybody is weird there, everybody except me. "They all have that morbid glow in their eyes," she said, "and those forced smiles! They make me sick. But you are different. You have a sincere and beautiful smile."

In Katrina's opinion the exclamations "Go, brother!" and "Amen, brother!" during the sermon are ridiculous and intrusive, and she considers our Saturday dates a perversion. But it upsets me that Katrina does not like my church and my brothers and sisters. At least she admits that Roberts is cute, but as she once said, way too righteous for having any fun.

133. I am having big crisis at home again. However, in the recent months I have been through so much that I seem to have developed immunity towards anything troublesome and unpleasant. My parents think that instead of attending the church services every night, I should rather look for some job, a part time job. In the times of economical crisis, as it is right now in our country, every student has some sort of a part time job, combined with his/her studies.

Of course it would not be a problem for me to find a job. I have experience at the Occupation Museum and ECAT, and my foreign languages skills are very demanded in Latvia at the current moment. Besides I have also basic computer skills. However, if I had a part time job, I would have to skip meetings, which I would gladly do if it only wasn't considered as putting something else first before God.

I was even offered a receptionist's position at some hotel. My work time would be evenings. I could do my home works there. Besides I would have some pocket money. I would be financially independent of my parents, who are giving away their last santims to provide me with everything necessary.

When I talked it over with my leader and later with Astrida, she said that by choosing the job I would have the wrong priorities. Astrida's words were, "You have a free choice, yet if you want to please God, you need to make the right choice. You know pretty well what God wants you to do, and I have full confidence that you will chose wisely; you will chose the meetings, of course."

I just cannot understand why God is so jealous of everything beside Him. How can He make me love Him if He is robbing me of all chances and pleasures? But maybe it is not God, maybe it is just the church who think they are doing God's will, but actually they are setting their own rules for everything and making people obey them by using God's word as a means of manipulation and intimidation. That is the way Dina described it.

I have managed to cast Roberts out of my mind, if not out of my heart, and I have started to pay more attention to my studies. I have even started to enjoy them. Frau Misinja seems to be satisfied with me. She thinks I should go to Germany for a year as an au pair. She has found a family for me again, some friends of hers, good and reliable people. I would have to look after two kids, four and six years old. They will pay me a weekly pocket money, plus my wage, free food and accommodation. That sounds attractive to me.

The Republic of Latvia offers more opportunities for young people than the Soviet times ever did, yet unfortunately that is not so for people after thirty-five, and that is why my parents do not like the new government. You have to think hard and to work hard to make your fortune, yet you have more opportunities. In Soviet times, the central planning thought for you, and you had no opportunities at all.

134. This morning I told my parents, "I refuse to go the school or to church or anywhere."

"What are you going to do then?" Mom inquired.

"I am going to sit in bed and stare at one point in the ceiling."

"That is not going to be acceptable."

"I do not care what is acceptable and what is not. I am tired of everything."

"Tired of what? Of hanging out every night, skipping classes and yelling at your parents? Is that what you are tired of?"

"I am not skipping my classes...ask Frau Misinja. I am just tired of everybody telling me what to do. I am tired of being controlled all the time! In the church, at home, at school! I want to think for myself sometimes. Alright?"

"Fine!" mother yelled. "Sit in bed, stare at one point! Who cares if you ruin your life? We are tired of all this crap too!" She slammed the door behind her.

I heard her telling Dad, "See what those sects do to kids. See what they have done. If I was in government, I would prohibit them with a law. I would wipe them all out of here with a shitty broom!"

Whatever.

135. Frau Misinja has called the family in Germany and they are ready to take me. All I have to do is to write them a letter—and yes, of course, I had to talk it over with my parents and my leaders. The German family lives not far from Munich. There is one Church of Christ in Munich. I could attend it there, which gives me a hope that the leaders in Riga will let me go. They say we are allowed to go anywhere abroad where the Churches of Christ are. If there is no Church of Christ near the place, we are not permitted to go there.

My parents kind of liked the idea of me going to Germany. Dad was a little reserved at first, but mother sets the rules and grants permissions in our family, and once she seemed not have any objections to my plan, Dad had no other choice as to agree.

The tough thing now is to talk to leaders. They are not as easy to persuade as parents.

136. They will not let me go.

First I talked to Zinta. She needed to ask Astrida. Then Astrida needed to ask Salvis.

Salvis's response to me was, "God needs you here in Riga. You are more effective for God here than you would ever be in Germany. Besides you are not spiritually strong enough to be away from us."

"But. . . ." I tried to explain my point, but Salvis cut me off.

"You *cannot* go anywhere! I clear enough?"

"No!" I said furiously. "It is not clear at all for me. Who are you to rob me off all my possibilities? It is my life, and I can do with it what I please to. I do not want anybody to mess with my life!"

"Your life does not belong to you anymore; it belongs to God. And talking like this just shows how much Satan has already managed to do with your heart. Do you know why Satan is in hell? It's because he is proud and rebellious. Just like you are right now. He also wanted to control his life himself. That is what he got. You have two options: either to stay here with the church in Riga and do God's will, or you can listen to Satan's alluring promises and follow him and do his will. You have those choices!"

Salvis was getting angry, but I persisted. "Why is it always like that? No matter what I want, all my desires are contrary to God's will for me."

"That's because human desires often are selfish and wicked. Now ask yourself, do you want to go to Germany because you genuinely want to help people there to find God, or because it is a great opportunity for you to go somewhere abroad where there is a better life?"

"I want to go Germany because I want to improve my language skills and because I could learn lots of things about life being there. It would be a unique experience. I would meet lots of people, make friends, testify them about Jesus. Since I would be far away from home I wouid need to trust in God more. Going to Germany could be even a spiritual test to me."

"I see," Salvis said after a while. "All your arguments are very logical and nice . . . yet I still have suspicions that you want to go there to seek your personal benefits, like language skills and money-making opportunities. Those are selfish desires, I must tell you. Besides, I can see that your heart is not for the lost but just for yourself."

"But in Germany there is also a church. I could learn many things from people there, and when I came back I would be more mature and more spiritual to help people here."

"Again, you say *you* would be more spiritual and more mature. You are thinking about your personal spiritual achievements and benefits."

"But being spiritual and mature I will be able to teach people and help them more than I am now."

"How do you know that you will definitely become more spiritual in Germany? Maybe it will be the other way around. What if you become weak in your faith and tortured by your constant doubts, and wander off God's path there?" Salvis was smiling wickedly . . . I knew he was trying to trick me, to corner me, so he would win the argument.

"But there is a church there too, where I could seek help. I will have a spiritual leader there, too. Besides, it is impossible for me to become less spiritually mature being away from home. I would have to learn to take care of myself. I would have to rely on God more than ever."

"That all sounds very nice, but are you sure you will be able to express yourself completely to confess your wrong doings in a foreign language?" Salvis was not going to give up. He had found a way to attack me from the other side.

"I speak fluent German; that is my major subject."

Salvis digested that for a moment; then he said, "I am totally convinced that your place is here in Riga. God has chosen you here. He wants you to start with your own country, your own people. He wants to see you accomplishing something here, in your own country, then and only then He will consider sending you someplace else."

"How can you be so sure about what is God's will for me?" I asked Salvis.

I saw a slight threat in Salvis's eyes: "I am your leader and you have to submit to what I tell you to do. That is what the Bible teaches you to do. I am not making anything up. I am just trying to follow the instructions of the Bible and live my life like a disciple of Christ, and you are supposed to do the same!"

With those words I was dismissed.

I cried the whole evening and half of the night. "I will go anyway. I will go! I am not going to stay in this cult any longer!" I screamed at the top of my voice.

Mom heard me and came into the room. "Cult . . . of course it is a cult! We have been telling that to you all the time," she said, trying to comfort me.

Dad was sitting in his room motionless.

137. Tonight was the first night I did not go to the meeting. My fury was so great that I even managed to forget about my fear of hell. I am mad at my parents for their lack of understanding, at my leaders for constantly messing with someone else's life, at God for making my life so miserable.

At 23.00 I received a phone call from Zinta. She was, of course, demanding explanations for my absence.

"I am sick and tired of you all!" I yelled at her and hung up. I know it was rude, but at the same time I felt a grim satisfaction for daring to say what I feel.

"You did the right thing," Dad said, patting me on the shoulder.

Then the phone rang again. I asked Mom to pick it up and find out who was calling. It was Sabine. "I just wanted to tell you that I am totally on your side. They were talking about you today. They think you are rebellious and disobedient. Anyway, you have my full admiration. Besides I do not think that it is God's will for us to spend all our lives in a rotten sect."

I told Sabine she was a real friend.

"You know, I am always there for you. I would do anything to help you," she promised.

She would, too. I know that. I just don't know why. She claims I have helped her a lot. I don't know what she means by helping—maybe surviving in the church. It would be tough if we were not there for each other. I guess we do not trust anybody else in the church except each other. We are loyal to each other.

The next call was from Kristine, now Salvis' wife and a church leader. Kristine is less scary than Astrida. It was nearly midnight.

"How do you explain your absence today to me?" she asked calmly.

"I did not want to come. I am fed up."

"Fed up with serving Christ?"

"Fed up with leaders making decisions about my life."

"Well, obeying leaders is a part of service to Christ, our savior." Kristine was trying hard to be patient.

I kept silent. What could I say? Leaders always know how to justify themselves, even if their justification does not make sense at times. They always find a way out by saying, "The Bible teaches us to obey our instructors."

"Do you think are you being obedient?" Kristine asked me in a soft voice.

"No, and I won't be from now on. From now on I will do just what I please."

"You know what happened to Satan when he refused to submit and obey God." Kristine's voice was still soft. She was talking to me as if I were an unreasonable child and she was a good mommy.

"Yes . . . and I do not care!" I yelled at her. How dared she preach at me, when she got baptized later than me? When we went to Moscow together she was nothing, she was as mature spiritually as I was at that point. Now that she's got big, fat husband, she feels big too.

"I see," she said calmly. "Have you been open with your leader recently?"

"No, and I do not feel obliged to."

"OK, it is late now. Could you come over to our place tomorrow so we cold talk?"

I agreed to come to their place tomorrow. Mother was getting angry. It was after midnight.

"Good night," she said sweetly.

"Good night," I told her.

Now what have I got myself in for?

138. I had long negotiations with Salvis and Kristine. I cried and yelled out my frustration, and then I was calm again. They, of course, proved me that I was wrong about everything, including my desire to go to Germany. I knew I was right and they were wrong, yet I was still too scared of being cut off and thrown into hell, so I agreed to stay here in Riga with the church and not to go to Germany. Salvis and Kristine were more than pleased with my decision. They both hugged me, kissed me on both cheeks and said, "You have made the right choice. God will pay you back for it."

I do not believe that, but whatever.

Aunt Olga had inquired Dad about the trip, and when he told her that I refused to go for God's sake, Olga got furious.

That very evening she called me and said, "Wake up! Do you realize what you are doing with your life? You are passing all the chances in your life. Instead of listening to your parents, you are listening to some asshole Salvis who is too lazy to work and earn honest money, so he chooses to lead a cult, brainwash fools like you, and destroy their lives. Let the Sect of Lunatics (that is how aunt Olga calls the Church of Christ) in the U.S.A. pay him his wage, which is not small I am sure."

I hung up on her, not being able to listen to anything that criticizes the church, for if the church is being criticized, my choice to be there is being criticized as well. Yet my aunt is right. Salvis does have a large comfortable apartment with furniture and all sort of equipment. The rent for the apartment, along with all of Salvis and Kristine's expenses, is being paid from the funds of churches in U.S.A.

139. Sunday, March 22. I will never forget today. I was getting ready to leave for my Sunday service. Mom had made breakfast for all of us: hard boiled eggs and potato salad. Dad was reading jokes from an old newspaper. I was trying to eat, but hard boiled eggs are difficult to swallow.

Mom seemed to be upset. I wanted to tell her something nice, to hug her, but I was shy. We had not been practicing it for so long. Showing affection after long years of not showing it is always a little awkward. I approached her and slightly patted her shoulder. "Are you all right, Mom?" I asked.

She turned away from the sink towards me. "Oh, yes. I am OK. I am OK." Mom's eyes were strange, distant. "I'm OK, thank you," she said and turned back to the sink.

Dad was getting ready to go visit his sisters in Ilguciems. He was already dressed and was waiting for me. I could not find my eye liner, and I definitely could not leave the house without putting on some eye make up. So I told dad to leave without me. "See you later!" I heard him saying. I heard the door cracking.

"You are slow like an old maid," Mom scolded.

"I can't find my eye liner!"

"I want you all out of the house today. I want to do the big clean up, and I do not want anybody in my way." Mom was getting impatient.

"Mom, it is Sunday. Why do you always have to clean on Sundays. Lie down, relax, watch TV or go for a walk." Mom is a workaholic. Whenever she has some free time, she uses it for cleaning or washing or ironing. She never rests. It drives Dad and me nuts.

"Of course, 'lie down, relax, watch TV,' " Mom mocked me. "It is easy for you to talk like that. But tell me please who is going to clean and wash? Are you? I have never seen you cleaning anything, just messing everything up!"

Mom cannot reconcile herself to the fact that I am not like her, that I am a different personality with different habits and different points of view about things.

I did not want to start a quarrel that morning, so I got dressed, grabbed my Bible, and left. It was a beautiful March day, sunny with clear blue skies. The smell of spring was in the air. I love that smell, even though it makes me a little melancholic.

I prayed in the trolley about my leaders, their health and welfare, about my non-Christian friends. Especially I prayed for Katrina, and about my parents that they would find Jesus and salvation one day.

When I got off the trolley, I saw dad standing at the opposite side of the street. "That's strange," I thought. "What is he doing over there? His stop for Ilguciems is in the old city."

Apparently he had been to the Market. He waved at me; I waved back and smiled. I was in a hurry. I was already a little late for the service. The sun was shining brightly over the roofs of the buildings in the old city. I was seized by an impulse to leave the half-dark hall with Salvis and all the disciples and to run outside, where I could inhale the fresh breath of spring with every cell of my body. But I did not. That day Salvis was preaching about the significance of evangelization. It's the same thing over and over again. "What a lack of imagination," I thought.

I did not hear a word of Salvis's sermon, either, but if somebody asked me what it was all about, I would be able to tell the content by heart. Salvis' repertoire has not changed a bit since last August. I did not see any of the people I had invited during the week. I sighed with relief, for that meant I did not have to stay long after the service and talk to them. This is a rotten attitude, but I stopped worrying about that already a long time ago.

I also wanted to visit Aunt Olga and Aunt Zelma. I needed them to help me to bake a cake for one of my sisters in Christ, who was having her birthday party the next day and had invited me too. Maija, my disciple, wanted to come with me. I did not like the idea. I was trying to find a way to get rid of her, which is hard because I have become almost a spiritual mother to Maija. She is one of those "holy innocent sisters" who know only to smile and submit. They always need to be told what they are supposed to do. They can never figure it out themselves.

Well, I had not choice but to take Maija with me. She wanted to pour out her heart to me, and I had no guts to send her "five blocks ahead." In fact, I was not at liberty to do that as her spiritual leader.

On the trolley Maija chatted all sorts of nonsense, mostly about her crush on Gintis, the brother she adores, who does not pay the slightest attention to her.

I paid no attention. When I arrived at my aunts' place, I rushed up the stairs and rang the bell. Olga, Dad's younger sister, opened the door.

"Hi," I exclaimed, and started to introduce Maija. Then my smile froze. Aunt olga was horribly pale. I could see the marks of tears on her cheeks.

"What's the matter?"

"It is a terrible tragedy. I don't . . . your father. . . ." She broke into sobs.

"Died?" I asked. My voice sounded unnaturally calm. Olga nodded, unable to confirm the horrible truth with words. I knew it would happen one day. I had been expecting it ever since I could remember. I knew he was incurably sick. All those years I had been living in constant fear of my father's death. Now it had happened, and I seemed not to feel anything. I just stood there and stared at my crying aunt. This was just another nightmare, of course. I have had those before. My life has been a series of nightmares. Then I wake up, and everything is all right again.

Aunt Zelma came out of the room. She embraced me and pulled me close. I pushed her aside gently, refusing to believe it. "It is not true!" I kept on telling myself in my thoughts.

I heard myself asking, "My mother—does she know?"

"We called her. She is coming," Zelma said faintly.

"Where is my dad?"

"In the other room. Do you want to see him?"

"No!" I shouted in sudden horror. "I don't." My mind knew, yet my heart refused to accept the horrible truth. I did not know how to face Mother. I was afraid that she would not be able to cope with life without Dad.

Maija took my hand into hers. She was as shocked and terrified as I was.

"Do you want something to eat, children?" Aunt Zelma asked us.

We both shook our heads, "No, thank you."

I felt sick. I was shaking. I wondered if the window was open. I was observing the naked birch tree outside the window. "Soon it will be green again. Tomorrow I have a grammar test by Mrs. Brigzna, who is slightly better than Mrs. Misinja. My aunts need a new wallpaper in the kitchen. Maija likes Gintis, but he does not like her."

Olga entered the kitchen. "Why don't you just go home?" she said quietly. "Your mom will come and help us."

The possibility of facing Mother terrified me; however, I could not run away like a coward.

"Are you sure you do not need any help?" I asked.

"You could go home and bring your dad's clothes," Zelma suggested.

"Okay."

In the hallway I stumbled over a bag of apples. Beautiful red and yellow apples. "Must be from abroad," I thought.

"Those apples your dad had bought for you," I heard Aunt Zelma's voice right behind me. She was giving me one of the apples. "Take that on the road."

Was somebody trying to choke me? I could not breathe. Hot burning tears blinded my eyes. It was good, I could breathe again. A memory of my dad standing at the opposite side of the street waving at me flashed through my mind—the last time I saw him.

140. Today I had to go to school to write my test with Mrs. Brigzna. The streets were full of sun and dust. It was an ordinary early spring day, busy people rushing up and down the streets, lots of brand new fancy cars causing traffic jams in Old Town. Dad always wonders—I stopped at the crossroad and bit my lip—I should say "used to wonder," where all those people got money for those cars in our poor, devastated country in transition.

It felt odd to use the past tense in thinking about my dad, when yesterday at this time he was still very alive.

Somebody pushed me accidentally. The sun was shining straight into my eyes. Any other day I would not have paid the slightest attention to such a trifle, yet I took his shove as personal offense. I was hurting. I wondered how many people in the world were hurting today just the same way I was. And how many were happy.

141. I did not do well on the test, but that does not seem to matter. I was sitting in the class, dumb and deaf towards everyone and everything. I was thinking about how we are going to live without Dad. Not only that we loved him, he also had a large pension (mostly because of his disease) which paid for a lot of our expenses. We will not be able to pay all the bills with only Mom's salary. We'll have to sell the apartment and seek a one-room apartment.

My father is dead, and I am thinking all sorts of crap about the apartment and the bills! I rebuke myself, yet I cannot force myself to think about him lying in my aunt's room dead. DEAD! The very word is horrible enough.

Mom is another tragedy. She can do nothing except cry, desperately, hysterically. She cannot cope with the situation any other way. I can't cry with her. Something inside me has broken and is blocking up the tears. They have swollen into a large painful lump inside my chest and are choking me. I do not know how to cope with my own situation, and I do not know how to comfort Mom.

142. The funeral was yesterday. A nice March day with light blue skies, dusky sun and muddy roads in the graveyard. Lots of people in the little chapel, my relatives, I guess. The scent of burning candles and flowers. Heaps of flowers on the coffin and around it. Mom crying aloud, I standing next to her, somebody holding my hand. The minister talking nicely about life full of hard labor and sacrifice for the welfare of others. Time for everyone to say a last good-bye to the deceased. People approaching the open coffin. Some just looking, some touching the deceased's hand or forehead. I say *deceased* because it is too hard to say *my dad*. How come my dad is among the deceased now?

Mom just standing at the coffin staring at dad, tears streaming down her cheeks, refusing to let others say good-bye, until somebody takes her by the arm and leads her aside. Approaching the coffin myself, shivering. Afraid to look, as if expecting to see my dad turned into some monster. Gathering all my courage and touching dad's forehead with my lips. Still refusing to believe that the cold, stiff figure in the coffin could be my dad.

A long line of people leaving the chapel for the burial. Mom and I right after the coffin, stumbling in the mud.

The gathering afterwards, squeezed between two relatives piling heaps of food on my plate. I unable to swallow anything. Thinking about Dad and wondering where he was at the moment. If he could see me and Mom and our relatives and friends sitting around the table eating, drinking and remembering him. The lump was letting loose, and I starting to weep. Not exactly unhappy, crying because my heart was too full of unexpressed emotions.

I did not even consider the possibility that my dad could go to hell. I was certain that he would not. Even if millions of disciples from the Church of Christ affirmed that he would, I would not believe them.

143. The saying "time heals everything" is not working in regard to me. Each passing day makes me more aware of our loss, and it hurts more than at first.

The living room seems empty and quiet without Dad in it. He always used to be at home during those last months. Nobody brings home fresh wheat bread from the Central Market anymore. Nobody is cursing the government anymore. I keep on thinking that he's gone to the country, and so does Mom. He used to go away for a couple of days. This time he seems to be away longer than usual. I keep on thinking he is coming back someday soon.

Why do we fool ourselves? The dead never come back. Never!

I hear a song on the radio, a love song. "How do I live without you? How do I breathe without you?" I hear this song constantly, and it makes me think of my dad.

144. I don't know why, but I have been appointed to be a leader of the women's Bible group, so naturally I am also being taught how to control and manipulate my disciples. How to make them give an account of everything they do. How to ask all sorts of embarrassing and intimate questions. How to intimidate them to make the mechanisms of manipulation more effective.

Being the Bible group leader also means I myself am no longer so controlled. Now I am the one who has the authority to control and manipulate. It is a pleasant feeling to have some sort of power, yet I do not want to mess with anyone's life. This is against all human rights. However, being a big leader I am forced to do it. By manipulating others, I go against my own conscience, which is considered a serious sin in the Bible, by the way.

I loathe giving accounts of "my girls," their struggles, their shortcomings, their intimate sins. Even more I loathe the questions asked by my leader afterwards, like, "What are we going to do with Kristina? She is overeating constantly!" "How about Anna? Can't she still wake up in the mornings?" "Is Zaiga still struggling with humility?" "Is Zinta still having impure thoughts?" "Has Aina become more organized recently?" "Does Inese still leave her umbrellas and her Bible in the hall?"

The mention of Inese forgetting her things makes me blush, for I also forget things in the hall quite often.

The poor girls and their sins are being discussed publicly behind their backs, and against my will I am forced to take part in those discussions. Often I try not to expose everything. I try to tell more about their success in spiritual area. However, I have to mention some of their sins every time. When I once told other leaders that it is not nice to discuss people's intimate sins behind their backs, their response was, "We are forced to discuss those things to be able to help our disciples to grow and overcome their problems. When we discuss it together we get clearer ideas, more support and advice from each other. We are doing everything possible to build up each other and our disciples."

145. We are having tough times at home. Mom is depressed. The factory where she is working at is going to be taken over by some large private company. There is no demand for air fresheners and hair sprays made by "Aerosols" anymore. This is all old fashioned stuff now: old Soviet facilities, techniques and recipes. So Mom's losing her job already for the second time in the independent Republic of Latvia. Naturally she's bitter and disappointed with her life. She studied hard at college, served our Soviet homeland faithfully, took part in meetings and demonstrations in 1989-1991 to help our nation get back its independence. She even stood on barricades in cold winter nights of 1990 and risked her very life for our country. All she gets back now for her life of hard work is her miserable 30 Ls pension, which is not enough to pay the rent, let alone to buy food. We all thanked God when she found a secretary's place in Aerosols. Most of her salary went for the rent and other bills. Her pension went for food. Dad's pension went mostly for my expenses. Now Mom's lost her husband and is also losing her job. If we cannot pay the rent, we will be put out on the street one day.

I guess Mom expects me to do something to help the situation. She assumes I am old enough to start taking care of myself. I can sense she is disappointed with me. She thought I would be as diligent, precise, and hardworking as she is. But I am not. Instead of being an outstanding student, mommy and daddy's pride, I have turned out to be a religious freak who knows nothing else as to sit in the church all day long. She often blames me: "You have no place for anybody in your life but your church leaders. You did not love your father. You do not care for your mother. The brothers and sisters are your family. The church is your home now!"

This is not true, and it hurts me very much when she says so. Maybe it appears that way to her, but it is not true. I did love my father. Maybe I did not show it very well, but I had to go to the church. For God's sake I still have to. I am still very scared of being in hell after my death. In the Bible hell is described as a horrible place.

I do not like the church or my new leaders. I have been praying God to change my mind on this, yet He does not. I cannot change myself or my way of thinking. It is God's job after all. I have been frustrated with my life (with the course it has taken) for a long time. Now, however, my frustration has reached its peak. I am sick and tired of spying on my girls. I am tired of Salvis's threats. I am sick of phrases like "God is disgusted with you! God is furious when you do not take all the chances for evangelization but let people go to hell! God will punish you on the Judgment Day."

146. On Tuesday nights I now have a class, so I have warned my leaders that I will not be coming to the church on Tuesday nights. At first they were against it, but when I told them that I am not coming regardless of whether they approved or not, they had no choice but to reconcile themselves to the situation.

The choice was between two evils: either sitting in the Hotel Riga conference hall listening to Salvis's never-ending story about the purpose of evangelization, or listening to Nietzsche's philosophy interpreted by Frau Nikogda—Frau Niemals, as we call her. I have chosen the latter, not because I really care, but because I want to prove to my leaders that they have no power to limit my choices anymore. I have become rebellious again, and very defensive. I do not let anyone dominate my life anymore. Once before I allowed them to talk me out of my independence, and I will not let them do it again. Would my country, after suffering so much in its fight against the Russians, suddenly decide to return to the Soviet empire? Never! If anybody, even a person from the church, tells me to do something one way, I will do it just the opposite way. Not that I think my choice is always correct. I just want to prove that from now on nobody will tell me how to live my life. I will make all my decisions myself. I am mad and frustrated with everyone in the world: with my crying mother, with the church leaders for not letting me go to Germany, with myself for listening to them, for giving in and missing the opportunity.

I am hurting all the time for my dad, and I feel guilty for letting him down, for not realizing his hopes for me. I tried to do what's best, I tried to make the right choice, yet it seems I have made the wrong one. If it was not for hell, I would have left the church and continued to live like most people do.

The Bible tells that salvation is free, yet I had paid a high price for my salvation. I gave up my freedom, my privacy, my personal choices. I am fed up with this life. I will stay in the church, but I will do things my way.

Yet what if they expel me from God's Kingdom? They have already taken away my leadership position, even though as the leader of a Bible study group I am still a pretty big authority figure and also a person the girls can trust. People love me in the church. Anna, Maija, and Rasma have made me their role model, and I am disappointing them with my rebellion and disobedience, but things are getting out of hand in my life, and I feel too tired to stop it.

147. The last three weeks have been rough on me. The spring session, tests every day, sleepless nights, mom's hysterical behavior, verbal abuse from the church leaders, total lack of support from Roberts, an absolute loss of faith.

On Monday morning I accidentally pushed my Bible off the desk. I stopped reading it when dad died. The Bible opened up somewhere in New Testament. I started to read. I had been reading for a while. Suddenly every scripture I read showed itself in a different light. It was as if somebody had taken a veil off my eyes. I was reading the scriptures

Salvis had been quoting after Dina left about false teachers being deceivers, wolves in sheep's clothing, about pharisees who make people carry burdens they cannot carry themselves, about those who put rules higher than a human being itself. All those scriptures, so many times read by Salvis for our own protection, he claimed, now turned against him. Salvis was constantly burdening us with all sorts of things we needed to do to become more spiritual. He was the one who forbade the brothers to take a bath because in his opinion it could lead to some sort of unwholesome, immoral thoughts, just because he himself, before he married Kristine, used to have serious problems in this particular area. He dictated how everything should be on Saturday night dates. He arranged extra meetings, like mandatory 7 a.m. prayer at Bastejkalns every Monday morning and evangelization activities every Saturday. He and Astrida were the first ones to approach a visitor in the church, claiming that we are a non-denominational church, simply Christians trying our best to live according the rules set by God himself. They are the ones who smile at the newcomers and flatter them, yet they do not warn people about mandatory meetings and the countless rules and regulations set by themselves until the poor victim gets tied up in Bible studies, which are all prepared in advance with standard questions and standard answers, and standard interpretations of Bible scriptures—Church of Christ version. They know how to persuade the poor victim to get baptized and join the church, either by heart-moving life testimonies or twisted Bible verses containing threats about hell and a God of wrath. They appear to be innocent sheep, yet once they get the prey in their claws, they turn into wolves ready to tear people apart. They use God's word to intimidate and manipulate others.

148. Yesterday I had my last conversation with the Church of Christ leaders Salvis and Kristine Teraudi. They have been calling me these last weeks non-stop. Other church members have been calling too, some to encourage me and sympathize with me, some to rebuke me and blame me for my cowardice and lack of love for God and other people. Oddly enough, their accusations do not affect me anymore . . . maybe Satan really has taken over my heart and I just do not feel anything, but maybe I am right and they are all deceived by Satan . . . deceived by some money- and fame-greedy sect.

My heart breaks when I see the gullibility and purity of heart of some of the church members, such as Marita, Roberts, Melita, and Lelde. I love them all dearly. They really do want to serve the Lord with all their hearts, yet are they serving the Lord or the whims of the power- and money-greedy leaders? I still wonder where I got the courage to tell Salvis that I am not coming to the church anymore. I used to be the mouse and he was the big scary cat who played with me and manipulated me into doing anything he wanted me to do. I remember staring straight into his ruthless blue eyes saying, "I am leaving and nothing, nothing, nothing in the whole entire world will convince me to do otherwise." I noticed anger flashing in his eyes as he pressed his both lips together to suppress a curse word. "I mean it, Salvis." My heart was beating so wildly that I could hear it echoing in my temples.

"Now you are acting like one stubborn, immature child. You want to leave because your daily cross has become too heavy for you. You want to leave because you have lost your focus and have given into self-pity. You have become so absorbed with yourself and your desires that you have stopped loving God and His people; you have stopped loving the lost. You have become one of those the Bible talks about, those who fall away for their own destruction."

Any other time Aivar's harsh reprimands would have made me break down and cry. Yesterday, however, I just stood there staring into his face, distorted with rage, waiting for him to finish. When he had half talked half yelled at me for half a hour still not seeing the desired results—my breaking down in uncontrollable sobs—he stopped. I felt I had won the fight. I cast a glance at Salvis and his wife, Kristine, hanging on his right arm. I could see she was torn between compassion for me and loyalty to the church and her husband. I have liked Kristine since the very first time I noticed her in the church. She came to the church two weeks after me. Kristine, the thin girl with honey wheat color hair, slightly freckled nose, huge silver gray eyes and that irresistible smile. Kristine, the girl with perfect posture and a waist so small like a child's, a future lawyer... . strong, confident, smart and beautiful. What was she doing here in this room? Why was she clinging to Aivar's right arm so tightly, as if she were not able to stand firm without clinging to her husband?

Aivar's husky voice interrupted my train of thoughts, "So you don't even have a word to say to us?"

I met his piercing gaze calmly. "I do. I do have a lot to say, but you will not listen. You accused me of being a little child. Well, you are right; I used to be one. However, I have matured rapidly... matured so much that since now on I will be making my own decisions instead of letting you make them for me. What concerns selfishness, you are wrong. I am leaving this church because I genuinely care for other people, including the girls in my Bible study, and I feel very guilty for leading them astray. Instead of calling me a coward, you should compliment me on my courage because I dare tell the truth about the International Church of Christ which recruits and manipulates young, innocent and God-fearing people.

Therefore, if any of the people in the church are going to ask me why I left, I will not hesitate a single moment to tell them the real reasons for my leaving."

My cheeks flashed from the excitement swelling inside me. For the first time in my life I was defending my cause, and I was zealous about it. Just as zealous as Apostle Paul used to be when defending his cause. God has finally lifted the veil of deception that was covering my sight and finally I can see again. How can I possibly keep it to myself!?

The room was silent for a while. Obviously Salvis and Kristine were not prepared for such an attack from my side. Then Salvis got up and said, "Satan has taken over your heart and your mind; therefore you are incapable of understanding God's words directed to you." He took his thick Bible in the leather cover and started rattling verse after verse to me. The verses that used to intimidate me just a couple of months ago, suddenly had a new meaning. I could see Salvis was twisting them and misinterpreting them. I could see that! I could also see something very insincere, even sinister in his eyes and the crooked smile he directed at me. I WAS capable of understanding! It was him who was deceived by Satan! Or maybe he knew he was serving Satan and was trying to manipulate me into believing him by intimidating me. What if he knew? I felt fear pressing like a heavy stone on my chest and choking me at my throat, depriving me of ability to breathe. I swallowed hard trying to maintain my composure and threw one quick glance at Kristine, the beautiful and sincere girl, the one I had always admired. Was she aware? I searched her gray eyes; they had lost their glow. Kristine looked pale and exhausted . . . and very, very sad. Was she sad because I was leaving, or was she envying me the way I used to envy those courageous souls who dared to leave? Was Kristine also trying hard to accept the Satan's version of God's kingdom? The proud, intelligent girl with a perfect body and a charmer's smile was blind, deceived and trapped maybe forever because she was tied to Salvis by the bond of holy matrimony.

"I've got to go," I said almost in a whisper; "our discussion is pointless; you will not convince me to stay. If you want you, can preach next Friday night about me in the church telling its members to beware of me, but I will be praying for them and you that your eyes may be opened one day." I grabbed my backpack and opened the doors to leave.

Salvis grabbed me by my arm and pulled me back. "Just remember you are risking your salvation . . . and if you ever want to come back call me."

"Thank you for your concern, but I won't call you." I closed the door behind me, took a deep breath, looked up at the dirty, spider web-covered ceiling, and whispered, "I made it. Thank you."

The bright sunlight and the noise on the street blinded and deafened me for a while. I stood at the corner of a street staring at the changing light for yellow to red. I could not believe I had made it. I used to be so scared of Salvis and his paralyzing gaze, yet I had gathered courage enough to break free. I am convinced I will never go back there. In fact I will do anything to get people out of there. I am still hoping that Sabine will leave too.

149. This morning I woke up realizing that I will never have to go to that church again. This was my very first completely free day after a long imprisonment. My life does not revolve around the church activities anymore, and now I can plan my days however I please. First I need to pass all my exams and get all good grades to please Mom; then I will try to get a summer job someplace, something not too boring and not to time consuming; my weekends I will spend in Jurmala visiting Sabine and listening to her whinings about not being married yet. On Saturday nights we will get all dolled up and go out to the bars. We will order vodka with grape or orange juice . . . about three or four servings as we already did once . . . and since I am not accountable to the church anymore, I can even look at some cute guys there. Not that I think I could find the love of my life at a bar, but maybe I will meet somebody. I love to be free and be my own boss again!

150. Last night I was already soundly asleep when Mom rushed in my room yelling "Phone! Tell your friends not to call in the middle of the night!" It was Sabine. She had just come home from the usual Friday night family time in the church. Even though she is prohibited any contacts with me, she is very loyal. Sabine wants to get out of the church because she is so beautiful that all guys in the bars drool over her; however, the church does not allow any kind of dating relationships outside it. The brothers in Christ avoid Sabine as much as possible because she dresses too sexy and she is not considered to be spiritual.

"Listen . . . I just had to tell you this!" there was excitement and indignation in her voice. "They preached a sermon about you tonight in the church!"

"I knew that! What did they say? Was it was as threatening as the one when Dina left?"

"Yeah. They told people that you have handed your life over to Satan and that they are prohibited to even say hello to you . . . and then Salvis started to rattle one scripture after another, I guess the same ones he used for Dina."

"What else did he say?"

"Well, he said that you have acted like a coward and have betrayed God and your brothers and sisters, and that it hurts him so much!"

"I don't think he is capable of feeling any kind of pain. I think he is just angry that I left and that he could not stop me."

"I guess so. He is never hurt, he is just mad. He has so much negativity inside. I think, despite his claim that he is the happiest person in the world, that he is not satisfied with something in his life and as a result he is trying to make anyone else miserable too." Sabine fell silent.

"I think you are right" I said.

"I am just so mad! How dare he preach about you like this, when he does not even know you? I know you, and I know that you love God and love people."

I knew Sabine was trying to cheer me up, yet I kept quiet. I am not really sure it I love God and love people. I am just not sure how to go on with my life from now on.

"You know I love you, and I believe that if I love you, God must love you too because the Bible says love comes from God." There was a silence again; I was contemplating Sabine's words. The flowers of the curtains in mom's room looked blurry. I swallowed hard.

"Thank you Sabine," I finally said. Sabine has been with me through the fire and rain. There is no doubt she loves me, but could it be true that God does too? Does He?

151. Sabine's place has become my second home—or more to say my weekend home. Even though Sabine technically is still in the church, she has become a real party animal, and I have started to party along with her. Surprise! The righteous ugly ducking has finally started to live life to its fullest! Every Friday night around eight we get all dolled up in front of Sabine's huge mirror in her tiny bedroom. After putting on large amounts of glittery lipstick and making our eyes smoky with jet-black eyeliner, we head out for Arabica—a bar near Sabine's place. Arabica is attended mostly by young Russian men, some of whom have spent five years in prison. The bar has an open spot in the middle (the square wooden tables and chairs are usually pushed near the walls) which resembles a tiny dance floor; even some lighting is installed for special effects. The lighting reminds me of streetlights: red turning to yellow, yellow turning to green, green turning to yellow, and so on. Primitive as it is, Arabica is good enough for us. No IDs are required; assorted drinks and cocktails are available for cheap, served by muscular and strikingly handsome bartenders; and the dance floor usually works fine to attract guys.

We have established a Friday night routine that we follow faithfully. As we walk into the bar, we throw a quick glance around to see what our chances are for the night. If the situation seems promising, we flash a couple of smiles at the single guys and then approach the bar. We always know what we want—a drink called skruve. It is supposed to screw you up, but actually it is quite healthy—only pure vodka with back currant juice. Usually we have to drink at least three skruves to feel some effect. After we get our skruve, the next step is to squeeze through the heavily intoxicated crowds to find a place to sit down. Sometimes we get snatched up half ways: some guy grabs our hand and we are dragged out on the dance floor. Since we are both extremely inexperienced in men matters, we try to gulp down some of our skruve before we start moving on the dance floor. If nobody snatches us right away, we go out on the dance floor by ourselves. We start moving, our eyes fixed on one another; we pretend that the rest of the world does not even exist. But we are not lesbians; we are just girls with little confidence pretending to be girls with a lot of confidence.

For a while we dance undisturbed, but then the crowds begin to part. Most guys stop dancing and retire to their tables, and soon we are the only ones on the dance floor. The men are clapping and shouting; the rest of the women are pissed, of course. But we just keep on dancing, unable to stop and afraid to look around. We are the dancing queens, and nobody has a clue how scared we are. Sabine dances like a maniac, her naturally blondee, long, straight hair shimmering in multiple colors of the disco lights; her super-mini skirt revealing two long, shapely and very sexy legs clad in black leather boots with six inch heels. She must have been born on a dance floor. I am crappy dancer. Maybe the problem is that I do not know how to relax. I am still mentally inside of the International Church of Christ. But after three or four skruves, my dancing usually improves. The bar owners and DJs are new Russians, who during the times of changes turned from crap into gold. They were shrewd enough to seize the opportunities, start some small business and make some money. They play the latest Russian disco hits, of course. Sabine is in love with Russian disco music. She knows all the popular songs by heart. Sometimes I get tired of only hearing Russian songs all night long, yet I've got to admit they have the right beat for dancing. And they are definitely better than Salvis's preachings.

After we have danced a while with each other, sooner or later some guy, completely unstable on his legs, tries to infiltrate between us and move his ass along with us. To get rid of the intruder, we move closer to each other, until the poor creature in the middle feels so crushed that he has to retreat before he falls down on the floor and gets stepped on by Sabine's six-inch heels. During these incidents we usually burst into loud laughter. Our laughing has a double purpose: it attracts attention and hides our lack of confidence. After all, we have to play cool to get noticed. After the drunk loser, completely embarrassed, leaves the dance floor, somebody more sophisticated usually comes up and asks one of us to dance with him. Usually Sabine gets the best shots and I get the second hands; nevertheless, sometimes it is the other way around.

After we both have paired up with some guys (it is big shame indeed to be a wallflower) we dance for a while, fast and slow dances, chat with our dance partners as much as it is possible under the beat of the music, and then go and sit down. Sometimes we are lucky enough to get a free drink from our dance partners, yet we try to be careful because women who are more experienced in the men matters have warned us not to accept anything from guys if we are not planning to give them anything in return. The thought that these guys, after buying us a couple of drinks, may want to have sex terrifies both of us. We are both still virgins at the age of nineteen. Our virginity is a big shame, and we try to keep it a secret. I guess the church-instilled hope that our husbands will be the only men in our lives still has not completely died yet. So at the bars we tease guys and make them want us, but we do not accept anything from them, especially no rides home. What if they rape us?

Yet even the prospect of being raped does not keep us away from Arabica. It's the place were we get attention and compliments, where we are finally appreciated as women. Sometimes I am afraid that Mom will find out about my Friday night adventures. Thanks God I used to stay at Sabine's a lot during my church years, so my mom is used to me being away on Friday nights and Saturdays. When Mom asks what we are doing every Friday night, I tell her that we usually eat liquor candies, cry on each other's shoulder, and then go to sleep. This was true in the church times, and Mom did not seem to mind, but now I am afraid that she will find out somehow. Sabine's mom does not seem to mind at all; she even encourages us to go to the bars and have some fun.

To please my mom and to appear a good girl, I still go to the church on Sundays. The church I attend now is called the Traditional Church of Christ. Like the International Church of Christ, they also teach that a person can only be saved through the water baptism. Unlike the ICC, though, the TCC does not force people to attend their meetings, so that is a plus. I can show up there after three missed Sundays and they still welcome me with their arms wide open. Overall, I think I am leading a well-rounded life between my school, parties, and churches.

Sometimes, though, like for example today, I feel really down and I cannot explain why. I am afraid that God is really mad at me and will punish me for my turning away from Him. I still go to the church, but I feel like a hypocrite. My heart is not in the church teachings anymore. I have stopped reading my Bible in the mornings, and I pray only when I feel scared of God or when something bad is about to happen. I go to church not because I love God or want to learn more about Him, but because I am afraid not to go. Today is just one of those days. As I am writing this, I am fighting back tears, but I have got to pull myself together because Mom's going to call me to the dinner in a couple of minutes, and if I want to escape her interrogation, I have to appear cheerful and smiley. I am so glad that those years in the I. C. C. taught me to wear a robot smile, the kind of smile that makes your cheeks hurt. So I will put on my smile and go to the dinner. To make the matters worse, Mom has invited one of her college friends over and also the plump neighbor lady Elvia. But I have got to spill my heart to somebody; I am so glad I have this diary.

152. Yesterday I was forced to attend one of those miserable family gatherings. They make me unbearably sad. Not that I do not love my relatives, only they are all so full of bitterness and fear of what the future holds for them. All they talk about is the hardships and hopelessness of honest working class people (especially if they happen to be old) in the post-Soviet Latvia. Honest, working-class people cannot get ahead in their lives because the government is corrupt. Everyone in the government is involved in some dirty business; everyone manages to steal some of the government's limited funds. Also, one gets ahead only if one has the right connections. The retired people—most of my relatives are either at that or close to that age—are the most affected by the thoughtlessness and selfishness of our new government leaders. The monthly retirement money is not enough to buy food for a month, let alone to pay for the rent and utilities, the prices of which have sky-rocketed in the recent years. Of course retired people are not allowed to work, and even if they were, at their age they wouldn't stand a chance of finding any kind of job. People who are unable to pay the rent are literally thrown out on the street, and they have nobody to go to and complain, for nobody cares for them. They have spent the best years of their lives bending their backs in the beet fields and milking the cows of the community farms; they have a work ethic and industriousness, but such their qualities are useless in Latvia today.

The poor, old, retired people have two choices: one is to pay the rent and slowly starve to death, because after rent and utilities are paid, there is nothing left for food. Or they can buy food to sustain themselves, but then most likely one day they will be thrown out on the street. Many of these people have become beggars. You can see them everywhere on the streets. The highest concentration of these beggars is around the Central

Station square and near expensive hotels. Those who are too proud to beg and do not have children to help them (or do not receive any help from their children) frequently opt for suicide.

In a couple of years Mom will be one of those people. After mom retires, all responsibility will lie on me. As her only child I must provide for her.

Such are talks at the reunions. My relatives like to remember the Soviet times with nostalgia. They loved those times because everyone had a job and a little bit of money to afford a black and white TV set and some ice cream on Sunday afternoons. Those two things were sufficient for the happiness of most of my relatives. They had laid their lives down working for the community farms; there was not much left in their bones or their minds, dulled by hard monotonous work, to ask more of life. It did not matter that they had to live in communal apartments sharing the kitchen, toilet and bathroom with nasty neighbors; it did not matter that they could not travel abroad (the sixteen republics of the Soviet Union were supposed to be enough to satisfy one's thirst for traveling). Neither did it matter that they could not think for themselves, act for themselves, or form any kind of opinions of their own. Pathetic as it may sound, they were comfortable that way. At least that's what they say now. No brain power was needed to exist in the Soviet Latvia, so skills such as independent thinking, decision making and creativeness remained severely underdeveloped. That explains why my relatives and their whole generation are so helpless, so utterly hopeless and so terribly depressed. They are like machines, robots, with no electricity to run their engines. They cannot move or act until somebody makes them. Neither are these people equipped with the necessary survival skills; they will never fight for their rights under the sun. Instead, they will let the tumultuous current of the events carry them along and at some point smash them into pieces at some rock in the river of life.

The only exception is my aunt Anna. Maybe because she is the youngest of all (she is the youngest sister of my dad), she has never succumbed to helpless depression by lamenting over her circumstances. She's got initiative, desire for growth (mental and spiritual) and a positive attitude. Anna has been like a second mother to me (sometimes I wish mom were more like her). Anna was the first one to notice that my front teeth were crooked and made me look ugly, so she started to nag my parents to bring me to the dentist and get braces before it was too late. My parents, so wrapped up in their own miseries, would never have thought of that. Anna was also the one who noticed my talent for languages and dragged me to the Grammar School of Nordic Languages. She was the one who encouraged me to continue my studies at the university afterwards. She also has helped me to find a couple of part time jobs. I always like to see Aunt Anna in these reunions. I love talking to her. Without her, these reunions would be completely unbearable

153. Last Friday as usual Sabine and I had planned a party night. This time, however, we invited one of Sabine's hot friends along with us. What a mistake! We all decided to meet at Sabine's place and then figure out where to go for the night. Arabica, of course, was not acceptable for Laira's refined taste, so we had to go someplace else. Good thing that Laira has a car.

When I got to Sabine's, Laira was already there, made up like a teenage model. Her long, skinny (a bit too skinny I would say) legs were clad in tight, cream color pants with numerous pockets, the latest fashion in Latvia. The white contrasted nicely with her tanned skin (solarium tan) and purple top, which revealed half of her breasts, which are not small, either. Her slender waist was embraced by a thick, brown leather belt with bizarre ornaments. Her full, baby-like lips were coated with a purple lipstick which matched her top perfectly. Finally, her already large brown eyes were accentuated with a purple glitter eye shadow and about a ton of mascara. My mouth dropped open as I took in all that beauty, but I recovered quickly. I could not just stand and stare at her for hours.
"This is my friend Laira," Sabine said; "come in and have a seat. We have got four bottles of wine. I got them at work. They were celebrating somebody's birthday, and they were all drunk under the table, so I took the four remaining wine bottles and left. They had had enough to drink anyway." Sabine was beaming. She was dressed up too, in a cosmo gray mini skirt and a black lacey top, which revealed a lot of what was underneath. I felt like a complete cake in my pleated miniskirt and my simple white top, which wasn't even tight. I looked more like a school girl than a disco diva.

We all sat down, and Sabine poured the red Moldavia wine in the fancy wine glasses she had taken out of her mother's buffet—without her mom's permission, of course. "Cheers!" We all looked at each other and burst into laughter. "Another Friday night, another spinster party," Sabine exclaimed. It is not common for women in Latvia to party and drink without guys, and Sabine is very concerned about getting married as soon as possible. Simply having a boy friend does not satisfy her. She wants to get MARRIED, and not necessarily to one of her brothers in the church. She is worried she will never get married, so she keeps visiting clubs every Friday night in hopes to meet her future husband. I am pretty skeptical about meeting my husband in a bar or a club. I still believe that meeting my better half is determined by destiny, or God, or whomever, and therefore it is not my task to search for him. If I am destined to get married one day, then I will meet him regardless of what I do or where I am; however, if I am not destined to get married, then going to all kinds of shabby places will not help.

"Want more wine?" Sabine asked. Despite its cheapness the Moldavian grape had already given me a pleasant buzz. Even though I do not like the sour taste of wine, I love that feeling of warmth in my stomach.

"Sure," I smiled.

After two glasses, I felt much better. Laira's stunning beauty did not seem so disturbing anymore. In fact, I even felt comfortable enough to chat with her. Sabine had already started the second bottle of wine. "Do you have anything to eat?" Laira asked.

"Just the chocolates," Sabine replied and put a huge box of Laima chocolates on the table. "I have got the liqueur candies too if you guys want some."

The rest of the evening is all covered in fog. I remember that we finished all four bottles of wine and ate all the liqueur candies. Sabine and Laira periodically went in the hallway to smoke, and I tottered along. Sabine offered me cigarettes with the vicious smile of a seductress. I shook my head out of habit, yet I must admit I had a real big temptation to try. Both Sabine and Laira looked so sexy with the thin, long Pierre Cardin menthol cigarettes clasped in their slender fingers. Bad as smoking is, sometimes it looks very classy. Well, maybe not classy, but definitely sexy.

One time when we were in the hallway again, I started laughing hysterically about something really stupid Sabine had said. I laughed so hard that I fell down. Everything around me seemed funny: the stupid ornaments on the hallway walls, and the broken lamp hanging down from the ceiling like a limp arm. My stomach muscles started to hurt, yet I could not stop laughing. I did not stop even when the door of one of the apartments opened and revealed an old grumpy lady's face. She looked so funny with those huge Russian blue rolls in her hair and a polka dot nightgown. I fell into a fresh fit of uncontrollable laughter.

"What the hell you think you are doing here in the middle of the night? Do you want me to call the police?"

"Yeah, go ahead, bitch," Laira answered calmly.

"Who do you think you are that you are calling me names, you slut?"

"Shut up, you stupid bitch," Laira snorted, turned to Sabine, and completely ignored the lady.

"If you do not disappear in a second, I am going to call the police," the lady threatened in a husky voice like a crow. I started laughing again.

The lady grabbed the broom that was there for the stairwell cleaning and threw it at us. The wooden stem hit Sabine's legs, and she shrieked like a banshee. Some other doors started to open.

"I am going to call the police," the lady threatened again. Another head with rolls and sleep-puffed eyes appeared in the door, and an older man in pajamas stripped like a prisoner's garment was coming from upstairs to check what the fuss was all about.

"I think we better get out of here," Sabine whispered to us. Even in my foggy condition, I could sense that things were getting serious. Laira pulled me up from the floor, and we ran into the apartment to grab our bags.

The smoky summer night was a perfect night for partying. We hopped in Laira's car. None of us was even slightly concerned about Laira's driving ability after the four bottles of wine. We were on a road with lots of bushes; the car was shaking and zigzagging like a snake, everything was spinning. "You are driving like a drunkard," I heard Sabine yelling.

"You want to drive?" Laira yelled back.

"Fuck you!"

"Fuck you back!"

Suddenly bright beams illuminated the windows, and a sound of horn came from somewhere. Sabine was screaming like a mad woman. I was too sick and too drunk to get worried. It was like in a movie!

A car passed us by, and a guy yelled at us something. "I must have been towards the middle of the road," Laira speculated.

"You almost killed us all, you stupid bitch," Sabine screamed at Laira. The next instant she slammed the door of the car and dragged me out of the back seat. Even in my drunk state of mind I appreciated her concern. We got out and started walking down the road. A couple of times we looked back. Laira's car was in the middle of the road, not moving. "We cannot leave her there, can we?" I asked. Sabine did not respond; she was mad and was probably sober by now. We kept on walking for a hundred meters, when Sabine stopped turned around and started going back. Laira was sitting in the car, sobbing. "We've got to get off the road!" Sabine yelled at her. "The Big Bamboo in not far from here. Do you think you can make it that far?"

Laira nodded. I was sober too by now, and I felt sick. So sick I have never felt in my life. Laira started the car.

As we arrived at Big Bamboo, the party was in full course. A crowd of people were outside the club smoking and laughing, among them Vladims, Laira's one of many boy friends, a foot taller than the rest. They have been dating on and off. Despite two missing front teeth, lost in a fight, Armands is considered the most handsome guy and thus the biggest heartthrob in the whole town of Jurmala. He was dating Katrina about three years ago, when he still had his two teeth. "What a small world," I though to myself. Although Laira is normally more show than go, Sabine claims she has seriously fallen for Armands. "What girl would not fall for Armands? He is a doll!" Sabine added dreamily.

Well, there was the doll standing in the middle of a bunch of girls, flashing his toothless grin. Laira cast a quick, suspicious look at the crowd, grabbed her handbag and rushed to the restroom to fix her shimmer-glimmer eye shadow, which tears had smeared all over her beautiful baby face.

"Are we going in?" I asked Sabine.

"Let's better wait for Laira," Sabine answered, scanning the crowds outside.

Laira was back in a second, and we headed towards the entrance. As one would expect, Laira got snatched half ways—well, to be more precise, right at the entrance. Some guy she knew grabbed her by the waist and dragged her to the dance floor. She laughed really loudly and flirted with him and the all guys around them. Soon she was dancing with a bunch of guys. She was pretending to be drunk, happy and careless, but I understood. Her flirting and her loud laughter was artificial, an attempt to make Armands jealous. Armands had also come in, yet he seemed undisturbed by Laira's success with the guys. Some tall, clumsy geek with glasses and curly hair was heading our way. My heart usually starts beating faster whenever guy makes a move somewhat towards my direction. I so much hate to be the wallflower that I dance even with an ugly person rather than support the walls. So what? Dancing is not kissing or marriage. My heart experienced that very familiar mixture of jealousy and self-pity, when the curly head and glasses asked Sabine to dance instead of me. Well, what could I expect, dressed in a pleated skirt and an ill-fitting top? "I should have borrowed one of Sabine's outfits," I thought to myself.

Since I was not dancing, I had plenty of time to scan the room. Big Bamboo has a huge dance floor and much better lighting effects than Arabica, but the entrance in Arabica is free, and here you have to pay one lat to get in. Sabine ran up to me, breathless from dancing, and dragged me on the dance floor despite my vigorous resistance. She was trying to be nice by not leaving me out, but I did not need her pity. I did not feel any better dancing in trio with her and the blondee sausage with glasses. I was thankful that a slow dance started and I could finally leave, because you cannot slow dance in trio. So I went back to supporting the walls. Everybody was dancing in couples, and there were no free guys left. Yet there were plenty of single women—most of them were really pretty—holding up the walls just like me. Statistics show a female overload in Latvia.

Since I was not dancing, I decided to get a drink. At the bar I bumped into Armands. I apologized, got my drink and retreated to the corner. As I continued to watch the dancers, my eyes met with Armands' a couple of time. "That cannot be real," I though to myself; "I am just imagining!" Yet as I looked at his direction a couple more times, he returned my stare and even grinned. I blushed. The biggest heartbreaker in Jurmala was checking out me! I was either drunk or dreaming. Armands was already parting the crowds of dancers and coming my direction. I looked around to make sure there was not another woman hiding somewhere in the corner whom he might have noticed. There was no one but me in my pleated skirt and ugly white ugly top.

"Would you like to dance?" asked a husky voice somewhere above me. I tilted my head and there he was: impudent, charming as devil, proudly displaying his toothless grin.

"Would you like to dance?"

"Sure," I said blushing. I was afraid that if I did not answer quickly, he would just walk way. But on the dance floor, I was suddenly stricken by an enormous feeling of guilt. I was dancing with Laira's love. I nervously scanned the crowd. I could not see Laira anywhere. Maybe she had left, or maybe she was somewhere making out with one of her other guy friends. After all, I had heard a lot of bad gossip about Laira. Armands was staring straight at me.

"Are you worried that your boyfriend will notice that you are dancing with me and then you will have to endure a jealously scene?" he asked with just a hint of sarcasm.

"I am not worried about that," I said, blushing again. I could not admit to Armands that I do not have a boyfriend—that I have never had even just one boyfriend in my nineteen-year life.

"What then?" he persisted

"I am looking for one of my friends?"

"Do not worry about your friend; you are not her baby sitter or anything. Let her have a little fun."

"It's not that. It's just. . . ." I got all tangled up in my words.

"What is it?" Armands asked mockingly.

"None of your business." I was getting annoyed.

Armands shut up for while. I kept on looking around, getting more and more nervous. Sabine had disappeared somewhere, too.

"Are you afraid of hurting Laira's feelings?" Armands asked suddenly.

"Well, I heard you and her are an item."

"Bullshit!" Vadmis exclaimed really loud. He grabbed me by my waist and started moving me along with him. I could feel his chest muscles and his thigh muscles, which was kind of pleasant. Yet at the same time I felt so absolutely clumsy, like an idiot. Armands let me go. "Have fun!" he said and left.

Humiliated but relieved, I decided to go outside and get some fresh air. Armands met me at the door and grabbed me by my hand. "I bought you a drink," he said smiling, this time without sarcasm. I shook my head, but he insisted. I took the drink and thanked him. He told me to wait for him outside.

I didn't know what to do, so I tried to locate Sabine. Could she have left too, with somebody? No. Sabine was not that kind of a girl. She never lost her awareness even when she was drunk. But where was she?

"Coming with me?" I heard a drunk male's voice somewhere behind me. Somebody roughly grabbed me by my shoulder. I turned around sharply, which made the drunk stagger a little.

"Get away from me," I hissed.

"Hey, you are one pretty woman, so why do your pretend to be such a goody goody girl?"

I found myself surrounded by a bunch of drunks, all grinning at me. As I attempted to push my way through and leave the crowd, another one of them grabbed me with an iron grip. I desperately tried to free myself but unsuccessfully.

"Let me go, you moron!" I yelled at him and bit him in his shoulder.

"You bitch!" he screamed, exasperated.

"What the fuck is going on here?" I heard Armands' husky voice coming somewhere from close above; "Let go of my girl, you bunch of assholes."

Had he said "my girl"? Maybe I misheard him.

The drunken crowd knew better than to mess with Armands. In an instant we were left alone. The glass with gin and tonic Armands had bought me lay crashed on the sidewalk.

"I am sorry I spilled the drink," I said to break the silence. What an idiot! Why did I need to apologize for the stupid drink?

"Yeah," Armands looked at me with that mocking gleam in his eyes, "you are a bad girl, getting yourself in trouble all the time."

I did not know what to say to that, so I just kept silent.

"I'll by you another drink."

"No . . . thanks . . . I really . . . I do not want another drink." I was remembering the advice of experienced women, and stories about men putting drugs in drinks at bars like this.

"Sure, you do. Come on."

"No, please!" Flattering as his attention was, my gut feeling started to send me warning signals. Enough playing with the situation. I had got what I wanted, a major vanity boost that would last me a year. I had danced with and even had been rescued by the heartthrob of Jurmala. But I did not want anything more.

"Come!" he almost ordered, which irritated me because I do not like to be pressured to do things against my will.

"No!" I jerked my hand away from his.

"You are acting like a little child," Armands hissed. "A little child" — that was the same phrase that Salvis had used. "Have a good life," he said and left.

I felt ashamed and a little disappointed. Maybe I had missed my chance. Chance for what? I went back into the club and sat down near the wall. Laira was back and was dancing with a new very handsome guy. Armands approached the couple and whispered something to Laira. They both left the dance floor for the bar. Armands was explaining something to her when she slapped him in the face and ran out. Then he came straight to my corner. "So have you made up your mind?" he asked without any introduction or explanation.

"Made my mind up about what?" I asked.

"Are you gonna come with me?"

"To where?"

"I don't know. To another club or a cafe or something."

"I am not going anywhere. I came here with my friends," I said, hopinh that my voicesounded firm and convincing.

"All right then, maybe we can dance and talk here."

"Why do you want to talk with me anyway?"

"Because I like you. You are very beautiful and different from the rest of the chicks here."

I felt my cheeks turn red. I never know what to say to things like that. I am not even sure if such words are meant as a compliment or as merely mocking.

"So tell me, what do you do?" Armands asked and sat himself next to me on the tiny bench.

I told him about school and my boring life. I had nothing much to tell, so I asked Armands about his life. He told me about how people judge him wrongly all the time (in reality he claims to be a very mellow guy) and how unlucky he had been with women so far; they were all bitches and none of them had ever been interested in him as a person. None ever asked him deep questions, the way I did. Armands also confided in me he is still looking for the meaning of his miserable existence and the he is afraid of death and the fires of hell. He seemed so open, so honest and vulnerable. "The bad boys have it tough too," I thought to myself. "They are as scared and as confused as the weak and the unpopular ones." And at that instant I realized that all humans without an exception are very vulnerable, constantly living under the doom of some upcoming disaster, be it a loss of job, disease, death of a loved one, abandonment, fire in the house or anything. All of us live in the shadow of death. All of us are consumed by different kinds of fears and concerns. I had not had such a deep and meaningful conversation in along time. Therefore, I did not even notice how we had gotten up and had started walking around the dimly lit streets of the city Jurmala. I was bewitched by the poignant confessions of this lost soul. I even thought that maybe I had been sent from God to help him. I came back to my senses only when we stopped in a completely dark corner.

"I guess we should be getting back to the club?" I suggested.

"Do you want to go back to those miserable drunk people there? To those sluts? What are you doing there anyway? It is not a place for you. What do you have in common with people like Laira and Sabine: low creatures with no education, no culture, no interest in anything serious. All they think about is how to get drunk and get laid. You, however, are like a person from a different planet, an abnormality in the regular public of Jurmala."

Even thought Armands' words sounded beyond flattering, I was indignant that he had called Sabine a low and shallow creature.

"I do not know about Laira, but Sabine is definitely not a low creature," I shouted angrily. She is a very smart, very deep and very loving person. She is my true friend and I will not let people who do not even know her put her down like this."

"Hey, you look really cute when you get excited like this," Armands smiled at me, a nice, almost gentle, toothless smile.

I blushed again and was thankful that the street was kind of dark. Armands had moved so close to me that I could feel his body odor: sweat mixed with the smell of alcohol and some mysterious cologne. He smelled . . . well, like a man, I suppose. I liked the way he smelled.

"Do you want to come over?" The question was like a thunder from clear skies. Nobody had ever asked me that before. Of course, I was not going to go to his place! I was too scared, too inexperienced, too dorky.

"What do you mean?"
Armands started laughing. "What's the matter? Are you really naïve or are you just pretending?"

"I am not going to your place," I said angrily. "I am going back to the club."

"You can go by yourself, then. I am going home."

The thought of going back to Big Bamboo through the dark neighborhood of Jurmala terrified me, yet I was too proud to show Armands that I was scared.

"Fine!" I said and started off the empty street, my heart in my throat.

After I had gone a block or so, I threw a cautious look over my shoulder. It seemed that no one was following me, yet since I am nearsighted I was not sure. I had about four more blocks to go into the looming darkness. All kinds of horror stories started coming back to me. I thought of my dad and how he had always warned me, trying to protect me. I felt helpless and scared. My head was throbbing; my heart was beating in my temples. To make the nightmare a reality, suddenly somebody grabbed me by my waist from behind and put a palm over my mouth. I frantically tried to free myself by kicking and biting. "Ouch! Stop it, silly! Fuck!" That was Armands.

"You idiot! You jerk! You scared the shit out of me!"

"I am sorry. I caught up with you by taking the side streets only I know. I could not let you go alone. Jurmala at night is dangerous."

I was touched by his concern, but I wasn't going to show it to him yet. "So maybe he really does care about me," I thought.

"All right. So you want to go back to the club?"

I just started marching down the street in front of him, pretending that I was still angry.

"Come on." Armands had a long stride. He was beside me, and he had even dared to put his arm around me. I tried to remove his arm, yet I was not succeeding. I did not know that it felt so good to be hugged. Nevertheless, I was anxious to get back to Big Bamboo, to Sabine and Laira. Tonight had provided enough adventures for about four months. We stopped at the gas station because Armands needed to pee. It was nice to be in a brightly lit and safe place after the dark streets.

"Do you want something to eat?" Armands asked. I shook my head, but Armands bought two packs of Chio Chips and handed one to me anyway. He also bought a couple of Crystal Vodka bottles and some orange juice.

"Why are you buying these?" I asked curiously

"So we have something to help us through the long night," Armands replied with a grin.

"Us?"

"You are coming to my place, aren't you?"

"I thought we were going back to Big Bamboo."

"You can go if you want to, but I am going home."

I started to hate his game playing. I was cold and I was anxious to get back to Sabine and Laira.

"Come on. You are not afraid of me are you? We have been in some really dark holes tonight; if I wanted to rape you, I would have done that already."
"Of course, I am not afraid of you," I lied.
"Then why don't you come?"
"I need to get back to my friends."
"We already have been through this. Let them get laid and have some fun." Armands was laughing. What was so damned funny?
"Hey, don't be a baby. Start acting like an adult. Let's go to my place, have some drinks and a decent talk. My parents are at home, for God's sake."

I did not want to go to Armands' place, but I was not going to show him that I was afraid of him. So I reluctantly agreed. Well, what the heck.

Armands' parents indeed were at home. They were still up when we came in, talking in their bedroom. I was relieved enormously. I do not think that I am attractive enough to be raped, but then men sometimes rape unattractive women too.

Armands showed me his room. It was a little square with aquamarine color walls and a black ceiling. The walls were decorated with posters of people and bands I had never heard of, except for the Madonna poster. She looked her usual self: an artificial blondee, elegant and impudent. Armands caught me staring at the poster and pointed out, "My favorite." I was not surprised. Katrina had told me that Armands is a huge fan of Madonna.

Armands did not have a real bed, only a queen size mattress with two black pillows and a shabby looking dark blue comforter. He did not have a desk or any chairs either; his only valuable possession seemed to be his stereo with humongous speakers.

"Sit down. I'll make you something to drink," Armands said. I did not know where exactly I was supposed to sit down. I certainly did not want to sit on the mattress. I simply stared at Armands making the vodka mixes. He seemed to enjoy the procedure: he slowly poured some vodka into a tea glass (a classic Russian way of drinking vodka), smelled it, clicked his tongue and then added the orange juice. As he was done, he sat down on the mattress, stationing the glasses on the floor in front of him.
"Hey sit down. Relax. Have some!"

I sat myself on the mattress a long ways away from Armands. He immediately moved closer and handed me the glass with the yellow drink.
"No, thanks!"
"Have some. It will be more fun that way!"

"What do you mean?"

"So you were not playing naive. You are naive! Why do you suppose I asked you to come over?" he asked, his gaze piercing my head.

"I am not sure. I thought you wanted somebody to talk to," I stammered and then added indignantly, "If you think I am that cheap, you are deeply mistaken. I do not have sex with my friend's boyfriend."

Vadmis laughed oddly. "Who said I wanted to have sex with you?" he asked.

I blushed again, like an idiot. "Isn't that what people do after they hook up at some bar or club?"

"So you are asking me because you do not know for yourself?" he asked teasingly. He was making fun of my innocence. He knew for sure that I am just an inexperienced virgin, at the age of nineteen!

"I have never had a one night stand because I consider myself too good for such kind of relations. Plus such relations are dirty and dangerous!"

"Too good, eh? A little Miss Innocence; we'll see how good you are." He grabbed me, pulled me close, and started kissing me. I could feel his tongue licking the inside of my mouth. All kinds of thoughts were running through my head. French kissing is supposed to make you dizzy and weak in your knees. I felt rather grossed out by it, so I tied to wiggle my way out of Armands' iron embrace, but I did not succeed much. He was squeezing me so hard that I felt like I was going to suffocate. When I gained my breath back I yelled, "Let go, or I will wake your par...." I could not finish my sentence because Armands put his palm on my mouth. "Stop, you crazy. We are just having a little fun, a little harmless fun!" His palm stank like smoke. I bit him. He shouted, but he did not let me go. I tried to kick him, but he was huge and very strong. He had pulled me underneath him. I felt like I was going to collapse; I could not move beneath his weight. His free hand was reaching beneath my skirt; he had already ripped my panty hose. I looked at him, my eyes full of despair.

"Hey, what's the matter?" he said suddenly. "I thought your resisting was some sort of a foreplay!"

A huge, warm tear ran down my cheek. Just then I was not even thinking of rape. I was thinking, "So this is my first kiss. I have never had any experience at love, not even a single kiss—and now this is it." And what else might happen? I had heard the stories of innocent girls getting raped. I had had been warned not to trust guys, especially not to trust the players. I knew! Yet I guess I am naïve, a believer in the goodness of other human beings. I had noticed something beautiful, something vulnerable about this guy's soul. I had trusted him, and now I felt like an idiot!

"I have never had never had sex before," I choked through the tears.

"You are acting like a child," Armands snorted. "I hate when grown women act like this. Well, I guess you are not really a woman then." He had finally let me go. I got up from the mattress and tried to straighten out my skirt and my blouse.

"Is there a bathroom?" I asked.

"Yeah, downstairs!" he mumbled hiding his head in the pillow.

"Downstairs where?"

"You'll find it!"

His attitude made me even more miserable. He did not even care! Of course, what had I expected! A special treatment from Armands, the player, the heartbreaker, the women hater, the king of one-night stands? I had been the bait for the night. I was no better than other woman he had had slept with. His telling me that I was special had been simply part of the strategy to make me trust him and then have sex with him. I had been told millions of times about these tricks, yet I fell for them anyway.

I found my way downstairs. It was pitch black there, and of course I could not find a switch. I stumbled over some piece of wood and knocked something over with aloud bang.

"Fuck, Armands, can't you be quiet?" I heard his mom's voice coming from one of the nearby rooms. My heart was in my throat again. I had finally found the door of the bathroom.

The bathroom looked very filthy. I looked in the mirror at myself. My eye makeup had left dark traces on my cheeks, my hair was tousled. My blouse was spotty and wrinkly, and my panty hose had tears everywhere. I was a mess!

I washed my face carefully and looked for some kind of a hand towel. There was none to be found.

It was getting light outside. I went upstairs to get my purse. Armands was asleep or was pretending to be asleep. I took my purse and was about the leave when he turned to me. "Where are you going?"

"To the first train!" I said in whisper.

He looked at me and said in matter of fact voice, "Have a good life! I hope you find some jerk who thinks like you."

I had nothing to say, so I left. I felt like vomiting. I called Sabine from the station.

She herself did not sound too good. She had been worried, and Laira was mad as hell. She knew everything. I told Sabine I would explain everything to Laira and hung up. My story sounded lame, and I felt pathetic. I wish I were either a hard-core party chick or a complete Puritan, not somebody with one foot in heaven and one foot in the disco. I was trying to be both a good Christian girl and a sexy vixen. It wasn't working out. The Bible warns us that we cannot serve two masters, either God or Satan. I am not sure which one to choose. I want to be with God, but at the same time I hate the church's legalistic rules. But I do not know how far I can go into the world without getting tainted.

There were quite a few people on the train. I looked dirty and cheap in my wrinkled blouse and pale face. Some people were staring at me, and everybody in that carriage knew that I had had a one-night stand. It was written all over my face. "Well," I thought to myself, "I did not really sleep with anyone, and I do not really give a shit what people think." I always tell myself that I do not care about how others see me, but that is not true. I care way too much what others think, even if they are strangers. I think all of us care what others think of us, some more and some less, but all of us do.

I got off at Sabine's station. Sabine met me with her arms wide open and her face pale and tear stained. Her eyes made me forget about my shame and my future and possibly unpleasant confrontation with Laira.

"What happened?"

"You know, I am really glad I am still alive," she said quietly. Tears started running down her cheeks again. I was at loss as to what to do or say, so I simply hugged her.

"What happened?" I asked.

"Come to my place. I will make you some coffee and tell you everything."

I glanced at my watch. I did not have a lot of time. I knew if I did not show up at my place around eight at the latest, Mom would make a real fuss and turn into this screaming, controlling mad woman and not let me out of the house anymore. But I really wanted to know what happened to Sabine and I also wanted to ask about Laira.

So we went to Sabine's flat, and I sat down on Sabine' couch. I felt sick, tired, drained. In a short time she had a steaming coffee pot and two cups. The smell of freshly made coffee filled the little bedroom.

Sabine poured the dark bitter liquid into cups and cuddled up on the coach drawing her knees near her chin.

"It all started like this. Remember that clumsy, blondee guy who asked me to dance first? I danced with the geek for a while, but then I got sick and tired of him; plus I had noticed some man around his thirties checking me out. Well, I wanted to be sure, so during one of my twists I stared right at him. Our eyes met, and I felt that quiver in my stomach. For the first time I was being noticed by a real man. He looked like some gangster from a movie: huge, tall and strong, and his eyes had a hard, gangster gleam. He was smiling; it was a mocking smile. It seemed as if he was making fun of all the young, poor and clumsy guys and girls with way too short skirts and cheap tastelessly put on make up. He definitely wasn't a Jurmala local.

You know how I play with men, tease them, then turn my back on them. My heart was beating like crazy, and my gut was telling me that I was about to play with fire, but I wanted to leave an impression that I am a woman, a seductress, not some nineteen-year-old virgin. So during my next twist I smiled at him. When the song was over, he came up to me and asked, "May I?" My geeky partner just rolled his eyes and stepped aside.

The next was slow dance. I loved dancing with him. He was so smooth, and you know he felt so warm and strong against my body. I was really sorry when the song was over and they started to play techno again. I guess my man was not a techno fan either, for he took me by hand and led me off the floor. I was so drunk and so happy that I would have followed this mystery man everywhere. You know, I was not drunk from the alcohol but from that awesome feeling that I had been chosen by a real stud. He led me to the bar and asked me what I wanted to drink. I said I was fine, but he insisted on buying me a drink. I do not even remember anymore what he bought me.

But I do remember how his arm hugged my shoulders. It was such a tight hug, you know.

"Let me introduce you to my friends," he said and led me outside where a bunch of guys dressed in khaki pants and suites had gathered around the big oak. A bit further ahead I saw some fancy cars parked. You know I really do not know the brands of the cars or anything. I am no good at that, but they looked fancy: huge, black, sleek. So I thought to myself, "Wow! What are those guys doing there in our miserable nightclub?" My surprise was even bigger when I noticed my ex-roommate Silvija among the crowd. One of the guys, almost as tall and handsome as mine (his name is Arvils), had his arm around her. I was introduced to everyone and greeted "warmly," so to say. One of the guys named Oljegs suggested that we go to some club in Riga. I was totally up for it. I am sorry, but at that moment I did not even remember that you and Laira still existed in the world. The next moment I was sinking in the soft seat of Arvils' Mercedes. We went to Pepsi Forums, which is not as breathtaking a place as we always thought it is. It's full of skinheads dressed in leather jackets, and swarming with prostitutes. You know, those tall, thin, incredibly blondee Russian girls. They seemed to be proud of themselves. Some of them checked me and Silvija out and turned away contemptuously. I guess we did not fit in there. But our guy friends seemed to like us a lot. Silvija told me that she had met her guy, Grisha, in Klub Kabata, and that is how she had met up with the rest of the crowd. Of course, the fact that Silvija knew the guys made me feel even more at ease. I was really enjoying my adventure. After all, how often do I get picked up by a handsome stud? Arvils and I gulped down cocktails and danced until we were ready to drop dead.

Towards 3 am, he suggested we go over to different club, which was fine with me. I was too drunk and too happy to notice where we were going. Somehow we ended up not in another club but at Grisha's place, a five-room apartment in one of those old, expensive and fancy downtown buildings near the Irish Pub. I am sure it was one of the ex-communal apartments. The living room was enormous, with a huge TV set, VCR and genuine leather couches. Silvija and I collapsed on the couches. You know, we had never sat our asses on leather before. It is quite the feeling! I was getting kind of sleepy by then. All the guys made a circle around us. They were laughing and blinking at each other. We started laughing too.

"So what's the deal here?" one of the guys asked.

"We are going to have some fun, he-he!" Grisha laughed.

"Right, right," Oljegs said and looked at me. There was something malicious in his eyes.

"So which one?" a guy named Artjom asked; "The blondee or the dark one?"

"How about the blondee," suggested Arvils. "I have been watching her all night; she's got a gorgeous body."

"Yeah, the blondee," someone added lazily. Drunk as I was, I did not like the conversation. Fear had started to sober me up. I looked at Silvija; she was totally out.

"Should we have another drink first?" one of the guys asked with a bottle of some expensive liquor in his hand.

I was starting to panic. Those guys were some mafia guys for sure, or Grisha would not have been able to buy a five-bedroom apartment. What if they raped or even killed us? I knew there was no escape. All I could do was sit on that wretched leather couch and wait for the inevitable to happen. I thought about you guys back in Big Bamboo. Artjoms had moved really close to me and wanted to put his arm around me, but I shrugged it off. "Hey, slow there!" Arvils yelled at him. "I have first right to the blondee. She is my girl. Are you my girl?" he grinned at me.

I gave him the genuinely silly smile of a drunk. I wanted them to think that I was still drunk, but my mind was working frantically. I decided to pretend that I was very sick and was going to puke, so I asked one of the guys where the bathroom was. I staggered in the bathroom and locked the door behind me. For a while I just stared in the mirror at my own

face. Then somebody knocked at the door. I did not respond. It was one of them. He knocked louder and then tried to push the door open. Suddenly I heard screams coming from the room. The guy let go of the door. I opened it carefully and tiptoed in the hall.
The living room door was open and I saw Artjoms threatening Arvils with a knife. "You son of a bitch, you cheated, didn't you?" he was yelling. Grisha was on the phone in one of the spare rooms.
I grabbed my purse and headed towards the door. Silvija had staggered out in the hallway. "Let's get out of here!" I whispered to her. She looked at me like I was weird. "They are some mafia guys, you know." She looked like she was drugged up or something. I took her by her arm and dragged her to the door. It was locked with one hundred locks, and I had no idea how to open it. There were buttons and buttons you know. I started pushing every one of them, and after a while the door opened. I closed the door behind us as quietly as I could and then like a mad woman, dragging Silvija along with me, dashed down the stairs. We ran towards the Monument of Freedom where some taxis had been parked. We took the taxi to Tornja Kalns station and sat there in the bushes until the first train came. All the way to Dubulti I was freaking out. Silvija had finally sobered up a little and had begun to realize the seriousness of the situation. God, now I am going to be scared to go to any clubs or pubs for a half a year! I am still scared. What if they find us? What if?" Sabine's face became pale again.

"Don't worry, silly!" I said trying to comfort her; "they are not going to come after you. But you know you are really lucky. I guess this crazy night was really a good lesson for us." Sabine's encounter with the mafia guys had made me forget about my own adventure with Armands.

"Hey what happened with you and Armands?" Sabine asked in a brighter tone. "Did you? Did he?"

"Yes, he tricked me to go to his place and tried to have sex with me. His parents were at home. I felt guilty all the time for being with him. I was flattered by his compliments, but I really did not want anything to happen between us."

"So what happened?"

"We talked and then he tried to French kiss me. I guess that was my first kiss, and it was gross."

"French kissing can be fun," Sabine said in the voice of a superior, more experienced virgin. She had kissed with a lot of guys.

"I do not know. I am pretty grossed out about that kissing thing. What should I say to Laira?" I asked anxiously.

"I will tell her that Armands is a jerk and that nothing happened between you and him. Nothing really happened, did it?"

"No, except the French kiss. Will she believe you? I doubt it. She will think that I am the slut and that I am to blame for everything." I felt crappy.

"Don't worry about what she thinks."

I finished my coffee and glanced at the clock. "I've got to get going. I have to translate today at church."

"You are going to church today?" Sabine exclaimed.

"Well, yes . . . to repent from my sins." I smiled, yet I wanted to cry so badly. Sabine's face darkened at me mentioning repentance. Deep down in our hearts we both fear that God has stopped loving us, and that we are going to hell after we die.

"Call me after you talk to Laira," I said and gathered my purse. Sabine saw me off till the front door and gave me a big, painful hug. "Take care!"

"You, too."

In a couple of minutes I was on the train again. Dozens of gloomy thoughts were going through my mind. Mother would be mad when saw me in this condition. What would I tell her? I guess I would have to lie again. She probably knows that I lie to her all the time. They say a mother can feel it. Besides I did not want to go to church. Since I left the I. C. C., I have started to go down so fast. From a righteous, pure Christian girl, I have turned into a bar hopper and a liar.

Of course I was a pretty pathetic interpreter for the poor missionaries from Alabama. I was so tired, I could not concentrate. I was not dressed for church, for I was wearing the brown miniskirt Katrina gave me a couple of months ago. I always wear a miniskirt to the church. It is way of demonstrating my defiance. All these godly missionaries with their bleached American teeth, their forced joyful smiles, their neat ties, fat bellies and logical arguments annoy me to death. It seems like they have never lived in real world, never experienced any kind of hardship, pain or disappointment. Everything is always so perfect with God and faith. I must come from a different planet.

154. It is another pathetic day and again I am sitting alone and jotting down my lamentations in my diary. Since the Big Bamboo night Sabine and I have become much tamer party girls. We pretty much do not go anywhere else but to Arabica. Laira never comes with us any more. She says she is not mad at me for Armands or anything; I suspect that she thinks we are too cheap and too inexperienced to be suitable company for her.

At Arabica we have a couple of drinks and then we dance and meet guys who try to persuade us to sleep with them, and we refuse. Many guys have told me that I am an idiot wasting my best years. Recently, I have even been lucky enough to get a couple of dates, but as soon as the guys find out that I am not an easy woman, they give up. Some more persistent ones have tried to manipulate me into sleeping with them by telling that men do not like inexperienced girls; they prefer women who have, so to say, the hang of it. So they in their "mercy" were offering me a chance for some learning experiences. As much as I want to get rid of my virginity and become experienced in sexual matters, I will never sleep with a guy I do not know or do not trust. To be able to take this huge step I need some foundation of trust and—yes, as cheesy as it sounds—love. But if I told this to the guys I occasionally date, they would laugh their asses off.

The clubs and bars are starting to annoy me. Why am I going there? To dance, to drink, to meet someone? I don't know. I guess I am tired of always being approached my drunks and asked for sex. I am tired of always worrying that nobody will dance with me. I am tired of all this mess. I wish I could renew my faith in the Lord. I try to pray, but my prayers are so pathetic. Actually my whole life is pathetic the way it is now. I am really tired and really sad and really sorry that there are no normal people left in this world. I mean people who have values and morals, yet who also know how to have fun without crossing the limits. I long for normal people who are not involved with sects and legalistic churches (one extreme) or drugs and one night stands (other extreme). Am I really the only such idiot in the world? Well, me and Sabine.

155.

Finally something is happening. Finally my club hopping has born some results. I have started to date a guy, Sergejs. We met at Arabica. I had never seen him there before; he is definitely not a regular. He asked me to a couple of slow dances and afterwards asked for my number. I, of course, was very happy because Sergejs is a fairly good looking guy; besides, he was nice and polite with me. He wasn't drunk or anything like the other Russian guys at Arabica. When he called me the very next day, I was ecstatic, of course. He invited me to go out with him the following Saturday. I was so dizzy with happiness that I did not even ask him where he was planning to go. We met at the Laima clock around 5 on Saturday, which is the time when the disciples of the International Church of Christ meet up for dates at the Laima clock. I wanted some of them to be there and see me meeting with a real guy and going to a real date, not some church-arranged, forced-upon parody of dating. There were indeed some disciples hanging around the clock waiting for their "dates" to arrive and eyeing me with white eyeballs. No doubt they saw Sergejs approach me smiling. What a satisfaction to feel their stares!

Well, our date went fairly well. We went for an ice cream, and we talked, and I had really started liking him, but then on our way home he stopped the car at some remote place and wanted me to make out with him. I let him kiss me (he is a fairly nice kisser), and then I told him I had some things to do, so I had to get home. He obediently drove me home and we parted with a kiss. He said he was going to call the next day, but he did not. Instead he called three days later and asked me out again. I was determined to be mad, but when I heard his voice I decided to change my tactics. I pretended to be simply indifferent, as if I had not even noticed his breaking his promise. (After all, he did not promise me that he was going to call the very next day; he could have simply said, "I will call you sometime again.") When he apologized, saying that he had lots of things going on at work, I just laughed and said, "That's OK; I have been very busy myself."

He asked me out again, and he showed up twenty minutes late! I was already on my way to the tram when he caught me. However, he had bought flowers for me, and when he gave them to me, my anger melted away like patchy snow in early April sun. I have such a soft heart with guys! But we had a terrific time just walking through the gray and misty parks full of fallen leaves. After an hour of walking and chatting, we warmed ourselves up with a cup of strong, bitter hot chocolate in one of the small and cozy cafes of the down town Riga. On our way home Sergejs wanted to make out a lot more than the first time. It was fun, yet it was sort of scary too. I did not want him to discover too quickly what a dork I am in love matters, I mean love-making matters.

156. After our second date Sergejs did not call for a whole entire week. I felt pretty sour about his neglect, because I had really started to like him, but then he called again and said that he had missed me and wanted to see me really bad. I was going to say that I was busy, but when he promised to take me to Cita Opera (a newly opened club in down town Riga), I gave in. Of course, I loathed myself again for my soft heart and lack of pride, but I really like Sergejs and maybe eventually our relationship will develop into something serious. I update Sabine regularly on my first real, long-term dating experience (I say long-term because up to now, I have never had more than one date with a guy). Sabine seems kind of sour recently, because besides the couple of lousy dates she has managed to snatch from the regular attendants of Arabica (she even went out with an ex-prisoner once), she has not had a decent date in a while. But as a true friend, she tries to be happy for me.

Our night at Cita Opera was not what I expected it to be. We had a couple of drinks and danced a little, but then Sergejs wanted to go to his dorm and wanted me to come with him. I knew what he meant. I like him a lot, but I am not ready yet for the big step, and I told him so. He got kind of irritated, so I told him that I have never had sex before. Sergejs almost dropped his gin & tonic, he was so surprised. So I guess I do not look that virginal, then, which is nice. I do not want guys to think that I do not know anything. That night we made out for a long time right there at the club (I think I am getting the hang of it, at least in kissing). Yet I refused to leave the club, since my experience with Armands is still fresh in my memory. The more persistent Sergejs got, the stronger my determination grew not to leave the club. In the morning, he drove me home in silence, and when we parted, he did not even kiss me. I was very sad because I do not know what that is about him that fascinates me and draws me to him despite the hurts caused by his careless attitude towards me. I really want to continue our dating relationship which for me is another step towards adult life. I hate, though, that he pressures me to have sex with him. Tempting as it is, I do not feel ready to sleep with him. We are not that serious yet, and I am not sure of his true intentions towards me. Sometimes I wonder if I am a fool, but I am really afraid of the big step. I think if I did it, something horrible would happen. Like I would not be the same person anymore, or something will change in my body. Anyway, after the fiasco at Cita Opera I am pretty sure Sergejs will never call me again.

157. Well, Sergejs called and invited me to a pool and sauna party. He wanted me to meet his friends. How thoughtful of him! Of course, I wanted to go. I had never been to a sauna party before, so it would be a whole new experience, another step towards the big life. If I want to look like a really hot and confident chick, I will have to work hard. I have to mill through thousands of different kinds of situations and circumstances, positive and disgusting like the one with Armands, to be able to learn, to gain experience, which apparently is a great virtue in men's eyes. At least in the ones I have met so far. When Sergejs invited me to his sauna party, I decided to throw off all the inhibitions I may have, and go and have some fun. Since I did not have a decent bathing suit of my own, I stole my mother's. She has an old one that is nice and small. She used to wear it in the days of her youth, but of course in the past fifteen years she has become too fat to wear it, so she has stashed it away on the last shelf of the dresser. I figured she would not even notice if I borrowed it.

The sauna party turned out to another disappointing experience which only deepened my general despair. Sergejs met me outside of the building where the party was supposed to be. We went inside and he pointed at the women's showers. I was supposed to undress and to shower before I got into the pool. I took a quick shower, put on my bathing suit and dared not to look in the mirror at my own body. Even though many people, including Sergejs, have assured me that I have a perfect body, I feel very self conscious because I know it has some serious faults. My boobs are too big, my chest bones are sticking out too much, my waist is too narrow and looks a lot like a male's waist, I have not enough curves, my stomach's got a weird shape, my thighs are fatter than necessary, my toenails are ugly from too much running and playing soccer in my younger years. Besides, I have not been wearing a bathing suit in front of men since my swimming lessons. My body has changed so much since then.

I was shivering when I left the shower room. Sergejs was already in the pool alone.

"Where are your friends?" I asked.

"Surprise! I rented this place just for the both of us. I knew that if I told you, you would chicken out and not come."

I was angry. Sergejs was out of the pool and coming towards me. "You look great, even though you would look even better without the bathing suit," he grinned.

"Would you like a drink? I have champagne, gin. . . ." I was not listening. "So this is it," I thought. "Is this going to happen now?" I was tempted to get done with it for once, but at the same time I was scared. Again I had that old feeling that something horrible would happen if I had sex with him. Well, I thought, maybe if I have some champagne. . . .

"Yes, I will have some champagne," I said and smiled at him. Sergejs led me to a shelf hidden behind a tiny wall at the back of the pool.

"Wow!" I exclaimed in surprise. There were at least three bottles of champagne, and all kinds of other drinks and fruit and sweets.

"This is so sweet of you!" I said. Sergejs poured a glass of champagne for me and then for himself. We drank and then he kissed me. I had gotten a buzz from the champagne, so his kiss felt great. We drank some more.

"Come on. Let's go swimming!" Sergejs said, dragging me towards the pool. We jumped in, but instead of swimming, we started making out. Water gave the whole thing a very special sensation. I had never been kissed in the water.

After awhile Sergejs whispered to me, "Do you want to go to the sauna?"

"I guess so," I said hesitantly.

"Come on." The sauna smelled like cider. Sergejs took off his swimsuit. "Come sit next to me," he invited. I sat next to him, but I avoided looking at him and I was not going to remove my swimsuit.

"What's the matter?" he asked in a concerned voice.

"Nothing," I said and sat down with my swimsuit.

"Aren't you going to take that off?"

"No!" I jumped up to my feet. "I know what you want, what you hope is going to happen, but I do not feel . . . I am not going to. . . . " I stopped, embarrassed.

"Why does it have to be so much work with you?" Sergejs asked, despair in his voice. "What kind of treatment do you need? What are you waiting for? You are a beautiful and passionate woman; why don't you use your assets?"

I did not know what to say. After a while I said, "Why does it always have to be about getting a woman to have sex with you?"

"Well, it is perfectly normal for couples to have sex," Sergejs said in a grave voice.

"So you consider us a couple? We have been out to about four dates. Three of them have been only make-out sessions, and you consider us a couple. I do not even know you!"

"How much longer do you think we should drag this out? I like you, you like me; I want you, you want me. So what's wrong with a little sex?"

"But what about the relationship?"

"Relationship? I am not ready for a relationship. I do not want a relationship. I like you and I really want you, but if you are hoping for a relationship, then I am the wrong person. I am a student and I am working part time. I have time for a little fun, yet I do not have any time for a relationship. Plus, I do not want to be burdened by a relationship. I wonder if all virgins are so stupid. I once slept with a virgin girl, and on our next date she asked me when I was going to introduce her to my parents. I almost fell over. Girl, it is not the nineteenth century anymore!"

"What happened to that girl?"

"Nothing. We parted and went into different directions. She got on with her life, and I got on with mine."

"But don't you ever long for a close relationship with someone? Having someone in your life whom you trust, having someone there for you not only for fun, but also in tough moments?" I asked Sergejs

"That's all cheesy bullshit you are talking. Of course, once I will probably settle down, have a family, a wife and kids, but honestly, that prospect terrifies me. You are such a child. You are looking for someone to trust, someone special. Hey, you have got to wake up to the reality."

In the church they told us that each one of us has a special other person. God has made that special other person for us, and we just have to be patient and wait for him. "Well," I thought to myself, "what bullshit were they teaching! How could I ever believe this?" The awakening has been hard. I gathered my towel and said to Sergejs, "I am sorry. I can't help being such a fool. I am really sorry for liking you and imagining that one day we could be something more than just make-out partners."

I heard his voice behind me. "Hey, don't... I am sorry too." I wanted him to run after me, snatch me by my hand, promise me the whole world. But he remained sitting.

Going home that night, I cursed myself all the way to my house for being an idiot and even entertaining the thoughts of having a serious relationship with Sergejs sometime in the future. Well, that's it, no more dating, no more clubbing, no more of the relationship bullshit, no more deceptive churches. This time I am resolved.

158. I have stopped going to the bars and clubs. I am trying to be a good and responsible girl by paying more attention to my studies. But I get distracted so easily. Instead of reading Goethe, I sit at my table, chew on my pen and immerse myself in a sea of gloomy thoughts. I guess I am going through one of my black phases, only this current one is more threatening than the ones before. I feel that I have lost all the ground under my feet. I am disappointed in religion and God, and I doubt I will ever find a way back to Him. I am disappointed in the world too for muddying up my white, girl's dreams. I have lost motivation and interest in my studies. What's the value of my diploma? The future looms in dark shadows.

During my preteens, my only concern was my ugliness and my status as a white crow. Now I am twenty years old and am not treated like a white crow anymore. In fact, many guys think I am beautiful. But am I happy? No! Beauty does not bring happiness, just a trouble. I always get stares and sex offers, so my vanity, which was so hungry and thirsty for prizes at the age of thirteen, is finally satisfied. But what's next? I have grown up. My opinions, values and expectations of life have changed. At thirteen, I could feed on one guy's smile or compliment for months. Now I want a quality relationship, a deep friendship with a guy. Am I really unrealistic? Am I a naive dreamer for wanting that one, special person with whom you are supposed to go through the fire and rain? Or do such relationships exist only in chick flicks and sultry novels? My going to clubs and social events has proven that men do not care about relationships, only about sex. I have started to realize that I want stability and peace in my life. Instead of being torn between all kinds of doubts and fears, I want certainty. I am tired of deceiving myself by accepting other people's religious convictions as my own. I want to have my own convictions, my own opinions about faith and God. But how do I know what's true and what's not? The more I search, the more confused I become.

Thinking about my career, I cannot help wondering what I am going to do with my degree in German Philology. Yes, I have learned a lot about

German language and culture. I have even read the *Niebelungen Lied* in *Altdeutch*. I am educated, but what good does it do to me? How can I use all this cultural capital? In the post-Soviet Latvia, only people with connections get jobs. I have no connections, no friends in highly respectable places. I am poor and unknown. My only option is to work at some high school as a German teacher and make just barely enough money to save myself from starvation. I know many girls who have graduated with my degree, and how many of them have found a good job? Only one, and only because her brother-in-law happens to work at the Ministry of Foreign Affairs. So there we are.

The Bible tells us not to worry and to rely on the Lord's providence. Well, it is easy to say, but in reality I do not have faith in the help of the Lord either. I do not have a church community where I belong and feel at home. I do not even have anyone to talk to. Mom and I were never close, and throughout the years of my growing up, we have drifted apart. I had never been able to tell my mother who I really am and what I think and feel. I mean, she has been a great mom to me. She has always given me the best she had. She has given up everything for me. She worried about me gravely when I was sick and hurting physically, but she never realized that there are pains and hurts that are not physical. Mom's old, and she is still broken up about Dad's death. I don't think she will ever recover. She works a lot and occasionally laughs, but her face is like a withered flower. I feel bad for not spending more time with her or helping her out more. I cannot explain why I avoid her company. I know my constant absence from home irks her, but evenings at home are unbearable.

    I spend my evenings outside the house wandering through the streets of downtown and wondering about my existence and God's purpose. Sometimes I go to movies alone. I always have been sort of a loner, but recently I have started to avoid even my closest friends. Sabine has been my best friend since my church years; she is my dearest friend, but she is even more down than I am. I always feel worse after talking to her. Katrina is my other best and dearest friend. When we are together we usually have a blast. We laugh a lot, make fun of everything and everybody. Being with her is like doing drugs: we laugh, we go places and do crazy stuff, but when I am back alone in my room I am unhappier than ever.

    Well, some people may say that I am just a whiner and a weakling that I simply do not want to bear my daily cross. But I would bear my cross, even if it were heavier than it is now, if I only had a cause to live for. But there is no cause in Latvia these days, and no cause in my life. The future offers no hope, no job, no way back to God, and no meaningful relationship.

Afterword

After that blackest of the black phases of my life, I did not open my diary for a couple of years. I was too confused, and was too grown up for my old friend, which lay buried in my desk drawer. I did not even reread what I had written, although remembering the troubles one has survived is always a great help in times of new troubles. Now that I find myself rereading my life, I regret ignoring my diary, both because of the many adventures I did not write down, and because of the reassurance it might have given me. I doubt that I will have much time to write in the future, but there are a couple of white pages left in this one. And since my last entry was quite gloomy, I decided to finish it up on a more hopeful note.

During these last years I continued to search. Many of life's mysteries remain unsolved, and I have not found peace or answers to all of life's puzzling questions. I still get sad about a lot of things, and I still feel sorry for the whole human race because we are all so vulnerable and so helpless. Nevertheless, I have come to a couple of realizations that help me maintain my sanity in the times when dark, stormy clouds seem to be covering the skies.

Number one, I have learned that every situation, no matter how horrible it seems, passes and life slowly returns to more or less normal flow. I have also realized that our future is absolutely and completely unpredictable. When we are miserable and unhappy, we see everything in extremely gloomy colors; it may seem that there is not hope for us in the days ahead. However, when our lives seem to be under control and we are satisfied with ourselves and the world, we think that our future shines bright and happy ahead of us. Yet one moment, one encounter, one missed train, one aimless walk on the streets, one "accident " or coincidence as people like to call such things (I do not really believe in accidents) can twist our life around, turn it upside down and inside out and make us take a completely different route from the one planned. The little "accident" or encounter can turn our hopelessness into a perfectly happy solution, or it can shatter our bright hopes and best plans into pieces. But that is the beauty of life. Each morning we wake up and we have no idea what the day will bring.

My next revelation is the fact that there is not a single absolutely right church on this planet. There is none! Because the body of the church is constituted by humans, who are all sinful and imperfect. So instead of running to different churches every Sunday morning and talking to all kinds of hypnotized, fanatic, brainwashed lunatics, I have started to listen to my own heart and my instincts. Slowly, one by one, the answers have started to come to me. No not all of them yet, but the ones I need for now have come so far. Besides, I am confident that one day God will give me all of the answers (maybe when I am dead).

I think that I am slowly starting to come back to God and my faith. Throughout my years of depression and desperate search; throughout those years of failures and the mistakes of my early youth, and throughout the years of idealism and naivete, God has been there for me. No matter how deep in trouble I got myself, he always provided a way out. I still argue with Him at times. I am a rebel by nature. For me it is necessary to understand why before I obey a law. So I have to experiment a lot and experience the consequences of my sometimes reckless experiments on my own skin to understand why. That is my way to wisdom and insight, my way to my self-discovery.

My next and the most comforting revelation is that there still are plenty of normal people left in this world who have morals yet who also know how to have some fun. During these last years I have met plenty of them (males included) and have made friends for life. By the way, one of these people is my husband whom I love deeply and passionately (even though he is far from perfect, but so am I) and with whom I have that meaningful relationship that I thought impossible after my rough encounters with the public of bars and pubs. Throughout our marriage we have seen the best and the worst of each other, and we have no unrealistic ideals about each other. At times we hurt and upset each other gravely, but through all the painful experiences our love for each other has matured and I have to admit that we have experienced moments of genuine happiness (although without the cheesy romanticism that I so longed for in my early youth). I am happy and content because I have a profound faith in the permanence of our relationship.

My last but not least revelation is that instead of frantically trying to figure out what our lives are all about, we should simply relax more and enjoy our lives as much as we can in the present moment. I am not looking for some ultimate purpose for my life anymore which, in the days of my early youth, I imagined would one day in some mysterious way be revealed to me and make me a hero, or a martyr, or a famous person. Instead, I have started to look closely at each day and find the purpose of my existence in little everyday matters, such as being effective in my professional life (doing my job as well as I can), loving my husband on daily basis, having children, using my spare time in doing things which make me happy, maintaining a few lasting friendships, continuing to educate myself on matters of arts, politics, religion. Oh, there are millions and millions of things which we can do to make difference in this world, from big things like running for election to seemingly trivial matters like helping a friend to move or decorating the house.

The bottom line is every single one of us is born to make a difference. Each one of us has the power to influence the lives of those around us on a daily basis (whether positively or negatively). We do not live secluded; instead we are all connected in many different ways. Our every action has consequences (positive and negative) which affect the other members of the chain that constitutes the human race. So ultimately every one of us makes some kind of difference and fulfills some kind of purpose, be it writing novels to enlighten millions of readers or shoveling the snow to make lives easier for the inhabitants of a single street. Not all of us were born to turn the world upside down (in fact very few representatives of the human race have succeeded into turning the world upside down, and in most cases the difference they made had very negative consequences, like Lenin, Stalin, and Hitler). Still, we can find our lives enjoyable, fulfilling and purposeful by making the best of each moment given to us.